# Values in Transition
## A Handbook

GAIL M. INLOW

Professor of Education

Northwestern University

*John Wiley & Sons, Inc.*

New York • London • Sydney • Toronto

# Values in Transition
## A Handbook

*Dedicated to*

Value builders everywhere
May uncertainty be their only certainty

# Preface

Three forces motivated me to write this book. One was a lifelong preoccupation with values: what they are, what conceivably they should be, and the ways in which they influence human behavior. Individual man and societies are, among other things, projections of values operating—sometimes overtly, many times covertly—to direct the course of mankind. Values tantalize with their complexity and diversity. They frustrate with their resistance to implementation and change.

The second motivating force was the so-called human condition at the time of the writing. Central in it, now as then, are the crucial choices that man faces in today's danger-laden world. Important among them are these: to continue to pursue materialism or to take seriously the summons of humanism, to be egocentric or altruistic, to let irrationality victimize or rationality redeem and, most fundamentally, to recover the environment and control man's power to destroy or pay the supreme price of failure. Choices as critical as these plead eloquently for man to make them in a value context. If this book contributes to that context in the slightest, it will have justified itself.

A third motivating force emanated from my interest in the field of curriculum. For years, curriculum theorists have been averring orally and in writing that curriculum grows out of educational objectives. While granting this, I believe that the values of a given cultural group are foundational to both. Thus I wrote the book to clarify my thinking about values and, in the process, to make my curriculum position more defensible.

I am not implying that schools should teach values didactically—far from it. I am saying, however, that formal education is remiss if students in too great numbers leave school without, at their levels of readiness, knowing what the governing values of the culture are. Knowledge of values is essential to an understanding of them, and both are essential to any assessment of them.

The audience for the book will, hopefully, be people outside the mainstream of formal education as well as preprofessionals and professionals within it. In colleges and universities, the book should serve the purposes of courses such as the following: Introduction to Education, Foundations of Education, Philosophy of Education, Social Foundations of Education, Politics and Education, Introduction to Philosophy, Sociology, and Man and Society. It should serve the purposes, additionally, of graduate-level courses in curriculum, philosophy of education, school administration, and educational sociology.

This project on values leads me to cite some value-oriented colleagues whose friendships through a few or many years have meant much to me. Among them are George Beauchamp, Walter Gregg, Joe Park, Jim Peterson, William Peterson, and John Wick. I cite also my sister, Muriel Olson, and my brother-in-law, Raymond Olson, Professor at Ball State University, with whom I have sharpened ideas many times. Nor can I forget the many acts of friendship and interest evidenced by Helen Beloungy, Orville and Flossie Matteson, Ruth Wilson, and Carla Palmer.

Finally I take note of the contributions, great and small, made by close members of my family: Joanne, Ron, Rick, Bev, Meg, Debbie, and Robbie.

GAIL M. INLOW

*Evanston, Illinois*

# Contents

*Values in Transition*
*A Handbook*

# 1

# Values in Perspective

The theme of this book is values: values that, for better or worse, have charted man's course in the past and are charting it today; values that serve, in part, to explain the nature of man and his behavior; values that have made, and continue to make, him human or inhuman. The fact that values and value systems, past and present, are many dimensioned and thus controversial is an understatement. Yet for that reason they challenge men of every generation—men of reason, of emotion, or of both—to plumb their connotative subtleties and assess their implications for behavior. The theme of values and value systems is important beyond debate. Very much in the province of debate, however, is the ability of any single individual, or even of mankind collectively through the ages, to do justice to the theme.

Values rise to their zenith of complexity in the process of prescription. In this connection, civilized history is an intriguing narrative of individuals who have impaled themselves on its horn. Moses, Plato, writers of the New Testament Gospels, the apostle Paul, Mohammed, Justinian I, authors of the Magna Carta, and many of our founding fathers are striking examples of such individuals. Although freely admitting to engaging in occasional value prescription, I have done so only incidentally, subordinating it for the most part to the processes of exposition and assessment. And even when prescribing, my intent has been more to motivate the reader to think reflectively than to accept any pronouncements verbatim.

## DEFINITIONS

At this early stage in the discussion, I raise the fundamental question: Just what meaning does the term "values" have? Lacking universal definition, it has been interpreted in a number of different ways. Jules Henry defines it as something that we consider good such as "love, kindness, quietness, content-

1

ment, fun, honesty, decency, relaxation, simplicity."[1] Carl Rogers, employing the term in its gerund form, says that "valuing is the tendency of a person to show preference."[2] Raths, Harmin, and Simon aver that "out of experiences may come certain general guides to behavior. These guides tend to give direction to life and may be called values."[3] Clough distinguishes between *ideal values,* which he depicts as being elusive if not actually unattainable, and *modal values,* which he views as compromises with ideal values.[4] And Coughlan, in a summary definition, states that "Values have been variously viewed as preferences, criteria, objects, and possessions, personality and status characteristics, and states of mind that are absolutes . . . , inherent in objects . . . , present in man . . . , and/or identical with his behavior. . . ."[5]

Values to me, simply stated, are the determiners in man that influence his choices in life and that thus decide his behavior. It follows then that the person who chooses beef over lamb, or pacifism over combat, or Occidentals over Orientals, or radicalism over conservatism does so, in each instance, in response to a given set of inner determiners called values. Relatedly, the person who kills, or makes love, or joins a social group, or actively campaigns for a cause does so, once again, in response to a set of inner determiners called values.

Values, as indicated, are inherent in individual man, but they are additionally inherent, although perhaps less definably so, in collective man—in a given culture, that is, or in a combination of cultures. The term culture, we note in passing, is descriptive of a life style that characterizes a given human society or group of societies. Whatever the exact nature of any human society, values exist in some form. In a primitive society, they customarily reside in the minds of individuals, handed down from generation to generation. In a developed society, they reside in written documents as well as in the intangibles of social mores and expectancies.

In respect to individuals and cultures, values are circular. Existing in individuals, they flow into and help to shape the culture. Existing in cultures, they condition, without categorically dictating, the values developed by individuals in those cultures. The point made here is an important one, namely, that all individuals habitually introject certain values from their respective cultures. Individuals who are more autonomous, however, are able to rise above at least many of the culture's values that impinge on them.

[1] Jules Henry, *Culture Against Man* (New York: Random House, Inc., 1963), p. 14.
[2] Carl R. Rogers, *Freedom to Learn* (Columbus, Ohio: Charles E. Merrill Publishing Company, 1969), p. 241.
[3] Louis E. Raths, Merrill Harmin, and Sidney B. Simon, *Values and Teaching* (Columbus, Ohio: Charles E. Merrill Publishing Company, 1966), p. 27.
[4] Shepard B. Clough, *Basic Values of Western Civilization* (New York: Columbia University Press, 1960), p. 9.
[5] Robert Coughlan, "The Factorial Structure of Teacher Work Values," *American Educational Research Journal,* **VI** (March 1969), p. 170.

These individuals, in fact, are usually the prime movers of progress. Endowed in some unusual way, they counter the prevailing beliefs and practices of a culture and, in the process, reshape it. The flat-earth concept, for instance was the accepted one until the Renaissance had almost run its course. Yet as early as 250 B.C., Eratosthenes, the Alexandrian, cast serious doubt on the concept's validity. However, it was not until almost two millennia later, that such early moderns as Copernicus (1473–1543), Brahe (1546–1601), and Kepler (1571–1630) dealt the concept a lethal blow. The fact that, until recent years, many were oblivious to the significance and implications of the blow detracts not at all from our point that autonomous individuals change the course of ideas and, thus, of history itself.

Some of our early forebears such as Roger Williams (1603?–1683)—in respect to religious freedom, Benjamin Franklin (1706–1790)—in respect to sense realism and inductive thinking, and Thomas Jefferson (1743–1826) —in respect to human rights, opposed established values and changed the world as a result. So too did Charles Darwin (1809–1882)—in respect to the origin of biological man, Karl Marx (1818–1883)—in respect to economic theory, Sigmund Freud (1856–1939)—in respect to psychic determinism, Albert Einstein (1879–1955)—in respect to relativity, and Martin Luther King (1929–1968)—in respect to the social rights of Negroes, as well as of all free men, in the United States.

## AVENUES TO VALUES

Individuals, singly and collectively, assume one of the following four stances in their attempts to formulate or change values and value systems. (1) In the manner of the deductivist, they postulate that truth is known a priori and thus needs only to be uncovered, understood, and applied. (2) Or in the manner of the pragmatist, they postulate that tradition, constantly tested, should guide human affairs. (3) Or in the manner of the existentialist, they postulate that individual man works out his own values. (4) Or, finally, in the manner of the Hegelian, they postulate that built into history is a dynamic force that guides human affairs. These will be developed only briefly here in view of their more extensive coverage later in the book.

### The Deductivist Position

Those who operate out of a deductivist position logically conceive of values as predetermined, sanctioned in advance either by some source of divine revelation or by the rationality of man. In the ranks of the first subgroup are religious fundamentalists who look to the Bible, to a church organization, or to daily revelation—one or all of these—for the pronouncement of truth. Fundamentalist Protestantism looks primarily to the Bible. Orthodox Catholicism looks to all three sources. Irrespective of origin, the following value essences emerge: A personal God, man, life endowed with meaning, and a cosmos subservient to divine will.

In the ranks of the rationalists are those who, like orthodox religionists, postulate, although much more tentatively, the existence of a priori values. The difference, however, is that they look to rational sources for authentication of their conceptualizations. Plato, historically unique in these ranks, drew on his own rational sources to prescribe, in a near-Utopian way, what man should be, what outcomes are good or bad, and what makes them good or bad. Plato's current counterparts, although not in exact kind, include such perennialists as Mark Van Doren, Robert Maynard Hutchins, Mortimer Adler, and Jacques Barzun.

### The Pragmatist Position

Pragmatists, unlike deductivists, reject the absolute nature of values, viewing them instead as ever emanating from the crucible of social living and social testing. That which is good (or a value), in effect, is that which works in the ongoing lives of men. What was good yesterday might not necessarily be good today, and what is good today might not necessarily be good tomorrow. To be more specific: If the brotherhood-of-man concept has validity, it is endowed with this quality not because the *New Testament* endorses the concept and not because rational tradition endorses it, but, rather, because the concept works—in today's pulsating, complex world. It is valid because a given social order decides that it is workable; even more, that it is working.

### The Existentialist Position

Unlike the deductivist or rationalist who assumes the existence of a priori truth, and the pragmatist who holds nothing to be true until it is validated in social living, the existentialist assigns individual man the responsibility to "work through to," "to agonize his way into," in effect, to create values by living them. As articulated by Jean Paul Sartre (1905–      ), the phenomenon of *being* precedes the outcome of *essence* (value, that is) or, conversely, essence is nonexistent until individual man in the process of living makes it so. The existentialist position thus commits every individual to live, to assess, progressively to define and develop values, and ultimately to forge a value system.

### The Hegelian Position

The Hegelian position is the so-called historist position that, in the words of Charles Frankl, "holds that there is a law of history in accordance with which the historical process as a whole tends to move in a certain direction."[6] The thesis is that history per se predetermines, or at least affects, man's destinies; and that it does so dialectically, pitting forces and counterforces against one another to the end of resulting syntheses. Individuals who espouse this position thus look to the dynamic forces at work in history to change the lives and values of man and cultures. However, they tend to beg the issue of exactly what those forces are and how they got there.

## SOME IMPORTANT SOCIAL CONCERNS

The following value categories receive chapter-length treatment in subsequent parts of the book: traditional cultural values, economic values, political values, scientific values, philosophical values, values of the New Left, values of the black community, and a value synthesis. Selected value issues supplemental to these will be covered here briefly. They include population, ecological abuses, and war.

### Population

Of the many perplexing problems that beset mankind, population is one of the foremost. Boulding, an economist, included it as one of the four traps that, if not controlled, might well keep man from completing his transition into the so-called postcivilized era. The other three traps that he identified were war, technology, and the nature of man himself.[7] The crux of the issue is whether man on a global scale can effect an equilibrium between the world population and his ability to supply its material needs.

*Some Statistics.* In the year 1968, 3,482,500,000 people inhabited the globe, contrasted with 3,005,000,000 in 1960, 2,517,000,000 in 1950, 2,295,000,000 in 1940, and 2,070,000,000 in 1930.[8] During the period 1960 to 1968, the increase for each year was an identical 1.9 percent.[9] In 1968, population figures by geographical areas were as follows.

| | |
|---|---|
| Africa | 336,000,000 |
| N. America | 309,000,000 |
| S. America | 180,000,000 |
| Asia | 1,946,000,000 |

[6] Charles Frankl, "The Relation of Theory to Practice: Some Standard Views." In Herman D. Stein (Ed.), *Social Theory and Social Invention* (Cleveland: The Press of Case Western Reserve University, 1968), p. 12.
[7] Kenneth Boulding, *The Meaning of the Twentieth Century* (New York: Harper and Row, Publishers, 1964), pp. 24–26.
[8] United Nations, *Statistical Yearbook, Annuaire Statistique,* 1969 (New York: United Nations, Nations Unies, 1970), p. xxvii.
[9] Op. cit., p. xxvii.

| Europe   | 455,000,000   |
|----------|---------------|
| Oceania  | 18,500,000    |
| U.S.S.R. | 238,000,000   |
| Total    | 3,482,500,000 |

The most densely populated nations of the world in 1967 were Mainland China with a population of 720,000,000, India with a population of 498,680,000, and the Soviet Republic with a population of 236,789,000.[10]

In 1969, the demographic statistics for the United States were as follows. Its population totaled 203,200,000 contrasted with 201,200,000 in 1968, 199,100,000 in 1967, and 180,700,000 in 1960. The population in 1969 included approximately 4,900,000 more females than males. The nonwhite population totaled 24,800,000, and the black population, 22,600,000.[11] Live births for selected years of the 1960–1970 decade were as follows:

| 1960 | 4,300,000      |
|------|----------------|
| 1965 | 3,800,000      |
| 1967 | 3,500,000      |
| 1969 | 3,600,000[12]  |

The United States population, by age range in 1969, was divided as follows:[13]

| Under 5      | 18,085,000 |
|--------------|------------|
| Under 21     | 82,400,000 |
| 15–24        | 34,341,000 |
| 65 and older | 19,500,000 |
| Median age   | 27.8       |

For females, the life expectancy at birth in the United States was approximately 74; for males, 67.[14]

The following conclusions may be deduced from the foregoing statistics. The world population is increasing at a rapid rate. Asia is the most highly populated continent. Mainland China and India are the most highly populated nations. And the United States, despite its 19.5 million people who are 65 or older, is basically a nation of young people.

*The Population Explosion.*   Since approximately 1600, the population of the world, with only short-term setbacks, has spiraled upward. Even the

[10] United Nations, *Demographic Yearbook, Annuaire Demographique,* 1967 (New York: United Nations, Nations Unies, 1968), p. 127.
[11] U.S. Bureau of the Census, *Statistical Abstract of the United States,* 1969 (Washington, D.C.: U.S. Government Printing Office, 1970), p. xiii.
[12] Op. cit., p. xiii.
[13] Op. cit., p. xiii.
[14] Op. cit., p. xiv.

current declining birth rate in the United States is merely a slowing of the population upsurge, not a reversal. According to one author, "The population of the world is increasing at the rate of about 180,000 people every 24 hours. In effect, we add enough people each month to make a new city the size of Chicago."[15] As stated by another writer:

> At present rates of population expansion it will take a little over three hundred years for the whole land area of the world to become a single city. It . . . will take seven or eight hundred years before we have standing room only over the whole face of the planet![16]

*Subsistence.* The problems brought on by almost four centuries of population acceleration have been many and serious, including the two important ones of subsistence and overcrowding. Unquestionably, a very important problem is that of subsistence—that is, of feeding the growing world population. The enormity of the problem is capsuled in the May 1967 report of the Panel on the World-Food Supply of President Johnson's Science Advisory Committee. "The scale, severity, and duration of the world food problem are so great that a massive, long-range, innovative effort unprecedented in human history will be required to master it." A statement by the Federal Agriculture Association in 1963 exposes in an even more disturbing way the enormity of the problem. ". . . some 60% of the people in the underdeveloped areas comprising some two thirds of the world's population suffer from undernutrition or malnutrition, or both."[17]

The human tragedy of the situation is that the world food supply, if properly located or distributed, is probably adequate to supply the needs of all people everywhere. But, unfortunately, despite the mammoth grain exports of the United States to needy lands during the past two decades, and the understandably lesser exports of Canada, Australia, and other first-rate but not-so-favored agricultural countries, hunger still stalks the world. In the last analysis, the food problems of the world cannot be solved by a few developed countries indefinitely exporting their food surpluses to underdeveloped lands. Geographical distance, cost, and the ultimate exhaustion of surpluses make this approach impractical. One recommended alternative is for nations with the greatest agricultural know-how to pass that on to potentially productive regions, such as Africa and South America, so that the total food supply can thereby be both increased and located more conveniently throughout the

---

[15] Louise B. Young (Ed.), *Population in Perspective* (New York: Oxford University Press, 1968), p. v.

[16] Boulding, op. cit., pp. 124–125.

[17] Tadd Fisher, "The Many-Faceted Food Problem," *Population Bulletin*, XXIV (December 1968), p. 93. This article I regard as the best on the topic of subsistence that I have seen. I credit Mr. Fisher with many of the ideas contained in this section.

world. A second alternative is for agriculturally favored nations to take steps to make more-or-less barren lands of the world more fertile. With today's scientific knowledge, even deserts are not totally without agricultural possibilities.

The issue of subsistence, as old as man and the world, became a controversial demographic one in the writings of the English clergyman and economist, Thomas Robert Malthus (1776–1834). The Malthusian postulate, a topic of continuous debate since its pronouncement almost two hundred years ago, is this: Man's potential for human reproduction always exceeds the earth's potential for food production. To the extent the postulate is valid, population control of some kind is essential if starvation is not to be mankind's perpetual legacy. Two modern Malthusians are William and Paul Paddock, who depict today's population explosion as a locomotive. With dramatic feeling they write that it is

> roaring straight at us . . . The unmovable landslide across the tracks is the stagnant production of food in the underdeveloped nations, the nations where the population increases are the greatest.
>
> The collision is inevitable. The famines are inevitable.[18]

Non-Malthusians, confident that the agricultural resources of the planet earth are sufficient to feed man for the unforeseeable future—provided man wisely uses the knowledge that he possesses—derive their optimism from the modern miracles of agronomy. These individuals substantiate their position by pointing to the dramatic impact being made by the so-called "Green Revolution" of the day.

The Malthusian postulate unquestionably depresses with its message of pessimism. The polar postulate, however, just as unquestionably disturbs with its possibly unwarranted optimism. A safer position than either extreme conceivably is one in the middle. From it would come the admonition: Continue to rely on the miracles of agronomy for increases, even vast increases, in food production, but at the same time redouble social efforts to control the world's human production.

*Overcrowding.* Inadequate subsistence, although a primary problem of the population explosion, is not the only one. A second important one is overcrowding which is making, with each passing day, increasing inroads on man's privacy. Overcrowding, a mounting threat to nonurban areas, is an acute affliction of urban ones. And because any large city is a microcosm of the world, the blights of one are the blights of the other, multiplied.

Travelers approaching large cities can count on a visual experience guaranteed to be dreary and grim, an olfactory experience guaranteed to be

---

[18] William and Paul Paddock, "Famine—1975!," quoted in Tadd Fisher, op. cit., p. 84.

repugnant even to the less sensitive, and an aural experience guaranteed to be cacophonous. Approaches to cities predictably are pockmarked with railroad tracks, broken-down box cars, unsightly billboards, antiquated commercial establishments, and rickety, unsafe hovels. Travelers who survive this experience sooner or later arrive in the inner city where they are engulfed by a web of towering commercial buildings, railway stations, traffic bumper to bumper, and people elbow to elbow. Then leaving the city for the suburbs, cloverleafs confront them with confusing options, traffic bewilders with its speed or, in case of road repairs or accidents, frustrates with its slowness, and noise once more jars sensibilities.

In his book, *1976: Agenda for Tomorrow*, Stewart Udall, discussing the combined problem of commercialism and overcrowding, zeroes in on "the mess that is man-made America."[19] He exposes the blights of city slums, of asphalt jungles, of architectural uniformity, of public highrisers that will be the superslums of tomorrow. He decries the ratio in American cities of fifty acres allotted for automobile parking to one acre allotted for public parks. And he pleads poingnantly for man to preserve the little bit of countryside that is left him, that "he retain his partnership with nature,"[20] that, above all else, he safeguard the human spirit.

*Reasons for Population Growth.* For almost four centuries, the population of the world has been on an upturn for reasons which include the following. One of the most important resides in the miracles wrought by medical science. Infant mortality has decreased and human longevity has increased with the passage of time. Specifically, medical science has brought under control such age-old killer diseases as small pox, malaria, diphtheria, poliomyelitis, tuberculosis, pneumonia, and others. The net result is more people. A second reason resides in religious belief. The admonition made in Genesis 1:28 "Be fruitful and multiply, and fill the earth" has been taken literally by many individuals and religious groups in the western world. A third reason resides in chauvinism. Until recent times, it was considered patriotic for parents to have large families, particularly if the children were male, as a contribution to the nation's military might. A fourth reason resides in the refusal of formal education, until recently, to get involved in matters of sex education. And a fifth reason resides in the slowness of medicine, until recently, to develop birth-control methods that would be reasonably acceptable to the masses.

*Controls.* Controls over population, like stimulants to it, are also many-faceted. Some reside in the natural order: for instance, uncontrollable dis-

[19] Stewart L. Udall, *1976: Agenda for Tomorrow* (New York: Harcourt, Brace and World, 1968), p. 17.
[20] Op. cit., p. 55.

eases such as cancer and heart disorders; pestilences such as the potato famine in Ireland in the nineteenth century; and holocausts of nature such as the droughts in the United States of the mid-1930's and the disastrous typhoon in Thailand in 1970. Other population controls are political, including war and restraints imposed by nations on food production and food distribution. Selected controls built into the social order include abortions, prostitution, mercy killing, and planned parenthood.

Dramatic advances in science and less dramatic ones in social responsibility have contributed to the population explosion by neutralizing heretofore effective, even though distasteful, population controls—disease and war, for instance. Planned parenthood may well be the only socially acceptable counter to the population explosion. Yet its effectiveness is limited. One reason for the limitation is that most people in underdeveloped countries, and many in developed ones, do not know about it or know too little about it. A second reason resides in the negative attitudes of many throughout the world toward the "pill," which, if it passes the many medical screens to which it is currently being subjected, promises to be the most effective method of population control yet conceived by man. In the words of Montagu, it

> ranks in importance with the discovery of fire, the development of the
> ability to make and employ tools, the evolution of hunting, the invention
> of agriculture, the development of urbanism, of scientific medicine, and
> the release of nuclear energy.[21]

If the pill passes its current tests, it unquestionably has the potential of (1) separating sexual activity for purposes of reproduction from sexual activity for purposes of pleasure, (2) neutralizing, or at least diminishing, the negative by-products of menstruation, and (3) protecting women from premarital pregnancies. The pill, conceivably, also has the potential of (4) diverting the attention of mutually interested couples away from an excessive preoccupation with the physical aspects of love to a balanced preoccupation with both its physical and psychical aspects.

Irrespective of other outcomes, the pill, if used widely and discerningly, is capable of resolving the population crisis of our time, a crisis that is becoming more critical with each passing day. The education of unenlightened nations in the use and effectiveness of the pill constitutes a serious but not an insurmountable task. The social-religious bias of certain cultural groups, however, may well constitute an insurmountable barrier, at least for the immediate future. The issue divides along lines of the following two questions. (1) When couples engage in sexual intercourse, are they divinely committed to accept childbirth as a possible consequence? If they are, the use of contra-

[21] Ashley Montagu, "The Pill and the Sexual Revolution, and the Schools," *Phi Delta Kappan* (May 1968), p. 480.

ceptives is immoral. (2) Or are couples, prior to the act of sexual intercourse, morally justified in using medicinal or mechanical devices to prevent conception?

The Roman Catholic Church has, historically, depicted sexual intercourse as a sacred act, indoctrinating participants with the importance of their accepting childbirth as a divine consequence. At the time of this writing, however, the Church is engaged in a reappraisal of its traditional position. Many within the Church, spearheaded by the younger and more liberal clergy, are speaking out forthrightly in defense of birth control by chemical or mechanical means. One of their theses is that life in an overpopulated world is not life in the true meaning of the term; thus population control, whether by observance of the menstrual cycle, use of contraceptive devices, use of chemical deterrents, or abortion may, in certain instances, be morally justified. Conservatives in the Church, nonetheless, including the older and still influential clergy, continue to be dominant.

I personally take the position that the world's population explosion has to be stopped and turned back some way, somehow. Thus I contend that morality lies on the side of those who are taking reasonable steps to halt population growth and turn it back. Admittedly, however, one man's rationality in respect to this point of view may be another's irrationality.

## Ecological Abuses

Any discussion of demography leads inevitably to a discussion of natural resources; the two, in fact, are functionally inseparable. Man, by the very nature of human existence, has to manipulate his natural environment in order to survive, but when he exploits it carelessly—without regard for long-term consequences, that is—he threatens his survival in the process.

The resources of land and sea have served man from his earliest origins. Plant life kept him alive when he had no other means of subsistence. Later he learned to hunt and fish, thereby broadening his subsistence base. Then, approximately ten thousand years ago, he learned the rudiments of agriculture. And as he became more proficient in agricultural pursuits, he ultimately learned the value of producing food beyond his immediate requirements. The resulting surpluses opened the door to civilization, providing time for the more knowledgeable and creative in advanced cultures to dream dreams, to make inventions, to refine or change political forms, to improve man's physical lot, in general, to make him more happy and more human.

As man's numbers have increased from an estimated 100 million in Christ's time to 3.4 billion today, with 60 billion having inhabited the earth throughout the period of man's life on it, the question of whether man has used, and continues to use, the earth's natural resources wisely is a germane one. The question resists answer apart from a satisfactory definition of the word conservation. Does it imply preservation only of arable soil, precious minerals, drinkable water, and breathable air—requisites of biological survival, that is? Or does it, additionally, imply preservation of esthetic beauty as found in Florida wildlife, Pennsylvania Dutch farms, Hudson River foliage, Indiana sand dunes, West Virginia hills, ocean shorelines, and other objects of beauty such as cathedrals, picturesque homes, covered bridges, and desert expanses? The term, to me, is properly descriptive only when broadly interpreted as in the latter usage.

By whatever definition, conservation is conceding perilously to exploitation, with water, air, and scenic beauty being victimized the most. In respect to water, Lake Erie, for instance, is a dying lake. Peter Schrag graphically tells of its possible death throes in the September 20, 1969 issue of the *Saturday Review*. To think about this dying lake, he writes, is

> to think . . . of all America, of our love-hate relationship with our technology, about our ambivalence about who we are and what we are, about the Hudson and the Missouri, about the Santa Barbara Channel and nuclear bombs . . . about DDT poisoned fish in Michigan—about all the things we value, often in contradiction—in our past and future.[22]

The federal government, says Schrag, has identified 360 sources of industrial waste that daily pours into Lake Erie. The city of Detroit is the worst perpetrator of this crime. Carbon dioxide is depleting oxygen in the lake, carp have replaced walleye and pike, and algae and oil deface the lake's beauty. And, ironically, the daily instances of pollution responsible for these abuses against nature violate the Water Control Act of 1965. Long in coming, it established and commissioned the Federal Water Pollution Control Administration to take action against violators. That the Administration has a gigantic task on its hands is understatement. Actually, it is a task that will be completed only when the country rises militantly against all violators.

Lake Erie's state of putrefaction is matched by the decomposition that characterizes all of our large rivers—the Mississippi, Missouri, and Hudson, as cases in point. And it only slightly exceeds the decomposition that characterizes Lake Michigan. Whether the oceans of the world will escape a similar fate, future generations alone will be able to determine.

If man's efforts to reverse the tide of water pollution are successful, he will still be vulnerable to the lethal effects of air pollution. In the United States in 1970, seventy-six million automobiles traversed approximately four million miles of roadway, helping to consume in the process the more than 3.3 million barrels of crude petroleum produced that year. In the same year, well over four hundred thousand factories combined with the automobile to spew

[22] Peter Schrag, "Life on a Dying Lake," *Saturday Review* (September 20, 1969), p. 19.

enough carbon monoxide into the air to kill, if properly concentrated, all of the country's inhabitants. The stratosphere fortunately absorbed most of the gaseous poison.

Yet in many urban areas, enough remained to make life barely livable for the more fortunate many, and unlivable for an unfortunate few. The mounting incidence of death from respiratory ailments, including emphysema and lung cancer, has to be blamed in great part on air pollution. This conclusion goes relatively uncontested by the medical profession.

An even more ominous outcome, or at least possible outcome, of carbon monoxide pollution is the effect it seems to be having on the earth's atmosphere. In this connection, the scientific community is evidencing increasing concern over the warming trend that during the past several decades has manifested itself in the atmosphere. Whether this actually is a trend or merely a cyclic phenomenon is moot. However, assuming the former, and further assuming the cause to be air pollution in the stratosphere precipitated by gaseous poisons in the earth's atmosphere, the ultimate danger to man is great. Global warming that melted the earth's ice caps and that changed vegetation in a significant way could prove cataclysmic.

Man's concern for his biological survival, important though it understandably is, should not obscure what should be an also important concern for the esthetic aspects of that same environment. Past generations admittedly may have overeulogized the pristine beauty of forest primevals, deep-blue oceans, snowcapped mountain tops, and daffodils. Conversely, however, many of the present generation, having been kept detached from nature's more appealing blandishments, may be unaware not only of their charms but even of their existence. Thus the need of the day is a marriage between the material and esthetic worlds. The two, even though different, are not incompatible. Practically speaking, however, man's esthetic interests are waging no more than a rear guard action against his material ones. Asphalt jungles of cities, receding countrysides, trees and shrubbery sacrificed to industry, and open space consumed by cloverleafs—all witness to the validity of this conclusion. And, ironically, the imbalance is occurring during a period when leisure time is on the increase. Possible antidotes to the imbalance will be a topic of the last chapter.

## War

The demographic threat of our time is of man's so overpopulating the earth that some of his numbers will have to die to enable others to live; or of people having to live so meagerly and incompletely they will exist rather than live. Whether those sacrificed will, in either instance, be victims of man's or nature's inadequacies is immaterial: unnecessary death and apathetic living, irrespective of cause, are unforgivable crimes against humanity. The *ecological* threat of our time is of man's polluting the environment to such an extent that it will become uninhabitable for some, many, or all; or so that it will become less inhabitable for those who live in it than man is capable of making it. And the threat is to man's psychological environment as well as to his physical one. The *war* threat, the third and last topic to be discussed in this section, is of man's exterminating some, many, or even all of his numbers; or of his making the environment for those who survive less livable than it rightfully should be.

War has etched an unforgettable mosaic into history's pages. The mosaic, in retrospect, takes on romantic hues more often than not, depicting noble men performing noble deeds in defense of noble causes. Thus high school youth, generation in and generation out, are exposed, and generally thrill, to the stirring epitaph of Leonidas, the fearless, obedient Spartan who, with 300 of his countrymen, died to save the homeland: "Stranger, go tell the Lacedaemonians that we lie here, obedient to their commands." Once again, many fall prey to the kind of logic expressed in John Davidson's "War Song" that "By war's great sacrifice, the world redeems itself." And who identifies other than pridefully with those heroes of World War II fame "The battered bastards of Bastogne" whose commander, General Anthony McAuliffe, answered "Nuts!" to the Germans' proposal that he surrender his forces.

Yet to many throughout the ages, and to a swelling host today, war is regarded as primitive and inhuman. Cicero decried that "laws are silent in time of war"; Montaigne, that "The clatter of arms drowns the voice of the law." To Dr. Johnson, it also drowned out the voice of truth: "Among the calamities of war may be justly numbered the diminution of the love of truth by the falsehoods which interest dictates and credulity encourages." (The Idler, No. 30). Francis Bacon in *Apothogems* let this coldly simple statement speak for itself: "In peace, the sons bury their fathers and in war the fathers bury their sons." Benjamin Franklin averred flatly that "There never was a good war or a bad peace." And Seneca in *Ad Lucilium* spoke out feelingly that "We are mad, not only individually but nationally. We check manslaughter and isolated murders; but what of war and the much vaunted crime of slaughtering whole peoples?" Attitudes toward war may vary widely from group to group, and from generation to generation, but the statistics of war are pretty much cold fact. The United States has engaged in nine wars: Revolutionary War (1775–1783), War of 1812 (1812–1815), Mexican War (1846–1848), Civil War (1861–1865), Spanish-American War (1898), World War I (1917–1918), World War II (1941–1945), Korean War (1950–1953), and War in Vietnam (dates undeterminable). Active participants of the United States in these nine wars totaled approximately thirty million persons, of whom approximately one million paid with their lives and another

1.5 million suffered wounds which, in technical language of the military, were nonmortal.[23] The greatest number of deaths occurred in World War II (405,399), the Civil War (364,511), and World War I (116,516).

With numbers the criterion, if wartime casualties of United States combatants repel, those of non-United-States personnel should repel even more. In World War II, for instance, "battle deaths" (these represented approximately 55 percent of all deaths of active participants) of United-States personnel totaled 291,557; those of all other national groups, 14,618,865. Comparable statistics in respect to personnel wounded were 670,846 and 25,899,562, respectively.[24]

War is costly in dollars as well as in human life. For the year 1969, the United States, with an income of 201 billion dollars, spent more than 79 billion on defense.[25] This constituted one and one-half times the amount spent by the total population that year on clothing, accessories, and jewelry; well over twice the amount spent for medical services of all kinds; over nine times the amount spent for private education and research; and over ten times the amount spent for religious and welfare purposes.[26]

In *Revelation*, the last book of the *Bible*, Saint John vividly depicts war as one of man's relentless enemies. *Revelation* is an apocalyptic account of the forces of evil matched to the finish against the forces of good. Satan commands the one group; God, the other. Forces of the former are led by the fear-inspiring Four Horsemen of the Apocalypse, colorful symbols of (1) war, (2) man's inhumanity to man, (3) famine, and (4) death. God's legions of righteousness oppose these forces and emerge victorious. John in a mystical way highlighted what countless others have done in a less dramatic way, namely, castigated war as a social scourge.

By any rational standard, war with the toll that it takes of lives and money mirrors grimly but authentically man's inability to live up to his professed values. The blame, in part, rests on the national state with its built-in commitment of defense against outside forces. Ironically, in this connection, the new nations of the world, profiting little from the mistakes of their older counterparts, have tended to think first in terms of national defense before thinking in terms of the economic and psychological needs of their citizens. Yet, because a national state is run by people, blame ultimately falls on man himself, revealing him as a creature unable to get along with his fellow creatures.

[23] Dan Golenpaul (Ed.), *Information Please Almanac, Atlas and Yearbook*, Twenty-Fourth Edition (New York: *Information Please Almanac, Atlas and Yearbook*, 1970), p. 794.
[24] Op. cit., p. 795.
[25] Op. cit., p. 189.
[26] Op. cit., p. 173.

The mental-health implications here are obvious, yet no less complex because obvious. Suffice it to say that antidotes to war reside more in man's psyche than in all the combined treaties entered into by nations throughout civilization's history. Whatever the antidotes may be and wherever they may reside, man, if he is truly civilized, has a mandate to rid himself of the social institution of war. Always horrible, war today is intolerable because it knows no bounds. It is an anachronism that man needs to treat as such or pay the consequences.

## A POINT OF VIEW

Man, indeed, is at the crossroads. He can continue to overpropagate the race and, in the process, make the good life unattainable for any single member of it. He can continue to pollute the environment and, in the process, make it unlivable. And he can continue to wage war on his fellow man and, in the process, destroy himself. Conversely, he can control his numbers, clean up his environment, and put a stop to war. These are man's choices. He will have to live with his responses to them.

# Bibliography

Battle, J. A., *Culture and Education for the Contemporary World.* Columbus: Charles E. Merrill Publishing Company, 1969.

Boulding, Kenneth E., *The Meaning of the Twentieth Century: The Great Transition.* New York: Harper and Row, Publishers, 1964.

Douglas, Paul H., *In Our Time.* New York: Harcourt, Brace and World, 1968.

Harrington, Michael, *The Accidental Century.* New York: The Macmillan Company, 1965.

Harris, Fred R., *Alarms and Hopes, A Personal Journey, A Personal View.* New York: Harper and Row, Publishers, 1968.

Henry, Jules, *Culture Against Man.* New York: Random House, Inc., 1963.

Michael, Donald N., *The Unprepared Society.* New York: Basic Books, Inc., 1968.

Mumford, Lewis, *The Human Prospect*, edited by Harry T. Moore and Karl W. Deutch. Carbondale, Illinois: Southern Illinois University Press, 1955.

Myrdal, Gunnar, *Challenge to Affluence.* New York: Pantheon Books, 1963.

*Population Bulletin*, published monthly by the Population Reference Bureau, Inc., 1755 Massachusetts Ave., N.W., Washington, D.C.

Price, Daniel O. (Ed.), *The 99th Hour: The Population Crisis in the United States.* Chapel Hill: The University of North Carolina Press, 1967.

Raths, Louis E., Merrill Harmin, and Sidney B. Simon, *Values and Teaching.* Columbus: Charles E. Merrill Publishing Company, 1966.

Schrag, Peter, "Life on a Dying Lake," *Saturday Review* (September 20, 1969), pp. 19–21, 55–56.

Stein, Herman D. (Ed.), *Social Theory and Social Invention.* Cleveland: The Press of Case Western Reserve University, 1968.

Theobald, Robert (Ed.), *Social Policies for America in the Seventies: Nine Divergent Views.* Garden City, New York: Doubleday and Company, Inc., 1968.

*Values in Transition*

Udall, Stewart L., *1976: Agenda for Tomorrow*. New York: Harcourt, Brace and World, Inc., 1968.

United Nations, *Demographic Yearbook, Annuaire Demographique*. New York: United Nations, yearly publication.

Young, Louise B. (Ed.), *Population in Perspective*. New York: Oxford University Press, 1968.

Weaver, Thomas and Alvin Maged (Eds.), *Poverty: New Interdisciplinary Perspectives*. Chicago: Science Research Associates, 1969.

# 2

# Traditional Cultural Values

As stated in the previous chapter, values are those determiners that tend to dictate man's choices in life and thus his behavior. A logical question for this chapter then is this: What are the traditional values that, in the western culture, have generally led man throughout his more recent history to make the choices that he has made and to behave as he has behaved? The modifying words, "tend" in the first sentence and "generally" in the second, underscore the truism that man has not always, certainly has not consistently, acted on the values that he has professed to hold. The chapter's discussion thus will reveal man as having gone counter at times, at other times as having conformed, to his verbally announced values. And because values are rarely, if ever, etched simplistically and uncontroversially into a culture, man has, on many occasions, acted of necessity in a state of value conflict or doubt.

In respect to the latter, what value for instance should guide a follower of the Mosaic Law when his father (theoretically to be honored) is an acting-out paranoid (practically to be feared and maybe despised)? Again, what value should guide a Protestant fundamentalist who, faithful to the Genesis story of creation, is suspicious of too much knowledge, but who, in the rationalist tradition, is led to believe that there is scarcely such a thing as too much knowledge? Or, as a third example, what value should guide the growing child who, while being indoctrinated with the sanctity of truth, witnesses a public figure being eulogized for having "lied" his way to a diplomatic victory over a so-called foreign power?

And if values are not consistently clear cut and discrete, man himself is not consistently rational and purposeful. Thus, not his intellect but his emotions—sometimes the more distorted ones—often motivate his behavior.

## SOURCES OF VALUES

The multiplicity of origins of values accounts in great part for the uncertainty of their status. And this status of uncertainty generally is no more or

19

no less multifaceted and complex than any given culture is multifaceted and complex. The values of the western world, particularly those of the United States, have been rooted traditionally in the following miscellany of sources. Each, because elaborated subsequently in the book, will receive only brief treatment here.

## Rationalist Tradition

One source is the tradition of rationalism: a tradition that holds the intellect to be supreme, that posits man to be conscious and discriminating, that remains skeptical before most affective responses.

## Judeo-Christian Ethic

An equally important second source is the collective traditions of Judaism and Christianity. The two converge in depicting man and the universe as endowed with ultimate purpose. The two diverge, however, with Judaism being concerned primarily with law, justice, and obedience; Christianity, with salvation and brotherhood.

## Anglo-Saxon Tradition

The rational and religious traditions join hands with a political one to broaden western man's value base. The political tradition is a potpourri of Anglo-Saxon institutions, beliefs, documents, and practices which extol individualism; which hold liberty and equality to be self evident truths; which advocate faith in the ability, and thus espouse the right, of the masses to govern themselves.

## Pragmatic Faith

Yet a fourth source of western values is the confidence, derived from a growing body of evidence accumulated throughout several centuries, that the combined rational, religious, and political base is a reasonably sound one— or at least a sounder one than the one from which most other geographical or national groups operate. The academic disciplines of the physical sciences and the social sciences lend strong support to this pragmatic faith. However, whether these disciplines merely reflect an entrenched status quo or possess an autonomy of their own is admittedly open to question.

Social happenings of the past several decades, particularly those pertaining to race and the distribution of economic resources, are making the latter question increasingly debatable. At the same time, they are serving to diminish, at least in some part, man's confidence in the inviolability of his long-cherished value base.

## VALUE TENETS

Forming this base are a number of tenets that have been dominant through the ages. A religious and secular admixture, they consist of the following. (1) Life has purpose. (2) Man is rational. (3) The individual is of supreme importance. (4) Material progress is important. (5) Certain basic social institutions are important. (6) Selected other miscellaneous beliefs and attitudes are important.

### Life and Purpose

A question as old as man, certainly as old as civilization, is the one regarding purpose. Does life have purpose, does it lack purpose, or is its purpose so indeterminable as to lie outside the province of rational contemplation and debate? Western man in the composite, although not without frequent and often strident minority opposition, has consistently held that life has purpose. Granted that its meaning might often have been obscure in respect to given events and circumstances, man's faith in it generally remained strong. This faith generally emanated from his belief in a supreme being or in the purposefulness of nature.

Individuals who subscribe to Orthodox Judaism or Christianity accept the reality of a personal God—the God of the Old and New Testaments, a God who is supreme, personal, noncontingent, and directly concerned with, and in, the daily lives and affairs of man. Individuals more liberal in orientation reject the simplicity of this orthodox view of God. Without necessarily rejecting the fact of a personal God, they hedge on the connotation of the word personal. Furthermore, some of them ascribe to nature, its laws, and order many of the attributes customarily ascribed by their orthodox counterparts to a personal God.

Within or without the frame of this oversimplified dichotomy, individuals have conceptualized life and purpose in ways too numerous for other than cursory comment here. Running through all, however, stated or implied, is the conviction that life is meaningful. To the Orthodox Jew, this conviction was manifested in God's leading the Israelites into the promised land. To the late Bishop Oxnam of the Methodist Church, it was manifested in "God's will . . . world law and order, economic justice, and racial brotherhood."[1] To the agnostic or skeptic, it is manifested when natural law operates in a predictable way. To at least one existential psychotherapist, Viktor Frankl, it is manifested whenever a client is able, in his own way, to read meaning into life. Therapy, says Frankl, is concerned

[1] G. Bromley Oxnam, *We Intend to Stay Together* (Chicago: Central Promotional Office of the Methodist Church, 1954), p. 15.

. . . not only with being but also with meaning . . . psychotherapy tries to make the patient aware of what he really longs for in the depth of his self . . . In other words, we have to deepen our patients' self-understanding not only on the subhuman but on the human level as well. The time has come to complement the so-called depth psychology with what one might call height-psychology.[2]

To another current writer, patently Hegelian in orientation, meaning is manifested in man's "faith in process."

. . . the stream of events which forms the substance of history is neither a random sequence nor a providential plan but is the result of process. Men, all organisms, all matter indeed, interact in accordance with laws which are imperfectly known but which are believed to be discoverable and assumed to be constant.[3]

Irrespective of orientation, western man has traditionally assumed life to be meaningful. And when hard pressed to reconcile such apparently contradictory phenomena as earthquakes, floods, famines, pestilences, disease, man's sadism, and death itself, he has fallen back on the explanations previously identified—or an agnostic one. One of the former is that ultimate purpose resides in God or in some natural order of events—a purpose that man, when unable to understand, has to accept by faith. A second explanation is that purpose, built into the natural order of the universe is capable, ultimately, of being understood by man if age in and age out he searches for it diligently. A third explanation is the agnostic one referred to above: Why try to explain the unexplainable? Explanations other than these generally go against the grain of purposefulness itself. A moot question in regard to the three proffered explanations, singly or collectively, is whether they raise more issues than they resolve. Each reader, obviously, has to answer this question for himself.

## Man's Rationality

Incorporated in the position that life is purposeful is the assumption that man is capable of understanding and explaining why, or in what way, it is purposeful. This assumption presumes man to be rational—capable, within given limits, of understanding life's mysteries. Early in the development of civilized man, the concept of rationality evolved into a cult of rationality —which is almost as prestigious today as it ever was. Its members, who are

[2] Viktor E. Frankl, *Psychotherapy and Existentialism* (New York: Simon and Schuster, 1967), pp. 1, 21.

[3] Sir Geoffrey Vickers, *Value Systems and Social Progress* (London: Tavistock Publications, 1968), p. 3.

legion, hold in almost reverential awe the associations evoked by such cognitive substantives as mind, intelligence, knowledge, ideas, reason, contemplation, and assessment and by such cognitive action words as thinking, knowing, reasoning, contemplating, and assessing.

The concept of man as a rational animal has been a topic of unceasing debate through the annals of history. The dialogue has revolved primarily around the relative importance of rationality instead of around the question of whether it is important. Most, conceding it a place of eminence, have assumed one of the following positions in regard to it: (1) that it holds a place of exclusive importance (a monistic stand), (2) that it shares a place of mutual importance with the soul (a dualistic stand), (3) that it shares a place of mutual importance with the body including affective components (also a dualistic stand), or (4) that it shares a place of mutual importance with both the soul and the body including affective components (a pluralistic stand).

In the province of philosophical traditions, each of the four positions has had many supporters. In the province of the Judeo-Christian tradition, the dualistic position has been the dominant one. In it, man, as part of a supernatural order, is depicted as a child of God—a soul committed, as a result, to obey rather than to reason. At the same time, man, as part of the natural order, is depicted as a creature of reason, committed, as a result, to reflect on life along its many dimensions. In the Judeo-Christian tradition, the emotions are depicted as subservient to reason. The first prong of the dualism is Hebraic in origin; the second, Grecian. The latter took on increased importance in the Middle Ages with the discovery in the Moslem world, around 1200, of some of Aristotle's lost manuscripts. These made the rationalist position much more substantial.

The Biblical admonition to man, generally, is to think reflectively (to reason, that is) within the prescribed bounds of absolute truth, divinely determined, but not to question absolute truth itself. However, the many problems raised by the controversial terms "absolute truth" and "divinely determined," have made this admonition overly simplistic, and thus unpalatable, to an increasing number of thinking people. These individuals, rejecting the symbolic interpretation of why Adam and Eve were expelled from the Garden of Eden, namely, for aspiring to "too much" knowledge, hold that there is no such thing as too much knowledge—provided it is "true," not spurious, knowledge. Relatedly, they hold that man's spectrum of contemplation should have no limits.

In the province of secular traditions, the phenomenon of reason has historically had a status of unparalleled eminence. Sense empiricism, its closest rival, has generally played a secondary role. In this connection, Plato in "Theaetelus" conceived one of Reason's primary roles to be that of assessing the validity of sense experience. To Aristotle, the *summa bonum* of existence was the contemplative life—the life of reason. Throughout history, individuals of diverse orientations such as St. Augustine, Thomas Aquinas, Francis Bacon, John Locke, Emmanuel Kant, Herbert Spencer, William James, Bertrand Russell, John Dewey, and George Santayana, just to name a few, probed reason both as a concept and as a process—and extolled its virtues. And, today, the rationalist tradition is very much alive, thanks to the support given it by such moderns as Jacques Barzun, Julian Huxley, Jacques Maritain, Mortimer Adler, Robert Maynard Hutchins, and James Bryant Conant.

Few would deny that the mind of man, his knowledge, his powers of reason, all combine to make him unique in the animal kingdom. These attributes have enabled him to peer more deeply into, and thus understand with greater clarity, many otherwise impenetrable mysteries of the universe. These attributes have endowed him with the wheel, the horse collar, printing, a comprehensive knowledge of nuclear physics, and modern technology. These have also, at least in part, given him access to the art of a Michelangelo, the music of a Beethoven, the literature of a Shakespeare. They have enabled him to perpetuate the cumulative knowledge of the ages. Their worth, awesome in scope, is beyond the power of human beings to assess.

Yet the rationalist position is vulnerable when overstated and unduly esteemed. It is one thing, for instance, for anyone to accord rationality a place of high status; another thing for him to accord it exalted status. Relatedly, it is one thing to hold all affective responses suspect; another thing to hold only the distorted and pathological affective responses suspect. If Marshall McLuhan[4] has overstated the case for the emotions, as I believe that he has, members ad infinitum of the rationalist school have, for centuries, overstated the case for reason. My contention is that reason and the emotions are interrelated, not discrete, entities—a point of view espoused by most biologists and psychologists of the present day. This is an organismic position which holds that the many systems of the human body—nervous, metabolic, digestive, reproductive, skeletal, cardio-vascular, respiratory, and endocrine—are interrelated and interdependent. Man so viewed does not have a mind or an intellect that functions discretely. Neither does he have emotions that function independently. Rather he has a mind and emotions that function interdependently with the other systems of the human body.

The rationalist position, vulnerable when overstated, is even more vulnerable when claiming reason to be the exclusive, or nearly exclusive, property of the intellectually favored; not at all, or very little, the property of the nonintellectually favored. Plato was guilty of such polarization when setting the philosopher apart from the less favored soldier and the unfavored slave.

[4] A good overview of McLuhan and McLuhanism may be found in Raymond Rosenthal (Ed.), *McLuhan: Pro and Con* (New York: Funk and Wagnalls, 1968).

Conant today, at least by inference, may also be guilty of such polarization: he virtually ignores the less talented 85% (an arbitrary figure) of most high school populations in his seemingly myopic preoccupation with the 15% who are, at least by comparison, more talented.[5]

The intent here is not to deprecate cognitive processes but to give them proper perspective. The Biblical adage, "Ye shall know the truth and the truth shall set you free" is no less majestic for reason of its mental-health implications. Truth, for instance, when filtered through the unhealthy emotions of disturbed individuals becomes untruth—for neurotics see not *what is* but *what they need to see*. The plea thus is for the society to assess values in a balanced way, endowing reason with the importance it justifiably deserves but refusing it exclusive billing.

With Ducasse, we

> regard the cognitive powers of man, his emotional capacities, his impulses and volitional capacities, his physical powers, his need of capacity for membership in a society, and so on, as so many aspects and dimensions of his nature. . . . They are present in different proportions in different men, and in some men a particular one of these ingredients . . . may come to occupy a ruling position. . . . But they remain parts of him nonetheless—parts which have a role to play in the total economy of his life.[6]

## Individualism

These many aspects and dimensions of man's nature, commented on by Ducasse, highlight the concept of man's individualism. And the latter, although a less venerable concept than reason, is an equally important and germane one. The thesis of humanism is that human nature is important. The thesis of individualism is that individual man per se is important: that the end of man on this earth is individual man.

The concept of individualism has roots in a number of cultural sources. One, as would be expected, is religion. Judaism and Christianity espouse it even though framing it in a context of eschatology and brotherhood. But the *Old* and *New Testament* portray God as having a one-to-one relationship with each of his children. And the *New Testament,* in particular, depicts God as agonizing over a lost human soul the way a shepherd might agonize over a lost sheep of his flock. Man is told that the very hairs of his head are numbered. And in Matthew 25, Christ informs him "As you did it [gave sus-

---

[5] James B. Conant, *The American High School Today* (New York: McGraw-Hill Book Company, 1959), pp. 57–64.
[6] C. J. Ducasse "What Can Philosophy Contribute to Educational Theory?" in *Harvard Review* XXVIII (Fall 1958), p. 290.

tenance] to one of the least of these my brethren, you did it to me." The *Bible*, indeed, dignifies individual man throughout.

A second source of individualism is Anglo-Saxon political traditions. Anglo-Saxon man, long subjugated by the heavy hand of absolute monarchs and lesser despots, ultimately struggled through to partial or total victory over them. The *Magna Carta* of 1215 stands as one of his early victories. The Bill of Rights of 1689 stands as a later one. Both became intrinsic parts of our own political institutions, documents, and traditions. And all combine to espouse the cause of individualism.

A third source of individualism is a hard core of political-philosophical documents. Some of these throughout the seventeenth, eighteenth, and nineteenth centuries made particularly significant impacts on individualism. Most were mirrors of existing or idealized political arrangements; a few, conceivably, were precipitators of political change. Irrespective of the status and impact of the treatises, the influence of the following ones on individualism continue in one way or another to be felt today. (1) Thomas Hobbes' *Leviathan*, 1651. This, primarily of historical significance, advocates the sacrifice of some of man's individualism for the good of the social group. Interestingly, Hobbes depicted a monarchial political arrangement as superior to an aristocratic or a democratic one. (2) John Locke's *Of Civil Government: The Second Treatise*, 1690. The theme of this work is that all men in their original state of nature were free and equal; that because they suffered socially for reason of their excessive individualism, they created a civil society; that they had the right to dissolve the society anytime that it turned against them. (3) Jean Jacques Rosseau's *The Social Contract*, 1762. The thesis of this work is that governments should come into being via social contracts, which are the products of individuals combining their wills into a collective or general will. This latter, endowed with sovereign status, has an inherent obligation to serve its constituents. The ideal government should be an elected body which, combined with the electorate, should be small enough to guarantee close and constant interaction between voters and leaders. (4) John Stuart Mill's *Essay in Liberty*, 1859. The central theme of this essay is that the only legitimate restriction on individual freedom exists in the rights and privileges of others. Within this single delimitation, individual men can unite around common causes, believe as they wish, speak as they wish, and indulge their tastes as they wish.

A fourth source of individualism resides in the life style developed by our early forefathers as they departed their homelands, founded a new land, stood up to its rugged challenges, and survived—often only by grace of nearly superhuman effort. And because many of these challenges pitted individual man against man or individual man against nature, rugged individualism took on unique status in the early days of our nation. It is a status that has diminished only slowly with the passage of time. Today's society may not have a Daniel Boone, an Andrew Jackson, a George Rogers Clark, or a Bill Cody to perpetuate the mystique of rugged individualism, but the mystique nonetheless is present. The reason probably resides in the psychological process of identification—a process that enables the average or below-average person to stand, in the manner of Walter Mitty, a bit taller when identifying vicariously with real or synthetic model figures of superior stature and prowess.

The assumption of individualism, whatever its sources and dimensions, is that individual man, because he is man, has inherent worth and thus merits both internal and external recognition and respect. In western civilization this assumption early took on the status of tenet or truism. And as an adulterated value it goes almost without question. By the term adulterated, we have in mind the change that takes place in the concept when it is juxtaposed against social practicalities. Individualism is one thing when Robinson Crusoe, except for his man Friday, stands alone and heroic beholden to no one. It is another thing when any of the two billion adults alive today has to define his identity in a social milieu. Faced with this challenge, without downgrading his self-worth or abdicating his individual rights, he has to adulterate his individualism so as to accommodate it to the worth and rights of others.

Thus individualism that passes the social test emerges as freedom within limits—as indicated in the first of the following two quotations; and freedom with a built-in social commitment—as indicated in the second of the two quotations.

Needless to say, the freedom of a finite being such as man is a freedom within limits. Man is not free from conditions, be they biological or psychological or sociological in nature. But he is, and always remains, free to take a stand toward the conditions.[7]

Freedom without moral commitment is aimless and promptly self-destructive. It is an ironic fact that as individuals in our society have moved toward conformity in their outward behavior, they have moved away from any sense of deeply-shared purposes. We must restore in both a vigorous sense of individuality and a sense of shared purposes.[8]

Freedom without limits and without moral commitment—unadulterated freedom, that is—is ominous in its possibilities for harm to mankind. In our free-enterprise economy of the nineteenth and early twentieth centuries, with

[7] Viktor E. Frankl, op. cit., p. 3.
[8] John W. Gardner, "The Ideal of Individual Fulfillment" in *The Education of Modern Man*, edited by Margaret M. Starkey (New York: Pitman Publishing Corporation, 1966), p. 183.

the doctrine of laissez-faire prevailing, individualism knew few bounds. As a result, power became the possession of an exclusive elite, prominent within which were such names as Ford, Rockefeller, Harriman, Morganthau, Morgan, Gould, Hearst, Duke, and Dodge. These and other entrepreneurs, including their families, literally controlled the country's financial and industrial, and, to a lesser degree, the country's political establishment. The private entrepreneurs of a past day have given way to the large corporate structures of today. These are financed both by affluent industrialists, many of whom are the entrepreneurs of yesterday, and by stockholders, who may or may not be affluent. The issue posed by these individual and organizational monoliths is whether freedom that is the disproportionate possession of a few is not freedom that is too little the possession of the many. If so, we have an instance of individualism operating outside the frame of defensible moral commitment.[9]

In a free-enterprise economy, individualism *without any* limits unquestionably implies at least a theoretical possibility of one person's controlling a large part of, or even the entire, economy of a country. In such an instance, he would actually control the country. Conversely, the same state of affairs implies the dubious possibility of a few or many of a given country's inhabitants living in a substandard way, or even dying, for lack of the minimum essentials of existence. Individualism *with too few limits* constitutes a major reason why more than two billion persons of the world's almost three and a half billion are hungry or starving, naked or poorly clothed, dying or preventably diseased, completely without shelter or inadequately housed. It is also a major reason why from twenty-five to thirty million of the inhabitants of the United States live a marginal economic existence.

Individualism, as will be developed in various settings throughout the book, is a combined religious-philosophical, humanistic, economic, political concept. As a religious-philosophical concept, it generally holds man to be important and commits him, in various ways, to arrive at his own value decisions. As a humanistic concept, it holds man to be important because he is man. As an economic concept, it generally stands in defense of a laissez-faire economy. As a political concept, it justifies the defense of individual man against the tyranny of centralized governmental power.

---

[9] This topic of the power elite and *who* runs *what* in the country is interestingly developed in the following important publications. E. Digby Baltzell, *Philadelphia Gentleman* (Glencoe, Illinois: The Free Press, 1958). Robert A. Dahl, *Who Governs?* (New Haven: Yale University Press, 1961). G. William Domhoff, *Who Rules America?* (Englewood Cliffs, New Jersey: Prentice Hall, Inc., 1967). Robert L. Heilbronner, *The Making of Economic Society*, 2nd ed. (Englewood Cliffs, New Jersey: Prentice Hall, Inc., 1968). Charles W. Mills, *The Power Elite* (New York: Oxford University Press, 1956). Talcott Parson, *Structure and Process in Modern Societies* (New York: The Free Press, 1960). Frank Tannebaum, *The Balance of Power in Society and Other Essays* (New York: The Macmillan Company, 1969).

Individualism unquestionably is a relative term and thus in need of careful definition whenever used. To me, it implies the intrinsic human worth of an individual; his right to live, and his obligation to help others live, adequately and decently; and his obligation to make and live with his decisions.

Individualism in today's world is becoming increasingly threatened by the adversaries of size, technology, and the many direct invaders of privacy. Size, the first of these threats, is almost too obvious to require comment, impinging as it does on the world of work, the nation's population, and its social problems. Detachment is a frequent product of size, and futility a product of detachment.

Technology, the second threat, has literally revolutionized business, industry, the military complex, and thus the lives of all people, because all people are affected by it. Technology, which is science applied, manifests itself across almost the entire spectrum of today's world. Its heritage to man includes industrial machines, production lines, airplanes swifter than sound, electronic computers, complex communications systems, lethal weapons of war, and an understanding of the universe unsurpassed in history.

To people who conceive of individualism as a contingent value that differs when viewed, for instance, in the context of a colonial town meeting, a western frontier society, or today's world, size and technology unquestionably constitute a serious threat to it. To those, however, who, like myself, conceive individualism to have properties which rise above context, the threat loses much of its seriousness. To me, individualism is a phenomenon of the psyche, its axis being the self-worth of a person. In this connection, I contend that because individualism is basically a product of personal and small-group influences experienced in a home, a school, and a local community, it is not as vulnerable, as many appear to think, to the forces that emanate from the complex society of the day. Although conceding that individualism is more difficult for anyone to achieve in a massive, technologically oriented society, I hold that it can rise above this obstacle.

The third threat to individualism resides in the growing practice of personal spying, a topic accorded widespread visibility in, among other sources, Vance Packard's *The Naked Society*, 1964. This practice of prying into another's private affairs has assumed in recent years the dimensions of big business, including in its operational personnel thousands of so-called investigators. According to Packard, the government alone employs, for purposes other than espionage, more than 25,000 of these investigators.[10] This total swells to even more alarming proportions when agents of the currently maligned military intelligence service, of unions, of business and industrial concerns, and of illicit underground organizations are included. And if

[10] Vance Packard, *The Naked Society* (New York: David McKay and Company, 1964), p. 5.

investigators themselves are numerous, the investigated are vastly more so. In this connection, Packard estimates that a single agency, the House Un-American Activities Committee, has "a card file of more than a million names."[11]

The dubious profession of personal spying casts its shadow over people of diverse walks and personalities. It includes in one category applicants for important positions in business and industry who lose much of their privacy in the process of their credentials being assessed. At the conclusion of an investigation, their potential employers know the nature of their organizational memberships, their political preferences, religious affiliations, social-drinking habits, gambling proclivities, sexual deviations, if any, from social norms, marital relationship, and financial status—these and others.

The profession of spying casts its influence over yet a second category of persons, namely, public servants, at such times as, in the opinion of some, their private lives need exposure. Teachers constitute a third category—and so on. Private and public investigators, broadening the scope of their operations by the year, are placing the personal rights of the country's citizens in increasing jeopardy, and thus are diluting individualism itself. And when electronic eyes, ears, and taped memories are parts of the investigations, concern understandably mounts. The issue of whether investigations that extend beyond generally accepted observational methods constitute both ethical and legal violations of personal privacy is undergoing heated debate today. I personally believe that they are.

## Materialistic Concerns

Western man's long espoused convictions that life has purpose, that reason should be a controlling guide of behavior, and that individuals, by definition, are important are framed in the tradition of idealism. A fourth conviction, namely, that material things have great worth, stands restively alongside the other three, very much outside the frame of idealism. Whatever the basis of justification, western man has, throughout his history, traditionally, and quite often paradoxically, accorded high esteem to material possessions— money, property, and heirship. And in according such esteem he has lent credence to the assumption that people of more material worth are also people of more intrinsic worth.

Thus man is trapped in a value paradox and a resulting behavior paradox as well. While espousing ideal values, he worships material ones. And, ironically, while the *economic haves* proclaim that life has purpose, the *economic have-nots* are often too hungry, or too cold, or too diseased to perceive it. Again, while the *haves* proclaim that all individuals are important, the *have-*

[11] Op. cit., p. 8.

*nots* realize full well that when material wealth is the criterion they are not important at all. To paraphrase a popular adage, if all people are equal, some are more economically equal than others. Faced with this conflict between value tenet and reality, western man has almost habitually looked to free will for explanation. The gist of the argument is that the masses, because possessed of the power of will, are capable of rising above their squalor. That this argument ignores the countervailing influences of biological and environmental determinism is obvious to a growing number today. Thus a case that might have been convincing when framed in a Puritan context of a century or more ago loses much of its validity when framed in a context of modern-day genetics, sociology, and dynamic psychiatry. Because this topic of materialism will be the central theme of Chapter 3, we pursue it no further here.

## Esteemed Social Institutions

Traditionally, the four institutions of family, church, school, and state have constituted the organizational hard core of western civilization's values. The family, since the end of the colonial period, has led the list, intimately related as it has consistently been with the cherished value of individualism. The family's central position in Roman Catholic dogma generally strengthened its claim to top position during this period. The church throughout colonial days assumed priority over the family in institutional importance, then lost some ground in the eighteenth and nineteenth centuries, and has lost even more ground recently. Today, it is reacting uncertainly to the combined assault continuing to be made on it by biological evolution, dynamic psychology (or psychiatry), and time, space and ideational relativity. The school has maintained a position of solid institutional stability throughout most of our country's history. Its stability, however, is being threatened today by student-activist groups.

In western civilization, the influence of the political state on man's values has varied greatly from period to period during the past several centuries. Absolute monarchies of the Middle Ages and early modern era subtly advanced the cause of individualism by breeding a hatred of authoritarianism. In the Anglo-Saxon countries, parliamentary arrangements, from the seventeenth century on, generally fluctuated from more to less centralized power depending on the social pressures of the time. Our own country, on becoming sovereign, reacted against its unsavory past experiences with authoritarian rule by militantly espousing the cause of individualism. In the opinion of many, it overplayed this role a number of times throughout its history leading often to individualism detached from social commitment.

A major issue of the present day is whether the people of the United States want their federal government to play a relatively strong or weak role in human affairs. When playing the former, as it did during the Kennedy and Johnson administrations, in matters, for instance, of race and education, the federal government interpreted and implemented the concept of individualism and individual rights more from a national than from a regional perspective. When playing a weaker role, as it has been doing during the Nixon administration, the federal government has tended to interpret and implement the concept of individualism and individual rights relatively less from a national and more from a regional perspective. A stronger federal role is generally played when the country has reached a reasonable consensus in respect to what a hard core of human rights should be. The reverse is true when the country is ambivalent about what the hard core should be. Our basic documents and the social tenor of the times are, in my opinion, definitely supportive of the first of these two approaches. The choice, once more in my opinion, is individualism for all versus individualism for just the favored. And even most who pay lip service to the slogan "The less government the better" are in favor of a government strong enough to guarantee the basic rights of all the citizens it serves.

We note in passing here that the best adjusted, most smoothly operating societies of the world seem to be those in which the four institutions of family, church, school, and state work in reasonable harmony. This outcome presupposes that the majority in those societies have somewhat similar values and aspirations. Russia is having problems today because the state, with only minority support (1 in 10 in Russia is a card-carrying Communist), has superimposed itself on the majority, and because the church has been crowded to the background. The United States is experiencing a problem today, although not yet a major one, because the family is in retreat and the schools are unable or unwilling to take up the slack.

## A Value Miscellany

To this point in the chapter, we have developed the tenets, supported by tradition, that life has purpose, man is rational, the individual has supreme worth, material things are important, and four social institutions are basic. At this point we freewheel a bit, identifying and briefly developing selected miscellaneous values, attitudes, and beliefs that have been, and that continue to be, parts of the fabric of our culture.

*The Golden Rule.* One of these values is the so-called Golden Rule of Matthew 7:12, one of several highlights of Christ's Sermon on the Mount. "So whatever you wish that men would do to you, do so to them; for this is the law and the prophets." This aphorism, unquestionably, is one of the gem's in western man's lexicon of values.

*Status of Authority.* The thesis that constituted authority is good and thus merits respect from those over whom it is exercised is yet another intrinsic part of our value code. Constituted authority is generally viewed as including parents, teachers, and some governmental agencies. The accordance of respect to parents finds its primary sanction in the fifth Commandment of Exodus 20:12—"Honor thy father and thy mother that thy days may be long upon the land which the Lord thy God gaveth thee." The accordance of respect to authority figures other than parents find sanction in Mosaic Law, political traditions, an extensive body of social theory, and empiricism.

A topic of continuing debate throughout man's history is whether institutionalized authority, irrespective of its nature and behavior, is automatically deserving of respect. Is a sadistic parent? A termagant teacher? An over zealous club-wielding police officer? A corrupt judge? And if these are not deserving of, and, as a result, do not receive, respect, what recourse does an offender have who is punished for withholding it. For civil offenses in authoritarian societies, he has no recourse. He has recourse in democratic societies through the courts, through public protest, and through the communications media. Certain radical activists today are electing the recourse of anarchy. The issue is one of deciding whether to attempt change within or outside the frame of the existing political "establishment." Those who elect recourse outside such a frame are not without precedent, our own Revolutionary War being one of many cases in point. Such an election, however, is always a radical one; thus should be made, most would contend, only after lesser attempts at redress have failed. This topic will be developed in greater detail in Chapter 7.

*Chauvinism.* A specific concept subsumed by the broader one of obedience to authority is chauvinism. It received its name from Nicolas Chauvin who fought and died militantly, bravely, and with fanatical zeal in the imperial cause of Napoleon Bonaparte. By definition, chauvinism is fanatical patriotism, unreasoning devotion to one's native land. In our own country, although still a respected value to many, it is less so today than historically.

Literature, classical and modern, is replete with references to it. Homer's eulogy of chauvinism stands as a classical precedent for the myriad of others that followed:

> A glorious death is his
> Who for his country falls (Iliad XV)

In most of our nation's schools, chauvinism has been a fixed curriculum star for almost two centuries. Rare, in fact, is the school that has not emotionalized over Nathan Hale's presumably authentic line: "I only regret that I have but one life to lose for my country." Rare, also, is the student who has not, at some time, memorized that part of Scott's *Lay of the Last Minstrel* which opens with:

> Breathes there the man, with soul so dead,
> Who never to himself hath said,
> This is my own, my native land.

During the past half century, the disillusionment resulting from four bloody wars has dulled much of Chauvinism's luster. Ernest Hemingway's cynical quotation from *Notes on the Next War* is illustrative:

> They wrote in the old days that it is sweet and fitting to die for one's country. But in modern war there is nothing sweet nor fitting in your dying. You will die like a dog for no good reason.

George Bernard Shaw's equally cynical passage from O'Flaherty V.C. is also illustrative: "You'll never have a quiet world til you knock patriotism out of the human race."

Anyone taking a stand on chauvinism should first have taken a stand on nationalism, the polar choices being these: nationalism viewed (1) as a purely organizational arrangement designed to expedite the management of social affairs or (2) as an esoteric arrangement designed to create within each separate group a mystique of superiority, thus setting it apart from other groups. Chauvinists, taking the second of these two stands, enshroud nationalism with an aura of sanctity. Nonchauvinists, taking the first of the two stands, perceive nationalism in a commonsense frame, viewing it as a means to given social ends. Nor should it be assumed that such individuals are not patriotic—because they may well be—in fact, generally are. However, they are patriotic within the bounds of rationality, very much conscious of the dangers inherent in blind patriotism, of man's long history of inhuman acts performed under its mistaken guise.

*Communism as an Evil.* Chauvinism which, in a direct way, accords love of country a place of supremacy in our nation's value system implies, in an indirect way, that other countries, particularly competitive ones, are inimical or, at best, should rarely be above suspicion. And because love of country implies supremacy of the social forms inherent in it, a skeptical attitude toward the differing social forms of other nations is generally a sequel. For approximately three decades, the Soviet Union as a country, and communism as a political creed and form, have been objects of opprobrium in our own country. And chauvinism, admittedly, is only one reason for the negativism. Other more important reasons consist of these substantive ones: communism's rejection of individualism, its philosophical grounding in materialism, its international bellicosity and, in general, its very real threat to the values and life style of the Western World.

Whatever the reasons, distrust of communism is a very real part of the fabric of our country's values. Nor is this state of affairs all good or all bad. Distrust may be justified when individuals make themselves well-informed about the dogma and practices of communism before assuming a position in regard to them. It can not be justified when individuals, devoid of, or with too little, knowledge and understanding, introject an inflexible position in regard to communism's dogma and practices.

Communism unquestionably is a reality of gigantic proportions. It controls approximately one billion of the world's inhabitants despite its limited card-carrying membership of not more than (and this is only a rough estimate) 30 to 35 million persons. Its creed emanates from two basic works: one by Karl Marx and Friedrich Engels, *Manifesto of the Communist Party;* the other by Karl Marx, *Capital.* My point of view in regard to communism is that it should be approached not on an all-or-none basis. The late senator Joseph McCarthy approached it in exactly this way and made the fifties frenetic as a result. The counter approach recommended here is for people to study it discriminately, understand it, and only then reject it in part or in toto or accept that part of it that can be defended. This, in my opinion, is the approach of the mature assessor of life's values.[12]

*Independence as a Controversial Value.* Such an approach, however, presupposes a high level of independence on the part of the person doing the assessing. And this leads into the fundamental question of what value status independence has in our way of life. Anything resembling a complete answer to this question appears one way when practice is the criterion, a different way when theory is the criterion.

In respect to practice, our culture generally rewards conformity more highly than it does independence. As indicated earlier in the chapter, constituted authority and authority figures have long occupied places of eminence in our culture; thus it follows that independence occupies a place of lesser eminence. Parents in their relationships with children, public officials in their relationships with fellow citizens, and business and industrial leaders in their relationships with subordinates—all hold the trait of conformity in high esteem.

In the world of business and industry, the increasingly accepted stereotype of the man on his way up is found in the following profile. He is an organization man first and foremost: loyal to the company and its management, an open advocate of company policy and procedures, and only mildly critical, if critical at all, of even obvious managerial misjudgments.[13] His personal

---

[12] I have elaborated the theme of communism in *The Emergent in Curriculum* (New York: John Wiley and Sons, Inc., 1966), Chapter 13.

[13] The organization-man stereotype received widespread visibility in William H. Whyte, Jr., *The Organization Man* (New York: Simon and Schuster, 1956).

values are consistently subordinated to company values. In effect, he is inconspicuous in his grey-flannel suit, unobnoxious in personality (until status allows him to become obnoxious), other-directed, and thus eligible for promotion. The amount of exaggeration in this profile is a matter of purely personal opinion.

In the world of formal education, despite protests to the contrary, rote learning has much more respectability than teachers will admit. Repetitive responses are more popular than creative ones. And independence truly worthy of the name tends to run headon into adult resistance.

Juxtaposed against these and other instances that might have been cited of conformity in practice is a body of theory that lauds independence of thought and action. The concept of individualism is part of that body. The concept of man's rationality is yet another part. So too is reflective thinking, a term more or less interchangeable with the kindred terms critical thinking and the scientific method.

Thus the society lives with the paradox of independence sanctioned in theory but resisted in practice. One reason for the paradox is that independence makes more demands on a culture than does conformity: the former is more unpredictable, more demanding of the time and energies of authority figures, and more threatening to fixed social patterns. Yet a culture begins to die when it becomes impervious to change—a product that independence alone can bring about. Because positive change seems to be the order of the day, I am personally convinced that independence in our culture is on the upswing.

## Sex Attitudes

The phenomenon of sex, including the many attitudes and values subsumed by it, constitutes the topic of this last section of the present chapter. The products of sex are an open book: (1) 204 million people in the United States, (2) the population upturn which started in 1942 to continue through the decade of the 1970's, (3) a declining birthrate since 1957 which today averages out to just slightly more than two children per couple, (4) a pill and abortion laws that are revolutionizing sexual behavior, (5) approximately 92 percent of all people in the United States currently or previously married, (6) a ratio of 100 girls aged 18–22 to 91 boys aged 20–24, and (7) a doubling of the divorce rate during the past 50 years. And these are but a selected few of the phenomena pertaining to sex that might have been presented.

The emphasis of this section, however, is not on the statistics of sex but on the values that people place on it. The early Greeks were quite casual about it, regarding it as merely one of the many basic life processes. Plato, in the

*Republic,* stated matter of factly that "There is no greater nor keener pleasure than that of bodily love—and none which is more irrational." Judaism within the frame of a complex body of rituals was quite forthright about it. New Testament writers projected sex into a religious setting. Mark's preachment "What therefore God hath joined together let not man put asunder" still constitutes a part of many, if not most, marriage ceremonies today. Paul was the most ascetic of all the New Testament writers in regard to sex, viewing it as competing with the "Lord's work" for the time and energies of man. Thus he gave this memorable bit of advice to the Church at Corinth:

> To the unmarried and the widows I say that it is well for them to remain single as I do. But if they cannot exercise control, they should marry. For it is better to marry than to burn.

In our present-day society, the primary issues in regard to sex are these: (1) Is sex a procreational activity, a recreational activity, or both? (2) Whatever its nature, to what extent should it be experienced outside the institution of marriage? In respect to the first of the two questions, the position taken by our culture, at least until recently, was that sex is primarily a procreational activity, only secondarily a recreational one—and only then to men, not to women. In fact, women who overtly enjoyed the intimacies of sexual activity were viewed traditionally as loose and wanton.

In regard to the second of the two questions, the traditional position taken has been that sexual activity that goes as far as intercourse is proper only when sanctioned by marriage. This position is defended by some on moral and religious grounds; by others, on practical grounds, centered in the question of who will (should) bear responsibility for the offspring which ensue from a given sexual union.

The advent of the pill requires no change of attitude on the part of those who defend premarital abstinence on moral and religious grounds. But it definitely makes for a change on the part of those who defend premarital abstinence on purely practical grounds. To at least many of these latter, the only legitimate controls over premarital intercourse consist of freedom from guilt and respect for the other person. As stated by Bertrand Russell in *Marriage and Morals* XI,

> Morality in sexual relations, when it is free from superstition, consists essentially of respect for the other person, and unwillingness to use that person solely as a means of personal gratification, without regard to his or her desires.

With little doubt, a significant change in sex values is taking place in today's society. And the direction of change is toward a liberalization of attitudes. Whether the change merits the designation of sex revolution is, however, debatable. We know that a militant number of the young are rebelling actively against the traditional sex code that, to them, bears the earmarks of hypocrisy and rigidity more than it does demonstrable workability. We know, also, that many, if not most, of the older generation continue to support, or at least to give lip service to, the traditional code.

The traditional code is vulnerable in that it denies sexual activity to late adolescents and young adults during a growth period when physical capacities and desires are at a peak. The resulting stresses in certain individuals border, at times, on the unendurable. However, no significant change can take place in the code until the society transports sex from its traditionally familiar moral-spiritual setting to a more natural one. In the latter setting, sensitivity toward a given sex partner and prevention of unwarranted childbirth would be the controlling factors. Psychological and social maturity would constitute the first control; birth preventatives, the second. What is needed to resolve the sex controversy is the perspective of time—a perspective that only a generation that has lived a decade or two with the newer conceptualizations in regard to sex and the newer methods of birth control can have.

# Bibliography

Allport, Gordon W., Philip E. Vernon, and Gardner Lindzey, *Study of Values.* Boston: Houghton Mifflin Company, 1960.

Bull, Norman J., *Moral Judgment from Childhood to Adolescence.* Beverly Hills, California: Sage Publications, 1970.

Clough, Shepard B., *Basic Values of Western Civilization.* New York: Columbia University Press, 1960.

Commoner, Barry, *Science and Survival.* New York: Viking Press, 1966.

Cornuelle, Richard C., *Reclaiming the American Dream.* New York: Random House, 1965.

Fromm, Erich, *Escape from Freedom.* New York: Avon Books, 1964.

Greeley, Andrew M., *The Hesitant Pilgrim: American Catholicism After the Council.* Garden City, New York: Image Books, 1969.

Halsey, Margaret, *The Pseudo Ethic.* New York: Simon and Schuster, 1963.

MacIver, R. M. (Ed.), *Great Moral Dilemmas in Literature, Past and Present.* New York: Harper and Row, 1956.

May, Rollo, *Psychology and the Human Dilemma.* Princeton: D. Van Nostrand Company, Inc., 1967.

Montagu, Ashley, *Helping Children Develop Moral Values.* Chicago: Science Research Associates, 1953.

Packard, Vance, *The Naked Society.* New York: David McKay and Company, Inc., 1964.

Starkey, Margaret M. (Ed.), *The Education of Modern Man.* New York: Pitman Publishing Corporation, 1966.

Vickers, Sir Geoffrey, *Value Systems and Social Process.* London: Tavistock Publications, 1968.

Waltzer, Michael, "Puritanism as a Revolutionary Ideology" in Barry McLaughlin, *Studies in Social Movements.* New York: The Free Press, 1969, pp. 118–154.

Whyte, William H. Jr., *The Organization Man.* New York: Simon and Schuster, 1956.

# 3

# Economic Values

In Chapter 2, it was argued that the values of our society constitute a paradoxical potpourri of the ideal and the practical. In respect to the first of these, the culture holds life up as purposeful, man as rational, the individual as supremely important, and the institutions of the family, church, and state as fundamental. In respect to the second, the culture holds the material things of life up as significantly worthy. Interestingly, few in the society are cognizant of the paradox, and even fewer are bothered by it. We comment in passing that man's tendency to compartmentalize life and live unperturbed by its contradictions is a civilization-old phenomenon. Irrespective of this issue, the purpose of the present chapter is to expose for scrutiny the country's economic system and its attendant values.

At this point in the discussion, we pause to define the axial term economics. Heilbroner suggests that "In its simplest terms, economics is the study of how man earns his daily bread."[1] And, he continues, man historically has earned his bread under one of three systems: the decentralized system of the family or clan, the centralized "command" system wherein a ruling force of some kind gives the orders, and the marketplace system. In the words of another economist,

> Economics is concerned with the activities of man in supplying his wants. Jobs, prices, production, distribution, consumption, buying, and selling are all, therefore, the subject matter of the discipline.[2]

The spectrum of economics is, unquestionably, broad, embracing a body of content that in part is discrete, that in other part is shared with a variety of other disciplines and social forces. To Gunnar Myrdal, economic problems

[1] Robert L. Heilbroner, *The Making of Economic Society*, second edition (Englewood Cliffs, New Jersey: Prentice Hall, Inc., 1968), p. 2.
[2] Don Paarlberg, *Great Myths of Economics* (New York: The New American Library, 1968), p. 3.

40

are at one and the same time moral ones involving human decency, moral living, Puritan ideas, poverty in the midst of affluence, and high-pressure advertising.[3] To Leon Keyserling, economic problems are inseparable from human sensitivities and values.[4] To the archconservative Friedman, economic problems become political by governmental interference with them.[5] The spectrum of economics can scarcely be other than broad, including, as it does, such complex phenomena or processes as demand, production, distribution, consumption, labor, finance, and the management arrangements that all of these entail.

## SELECTED STATISTICS

The following miscellany of facts and figures about the nation's economic establishment tells an interesting story. It is a story about the most affluent social group in the world whose Gross National Product rose to an incredible 900+ billion dollars in 1969.[6] This amount, with the 1954 dollar value used as the computational base, represented an increase of 400 percent over the G.N.P. of 1929. The G.N.P. derives from the following formula: Total consumption goods + Domestic and foreign investments + Governmental expenditures on goods and services.[7]

Other indicators of the nation's affluence include these. The United States, with about 6 percent of the world's population, controls nearly 50 percent of its wealth. Of its population of 204 million, approximately 80 million are employed. In 1969, the median family income per year was approximately $8500. Personal savings exceed 60 billion dollars yearly, we produce far more than we can eat, we produce one-fourth of the world's petroleum, and 60 percent of all dwelling units are inhabited by their owners.

## POVERTY AMIDST PLENTY

In this majority culture of plenty, there exists, however, a minority subculture of poverty, the magnitude of which, although only approximately known, is considerable. Most recent estimates place it at about 30 million

[3] Gunnar Myrdal, *Challenge to Affluence* (New York: Pantheon Books, 1963), p. 7.
[4] Leon H. Keyserling, "The Problem of Problems: Economic Growth" in Robert Theobald (Ed.), *Social Policies for America in the Seventies: Nine Divergent Views* (Garden City, New York: Doubleday and Company, Inc., 1968), p. 6.
[5] Milton Friedman, *Capitalism and Freedom* (Chicago: The University of Chicago Press, 1962), pp. 16, 28.
[6] Dan Golenpaul (Ed.), *Information Please Almanac, 1970* (New York: Information Please Almanac, Atlas and Yearbook, 1970), p. 172.
[7] Paul A. Samuelson, *Economics, An Introductory Analysis*, seventh edition (New York: McGraw-Hill Book Company, Inc., 1967), p. 178.

people, the most fortunate of whom, if part of a family of four, share an income of $4000, the least fortunate of whom share, on the same basis, an income of $2000 or less.

A variety of categories and types makes up this subculture. Ethnically, it includes a significantly greater proportion of nonwhites than whites. Vocationally, it includes the majority of the 5 to 6 percent of the nation's population who, in 1971, were unemployed. Educationally, it includes individuals who dropped out of school early—as early as legally permissible in many instances. The following table reveals the close relationship that exists between these two factors of income and formal education.

TABLE 3-1

| Years of Formal Education | Annual Median Income 1966, of Males 25 Years and Older |
|---|---|
| Less than 8 years | $ 3,520 |
| Elementary-school graduate | 4,867 |
| 9 to 11 years | 6,294 |
| High-school graduate | 7,494 |
| 13 to 15 years | 8,783 |
| College graduate | 11,135 |
| 17 years or more | 12,563 |

*Source.* Kenneth A. Simon and W. Vance Grant, Digest of Educational Statistics, OE-10024-69 (Washington, D.C.: U.S. Department of Health, Education and Welfare, 1970), p. 13.

Geographically, the miscellany includes people from the Appalachian Mountains of the east to the fruit orchards of California, from the wastelands of the Dakotas to the bayous of Louisiana. Genetically, it includes people whose parents were, more likely than not, also members of the subculture.

The tenacity of poverty is, in fact, one of its most insidious characteristics. As stated in one of the Council of Economic Advisers' several reports to President Johnson,

Poverty breeds poverty. . . . A poor individual or family has a high probability of staying poor. Low incomes carry with them high risks of illness; limitations on mobility; and limited access to education, information, and training. Poor parents cannot give their children the opportunities for better health and education needed to improve their lot. Lack of motivation, hope, and incentive is a more subtle but no less powerful barrier than lack of financial means. Thus the cruel legacy of poverty is passed from parents to children.[8]

George Bernard Shaw in *Major Barbara* capsuled with biting realism England's attitudes toward, and treatment of, the poor—which, at least in certain instances, are no different from our own. If a man is poor, said Shaw,

Let nothing be done for . . . [him] : Let him be poor. . . .

Now what does this Let Him Be Poor mean? It means let him be weak. Let him be ignorant. Let him become a nucleus of disease. Let him be a standing exhibition and example of ugliness and dirt. Let him have rickety children. . . . Let his habitations turn our cities into poisonous congeries of slums. . . . Let the undeserving become still less deserving.

Michael Harrington, writing in a political vein, is no less caustic.

The nation's spokesmen proclaim that they seek only to abolish war, hunger and ignorance in the world and then follow practices that make the rich richer and the poor poorer, and incite the globe to violence. The Government says that it will conduct an unconditional war on poverty and three years later announces that life in the slums has become worse. And supposedly practical people propose that the country make a social revolution but without the inconvenience of changing any basic institutions.[9]

Poverty in the United States has a history that goes back to the time of the earliest settlers, some of whom were rich, others poor. Policies of open immigration perpetuated the tradition of an economic mix. And the "devil" of individualism condoned inaction without guilt by the affluent when they were confronted with the problems and needs of the poor. The logic supporting this inactivity was that the poor, because they were lazy freeloaders, did not merit outside help. Not until the Great Depression of 1929, which lasted more than a decade, did the country take poverty seriously. The stock market crash, the closing of banks, the evaporation of fortunes overnight, the loss or freezing of the "little man's" savings, unemployment that affected one worker in four —these and related events led not only to deep despair but to a new sensitivity to the plight of the poor. This sensitivity found expression in the New Deal program of Presidents Roosevelt and Truman, the Great Frontier program

[8] Sargent Shriver, "Poverty" in Thomas E. Linton and Jack L. Nelson (Eds.), *Patterns of Power: Social Foundations of Education* (New York: Pitman Publishing Corporation, 1968), p. 110.
[9] Michael Harrington, *Toward a Democratic Left* (New York: The Macmillan Company, 1967), p. 1.

of President Kennedy, and the Great Society program of President Johnson.

Yet despite these and the less dramatic, or, at least, less publicized welfare programs of President Eisenhower's and President Nixon's administrations, poverty still constitutes a way of life for millions in the country. We grant that the poor, collectively, are not as poor as their counterparts were during the Great Depression, or even twenty years ago—for their economic status, on an absolute basis, has improved through the years, albeit painfully slowly. Nonetheless, three facts of economic life stand out. One is that millions in the United States are, at best, living marginal existences: they remain alive but become increasingly less than human from bearing the cumulative burden of poverty. A second fact of economic life is that people in greater numbers than most are willing to admit are actually dying from lack of adequate food and medical care. A third fact is that the status, relative or absolute, of the very affluent changes little from year to year. This allegation will be supported in some detail later in the chapter.

The elimination of the subculture of poverty in our country would, unquestionably, be a costly venture. Heilbroner, in 1966, placed the cost at 10 to 12 billion dollars;[10] Keyserling, in 1967, placed it at 11 to 13 billion dollars.[11] If these estimates are reasonably accurate, another billion or so would need to be added today to offset the recent inflationary spiral. Such a total output would, in the opinion of Heilbroner, add $1000 to the tax burden of the person with an income of $16,000, and proportionate amounts to the tax burdens of persons with greater or lesser incomes. Yet if the elimination of poverty significantly increased employment and, conversely, significantly lowered welfare expenditures, immediate debits would in the future turn into sizeable credits. This is the deduction made several years ago by A. Philip Randolph when he was chairman of the White House Conference on Civil Rights. He concluded

> that if the Administration would make a serious effort to end poverty, the resultant full employment would add between $2.3 and $2.4 trillion dollars to the G.N.P. to what it would be if the 1965 rate prevailed over the next decade.[12]

The status of poverty in the United States is essentially this. Its existence is an unquestioned reality. Most, however, who know about it know about it only academically; few are acquainted with it from first-hand experience. During the greater part of the past half century, the society, possessed of the means to eliminate it, has elected instead merely to ameliorate it.

From the foregoing status picture, the following principle emerges—and it

[10] Robert L. Heilbroner, "The Future of Capitalism" in *Commentary* (April 1966), p. 26.
[11] Leon Keyserling, in Theobold, op. cit., p. 21.
[12] Quoted in Michael Harrington, *Toward a Democratic Left*, op. cit., p. 135.

has moral as well as economic overtones. *The principle is that our culture places a higher value on materialism than it does on humanism.* While paying lip service to the "good life for all" concept, it refuses to pay the cost required to bring it about. The country's position in respect to this principle— whether to continue paying allegiance to it or to change stance in regard to it—will have consequences that reach far into the future.

## THREE ECONOMIC ERAS

The United States has passed through two economic periods and is living in a third, each of which has conditioned its values in a significant way. The basic economic conceptualizations of each of these three periods, along with their practical impact on the society, constitute the subject matter of this section.

### Laissez Faire Period

The year 1776 commemorated the publication of two political-literary treatises that in different ways made deep and abiding impressions on the Anglo-Saxon world. One was *The Declaration of Independence*, which set a new political course for the fledgling American nation. The second was Adam Smith's *Wealth of Nations*, which set an economic course for both Britain and the Colonies. The central theme of the treatise was that in a market economy, private effort leads, in an almost one-to-one ratio, to public welfare; that the public sector profits most when individuals serve their self-interests. In the words of the document itself,

> Every individual endeavors to employ his capital so that its produce may be of greatest value. He generally neither intends to promote the public interest, nor knows how much he is promoting it. He intends only his own security, his own gain. And he is in this led by an invisible hand to promote an end which was no part of his intention. By pursuing his own interest he frequently promotes that of society more effectually than when he really intends to promote it.

The *Wealth of Nations* ushered in the so-called laissez faire period, which lasted in Great Britain until the Great Factory Acts of the 1830s and 1840s, and in the United States until near the end of the nineteenth century. During this period, the role assigned to government was to interfere little, if at all, in economic affairs. In the words of Jeremy Bentham, English philosopher and political scientist, the government was to "Be quiet." Conversely, the role of the private economic sector was to "Be active"—by formulating and enforcing policies in respect to rules of competition, conditions of labor, prices of commodities, and related economic issues. Competition's only major limits in the laissez faire economy were preservation of private property and freedom of contract.[13]

The laissez faire economic arrangement was tailor-made for the Puritan-oriented society of the time. It had its center in individualism, encouraged industriousness, justified private wealth on semiphilanthropic grounds, and assuaged guilt about poverty by attributing the latter to disinterest and sloth. Nor is laissez faireism completely dead today: its impact has only lessened. Government interference is still regarded by many as a necessary evil. Most people tend to oppose it unless they themselves are direct beneficiaries of it.

Yet because of government's failure to interfere in the business affairs of the nation during the laissez faire period, which lasted until around 1890, the democratic system itself became threatened. The reason resided in the growing concentration of too much economic power in the hands of too few. Power, we note in passing, is the capacity of a person or group to achieve its intentions.[14] It is that social force in life that enables men who have it to impose their wills on others who either do not have it or have too little of it.

The laissez faire economy of the nineteenth century bred the giant entrepreneurs of industry—John D. Rockefeller, Sr., J. P. Morgan, Andrew Carnegie, and Andrew Mellon, for instance. At the century's end, a small group of individuals were on the verge of achieving, or actually had achieved, monopolistic control over important aspects of the nation's economy. The immediate victims were the masses of have-nots in the country. The ultimate victim, conceivably, might have been the country itself. The government took action, however, as we shall soon see, to dull at least some of the excesses of economic power. Whether the action was too little and too late has been a topic of controversy ever since.

## Government Intervention Period

Late in the nineteenth century, the laissez faire period eased into the government intervention period. The move was away from economic individualism unlimited (or almost so) toward economic individualism selectively policed by the central government. Thomas Jefferson, in effect, was conceding to Alexander Hamilton.

The landmark that denoted the end of the one era and the beginning of the other was the Sherman Antitrust Act of 1890. Its target was monopolies in

---

[13] Lord Franks, "The Evolution of Twentieth-Century Capitalism" in National Industrial Conference Board, *The Future of Capitalism* (New York: The Macmillan Company, 1967), p. 9. I credit Lord Franks for much of the content of this section.

[14] Melvin Tumin, "Captives, Consensus and Conflict: Implications for New Roles in Social Change" in Herman D. Stein (Ed.), *Social Theory and Social Invention* (Cleveland: The Press of Case Western University, 1968), p. 95.

general and monopolistic restraints of trade in particular. The fact that the act for several decades served as an instrument of harassment to labor unions detracts little from the historical impact it had on the nation.

In the new era, the federal government, on many fronts, intervened selectively to prevent privileged individuals and organized groups from unduly imposing their wills on their less privileged counterparts. The government, for instance, intervened to protect unions from management by enacting the Clayton Antitrust Act of 1914, the Railway Labor Act of 1926, and the Norris-LaGuardia Act of 1932. Then it moved to protect management from labor by passing the Taft-Hartley (Labor-Management Relations) Act of 1947. It intervened against poverty via the welfare legislation of Franklin D. Roosevelt's administration, the Social Security Act of 1935 being particularly noteworthy. During the 1930s and 1940s, it moved in a number of legislative instances against unfair employment practices. None of the acts would, in all probability, have been passed if the laissez faire era had not undergone modification.

## Government Management Period

The second economic era merged into the third one in the middle 1940's. This third era has been one in which the federal government has assumed responsibility for safeguarding the economy as a whole. The government compiles economic statistics to guide efforts aimed at preventing seriously debilitating periods of recession and inflation. It controls balance of payments and establishes needed floors or ceilings for prices, income, and interest rates. The Employment Act of 1946, which brought into being the Council of Economic Advisers in the executive office, is generally credited as ushering in this third economic era. President Kennedy's intervention in the steel disputes of 1962 and the tax cuts of 1964 designed to stimulate the nation's economy are instances of specific government intervention in behalf of the economy as a whole. So too were Phases I and II, so-called, initiated and implemented by the Nixon administration.

We hasten to interpolate here that the government management period has nothing to do with socialism. The distinction is one between government *surveillance* and general *superintendence,* on the one hand, and government *ownership* of sources of supply and means of production, on the other. The role of government in this third period is definitely not to own but to oversee, definitely not to control in a highly systematic way but to intervene, as required, in a highly selective way.

Governmental power has increased in part, as hitherto indicated, in response to the monopolistic potentials inherent in big business. It has also increased, however, in response to the mounting complexity of life itself manifested in such phenomena as the Great Depression, the corporate business structure, the scientific estate, technology, urban decay, population growth, environmental pollution, depletion of natural resources, and the social revolution. These are phenomena that the total society in great part through its central government is increasingly having to face. Gone, probably forever, are the "good old days" of weak government, simplistic living, and rugged economic individualism with every man a potential king. And, if the truth were known, the days were probably not that "good," weak government was not very effective, living, if simple, was also arduous, and many people were paupers, few were kings.

This flight into subjectivity leads to the following value judgment. *The American culture, because it has no other choice, is becoming increasingly receptive to the reality of a strong central government as the best answer to the complex economic problems of the day.* The choice, admittedly, is grudging, enamored as the culture is of rugged economic individualism. The above value statement, to the extent it is factual, causes distress in the ranks of such conservative economists as Milton Friedman, F. A. Hayek, and Frank Tannebaum who are basically laissez faire theorists at heart.[15]

## FREE ENTERPRISE PRINCIPLES

The purpose of this section is to identify and briefly elaborate the principles (or values) basic to any traditional capitalistic economic system. These have discrete status because of their historical and operational significance. They have contingent status because of the light they shed on the theme of the next section, which is the corporate economic structure. A certain amount of duplication is inevitable here, but we shall hold it to a minimum.

### Private Ownership

The principle of private ownership is intrinsic to the system of free enterprise. Most tangible property (land, factories, office buildings, equipment, and goods) and most intangible property (stocks, bonds, savings, and so forth) are owned directly by some individual or some collective body of individuals. The exception is government-owned property which constitutes a minority part of the total property owned in the country. In our economy, a title of ownership guarantees its legal possessor the right, within limits, to

15 Milton Friedman, *Capitalism and Freedom* (Chicago: The University of Chicago Press, 1962) ; F. A. Hayek, *The Road to Serfdom* (Chicago: The University of Chicago Press, 1944) ; and Frank Tannebaum, *The Balance of Power in Society and Other Essays* (New York: The Macmillan Company, 1969).

use the property as he sees fit, to receive legal protection against would-be dispossessors, to earn profits from it, and to sell or give it away. Traditionally, an owner had the right, implied or stated, to protect his property, by force if necessary, against invaders. Today that right is conceding gradually to the concept of human rights before property rights. Thus, for instance, a house owner who, unthreatened, shoots a fleeing burglar may conceivably be held criminally liable for that act.

## Production for Profit

The right of individuals, singly or collectively, to produce goods for personal profit is a second principle inherent in the system of free enterprise. Whether the source of production is land, technology, capital, or labor is immaterial. Every bit as important as the principle per se is its antithesis, namely, that social utility does not have to be the motivating force behind production and management.

## Competition

The free enterprise system is a competitive one. Producers compete against other producers on two fronts. One is the retail market which merchandises the thousands of wares purchased by individuals day in and day out in their normal course of living. The other is the wholesale market which is a veritable hotbed of competition among retail firms for goods, equipment, methods of production, and labor.

Imbedded in the phenomenon of marketplace competition is the assumption that material things are of greater importance than the sensitivities of people, profit than quality of product, and winning than the methods employed to win. Within the letter of the law, few holds need to be barred—so the operational thesis goes. It is in this arena of competition that free enterprise practices conflict most noticeably with such cherished cultural ideals as cooperation, brotherhood, and altruism. This constitutes further proof, then, of the validity of the assertion made earlier in the chapter that our culture places a higher premium on material things than it does on human values.

## Uneven Distribution of Economic Resources

The three previously discussed principles—private ownership, production for profit, and competition—lead logically into this fourth principle, namely, that it is legitimate for the economic wealth of the nation to be unevenly distributed, even to a point of distortion, among the population. The economic have-nots were the center of attention in the first part of the chapter. The affluent, or the so-called power elite, constitute the center here. In the middle are the masses of middle class humanity who live comfortably but not sumptuously, save a little out of their paychecks without ever amassing more than a modest estate, climb the ladder of upward mobility when opportunity beckons, live life with at least a modicum of confidence, and face the future with reasonable assurance. On a comparative basis, members of the middle class in the United States are better off economically than any comparable group in the world.

So too, on both absolute and comparative grounds, are the nation's power elite. These are the possessors of great wealth in the country, the shapers of the nation's economic affairs, and the direct or indirect shapers of social and political decisions.

The phenomenon of social stratification elicits the following realistic appraisal from Mills, an early apostle of the New Left.

> The top of modern American society is increasingly unified, and often seems wilfully coordinated. At the top there has emerged an elite of power. The middle levels are a drifting set of stalemated, balancing forces; the middle does not link the bottom with the top. The bottom of this society is politically fragmented, and even, as a passive fact, increasingly powerless; at the bottom there is emerging a mass society.[16]

The power elite in our society have been objects of increasing study during the past several decades. Mills categorizes them as "simply those who have the most of what there is to have . . . money, power, and prestige—as well as the ways of life to which these lead."[17] Wealth is their most dominant characteristic. By general consensus, John D. Rockefeller topped their list in 1900, Henry Ford in 1925, and H. L. Hunt and Hugh Roy Cullen at midcentury. In the opinion of at least some, Howard Hughes tops the list today.

As will be developed in the next section, the power elite, although owning much of the wealth of the country, do not manage it. Thus they probably are somewhat less powerful today than they were in the days of precorporate capitalism. Yet ownership by its very nature breeds a certain amount of control, and the latter, in turn, breeds power. Thus even though the very affluent may have lost a little of their power during the past few decades, who can doubt the economic influence of, as just one example, the Andrew Mellon complex that controls the Mellon National Bank, Gulf Oil Company, Westinghouse Electric, Aluminum Corporation of America, and a number of lesser industries?[18]

[16] Charles Wright Mills, *The Power Elite* (New York: Oxford University Press, 1956), p. 324.

[17] Ibid., p. 9.

[18] G. William Domhoff, *Who Rules America?* (Englewood Cliffs, New Jersey: Prentice Hall, Inc., 1967), p. 49.

The majority of the power elite—approximately seven in ten—come from upper (or upper-upper) middle class homes. Only the occasional one in ten, in the manner of the Horatio Alger hero of bygone years, has risen from the ranks of the lowly. Most, Jews and Irish Catholics often excepted, are listed in the Social Register, which contains the names of 108,000 individuals and 38,000 families. Most attended private schools and universities. Most belong to exclusive private social clubs. Most engage in extensive charity work. Most are conservative in respect to social and political issues.[19] And most of their daughters make debuts into society. The latter, says Cleveland Amory, is a nineteenth century word in a twentieth century world.[20]

The elitist structure of economic power is a tremendous force in our culture, and one that strongly resists social change. In this connection, Heilbroner, in a thought-provoking article of several years ago, poses the questions: What elements constitute the hard core of capitalism? What are the irreducible limits from which it will not retreat? He concludes that the limits are threefold: (1) production for profit, (2) private ownership, and (3) capitalism as a system of privilege. The concept of privilege, he says, is so ingrained in capitalism that the two are inseparable.[21] A frequently offered defense of privilege is that by playing the role of forward-looking pioneer, it clears the path of opportunity for the less privileged who follow in its wake. This is the position of Hayek who holds that economic inequality on the part of the few ultimately opens the door of promise for the many.[22] Nor is this position necessarily specious when it avoids extremes. In the latter instance, the issue is not one of privilege versus nonprivilege, but of what the reasonable limits of privilege should be. If these limits are so wide as to permit the unprivileged to become dehumanized, the system has to be faulted on humanistic grounds. If they are kept flexible enough to guarantee for all the essentials of humanity, the system cannot be as seriously faulted, if even faulted at all.

## THE CORPORATE STRUCTURE

To this point in the chapter, the country's economic system has been presented as a mixed arrangement, grounded in individual initiative but dependent on the services of government to protect against monopolistic control and cyclic economic upsets. Under this system, equilibrium—which exists when production, labor, income, consumption, and investments are in

19 Ibid., pp. 13–28.
20 Cleveland Amory, *Who Killed Society?* (New York: Harper and Row, Publishers, 1960), p. 11.
21 Robert L. Heilbroner, "The Future of Capitalism," op. cit., pp. 23–25.
22 Frederich A. Hayek, *Road to Serfdom*, op. cit., pp. 43–45.

proper balance—is the desired ultimate outcome. At this juncture, the chapter's focus shifts to the corporate structure of the economy.

## Definitions

We open the discussion with a few selected definitions. A *corporation* "is an association of persons into an autonomous legal unit with a distinct legal personality that enables it to carry on business, own property, and contract debts."[23] In a corporate structure, then, power resides not directly in persons but in a legal unit. General Motors, Montgomery Ward, and Jewel Tea Company are, for instance, three such legal units. And each is one of only a few corporations that manufacture and sell their respective products; thus, each, in business parlance, is known as part of an *oligopoly*—a term denoting only a few sellers. *Monopoly* which, as previously indicated, is even more restrictive denotes only one seller. Its kindred term, *monosopony*, denotes only one buyer.

## Giant Corporations

In 1968, the 10 largest industrial corporations, in order of size, consisted of General Motors, Standard Oil (New Jersey), Ford Motor, General Electric, Chrysler, International Business Machines, Mobil Oil, Texaco, Gulf Oil, and U.S. Steel. The range of their sales was from $22.75 billion to $4.5 billion, and of their assets, from $14 billion to $6.4 billion. Their combined assets totaled $86 billion. The 5 largest commercial banks were Bank of America, First National City Bank, Chase Manhattan Bank, Manufacturers Hanover Trust, and Morgan Guaranty Trust. The range of their assets was from $26.6 billion to $9.3 billion. Their combined assets totaled $83.1 billion. The 5 largest utilities were American Telephone and Telegraph, Consolidated Edison (New York), Pacific Gas and Electric, Southern California Edison, and Commonwealth Edison (Chicago). The range of their assets was from $40.1 billion to $2.6 billion. Their combined assets totaled $53.1 billion. And the 5 largest insurance companies were Prudential, Metropolitan, Equitable Life, New York Life, and John Hancock Mutual. The range of their assets was from $26.6 billion to $9.3 billion. Their combined assets totaled $85.4 billion.[24] The composite assets of these 25 giant corporations totaled $307.5 billion in 1968—an incredible sum, to say the least.

Our economic system is one of collective capitalism. It is a system of domination by corporations, particularly by the very large corporations. In

[23] Harry G. Guthmann and Herbert E. Dougall, *Corporation Financial Policy* (Englewood Cliffs, New Jersey: Prentice Hall, Inc., 1948), p. 9.

[24] Dan Golenpaul (Ed.), *Information Please Almanac: Atlas and Yearbook, 1970* (New York: Information Please Almanac, 1970), p. 183.

1962, according to a government source, 500 of the largest corporations controlled over two-thirds of all manufacturing assets.[25] In 1960, four corporations carried on 22 percent of all the industrial research and development contracted for that year.[26] And in 1965, "three industrial corporations, General Motors, Standard Oil of New Jersey, and Ford Motor Company, had more gross income than all of the farms in the country."[27] As stated by Mills,

> The economy—once a great scatter of small productive units in autonomous balance—has become dominated by two or three hundred giant corporations . . . which together hold the key to economic decisions.[28]

### Corporation Ownership and Management

Ownership of the country's corporations resides in two categories of persons: (1) affluent individuals and families who own controlling blocks of stock in the larger corporations, and (2) less affluent or nonaffluent stockholders who own noncontrolling blocks in the larger corporations, but who sometimes own controlling blocks in the smaller ones. In the affluent category are descendants and families of many of the entrepreneurs of yesteryear—Rockefeller, Ford, and Morgan, for instance.

In fact, the most affluent two percent of the nation's families own from two-thirds to three-fourths of all corporate stocks.[29]

It is management, however, not ownership, that makes corporations unique today. Until slightly more than a half century or so ago, these two functions —ownership and management—tended to reside in the same individuals. The corporation was an exclusive instrument of its owners, the lengthened shadow of their personalities, the projection of their values and life styles. Henry Ford, for instance, not only *owned* Ford Motor Company, he *was* Ford Motor Company, and he ran the show his own way. This is not to say that the company was not staffed with reasonably capable second and third level personnel, for it generally was. But it is to say that all major decisions, and even many minor ones, emanated from the person of Henry Ford himself. Such a unitary arrangement was possible because of the simplicity of the

25 Hearings before the Subcommittee on Antitrust and Monopoly of the Committee of the Judiciary, U.S. Senate, Eighty Eighth Congress (1964), p. 113 (Cited in Galbraith, p. 75, see Footnote 26).
26 Hearings before the Subcommittee on Antitrust and Monopoly of the Committee of the Judiciary, U.S. Senate, Eighty Ninth Congress (1965), pp. 1139–1140 (Cited in Galbraith, see Footnote 27, p. 15).
27 John Kenneth Galbraith, *The New Industrial State* (Boston: Houghton Mifflin Company, 1967), pp. 75–76.
28 Charles Wright Mills, *The Power Elite*, op. cit., p. 57.
29 Robert L. Heilbroner, "The Future of Capitalism," op. cit., p. 26.

Model T Ford, which, in turn, reflected the simplicity that characterized the planning, manufacturing, promotion, and selling phases of the operation.

As technology increased in complexity, so too did the requirements of management. The result was that owners ultimately had to choose between continuing to manage what would soon become failing enterprises, or delegating to more qualified individuals their erstwhile managerial responsibilities. Most, because their business empires, and thus their fortunes, were at stake, elected the second option. This shift in power from entrepreneur owners to specialist managers was a *major* breakthrough in the nation's economic order. Historically, power resided in land. Next it shifted to capital. For a half century, now, it has resided—if not exclusively, at least more than ever before —in the collective intelligence of management. And, as stated by John Galbraith,

> This shift in power has been disguised because, as was once true of land, the position of capital is imagined to be immutable. . . . It [power] has not passed to labor . . . [for] the latter still tends to abundance.
>
> Power has, in fact, passed to what anyone in search of novelty might be justified in calling a new factor of production. This is the association of men of diverse technical knowledge, experience, or other talent which modern technology and planning require. It extends from the leadership of the modern industrial enterprise down to just short of the labor force. . . .[30]

The need for sophisticated managerial know-how in business and industry derives from the following three sources. One, as previously indicated, is the *technological demands of modern industry* which are increasing in complexity almost by the day. These run the spectrum of the pure sciences of physics, chemistry, biology, and metallurgy; and the applied sciences of engineering, quality control, production management, labor relations, finance, advertising, and sales.

A second source is the *demands placed on management in the area of corporate planning*. In the not too complicated world of the nineteenth and early twentieth centuries, planning for a future product—whether a crop by a farmer, a die by an engineer, a bookkeeping system by an accountant, or a layout by a production manager—was a relatively simple matter. The lapse of time between planning and production was rarely extensive, and the monetary cost was generally not excessive. Galbraith reveals, for instance, that the manufacturing plant of the Ford Motor Company was completed on

[30] John Kenneth Galbraith, *The New Industrial State*, op. cit., pp. 58–59. I found this entire book to be highly informative, and lucid. It is very worthwhile, even though heavy reading.

June 16, 1903, and the first car reached the buying market in October of that same year. This outcome was achieved by a work force of 125 men employed by a firm with an authorized capital of $150,000. Such a phenomenon would be impossible in the 1970s, for planning today is a complex and expensive process. The Mustang, in contrast to the Model T Ford, required three and a half years of production time before it reached the buying market. Furthermore,

> Engineering and "styling" costs were nine million dollars; the cost of tooling up for the production of the Mustang was fifty million dollars. In 1964, employment in the Ford Motor Company averaged 317,000. Assets were approximately six billion dollars.[31]

A third reason why management is an increasingly important commodity in business and industry resides in the process of coordination. With planning and production customarily dependent on the knowledge of many specialists who vary widely in orientation and skills, their efforts need to be carefully integrated if the finished product is to be successful. Management constitutes the catalyst of this coordination process.

## Size and Power of Corporations

The increase, during the twentieth century, in the size of individual corporations and of the corporate structure as a whole has been nothing short of phenomenal. Nor has the increase been an unmixed blessing. On the positive side of the social ledger, size in many, if not in most, instances has resulted in greater efficiency on the part of management and lower costs to the consumer. Few would doubt, for instance, that the typical housewife pays much less proportionately for a better product when buying today at the Great Atlantic and Pacific Tea Company (the largest grocery chain with sales of five and a half billion dollars annually) than her counterpart did when buying in 1900 at the privately owned grocery store "down the street." And the husband of this typical housewife who bemoans not being able to "own my own business" because the "big guys would only crowd me out" is generally better off today, at least financially, when working for big business than his counterpart was in 1900 when working for himself.

On the negative side of the ledger, corporate size has, undoubtedly, narrowed the range of ownership possibilities for the individual. Furthermore, it has narrowed the limits of his control over what is to be produced and what the immediate and ultimate social consequences of its production will be. Individual man, for example, may want an exhaust-free automobile, and

---

[31] Ibid., pp. 11–12.

science knows how to produce it, but he will not get it until corporate power, with or without government pressure, creates it.

Also on the negative side is the control that large corporations are increasingly exercising, directly or indirectly, over sources of supply, pricing, and competition. The logic of this phenomenon is understandable: If Ford Motor Company is to invest fifty to sixty million dollars in planning and tooling for a product such as the Mustang, it must have reasonable guarantee in advance that steel and labor, for instance, will be available when needed. Relatedly, it must have assurance in advance that no big rival such as General Motors or Chrysler will preempt its resources. The logic of corporate control, however, is offset in great part by its monopolistic dangers.

Control is a function of organizational size, commodity diversification, reciprocity among large firms, and government cooperation. The first of these, organizational size, gives the large corporation certain market advantages not possessed by its smaller rivals. Volume buying per se gives a large corporation priority status—and thus a disproportionate amount of market power. Furthermore, a large corporation, if dissatisfied with conditions surrounding a given source of supply, can often, because of its size, develop and thus control its own source of supply. The second control, commodity diversification, easily leads to organizational conglomerates which carry in their wake the unsavory possibility of monopolistic control. If Corporation X, for instance, operates several large coal mines, a hydroelectric plant, a steel manufacturing firm, a leather processing outlet, a rubber processing firm, and a synthetic fabric plant, these may lead collectively to the outcome of *too much* control—to monopolistic control, that is.

The third method of market control, reciprocity, generally casts two large corporations in a reciprocal arrangement, each extending the other designated economic guarantees. A given steel firm, for instance, might, over a five-year period, guarantee a cooperating automobile firm so many million tons of steel at a prearranged price in exchange for priority rights to certain mining properties owned by the automobile firm. Such an agreement, by delimiting production uncertainty and financial risk, would permit each of the two firms to engage in long-term planning and development activities.

The fourth method of market control, government cooperation, casts the federal government in certain situations in the role of guaranteeing market stability to given individuals or corporations. The government assumes this role when, for instance, it sets commodity prices for farmers, when it enters cost-plus agreements with designated firms for performing specialized research, or when it agrees to buy from a given corporation all of a certain commodity produced. In these instances, the government operates outside the frame of supply and demand market conditioners. And, in so doing, it usually enhances the power of the corporations involved.

The large corporation, because a creation of technology, is here to stay. Relatedly, despite nostalgic regret on the part of many, the small business and business man of a generation ago are on their way out. And the traditional market economy, which featured production as an outgrowth of consumer demand, is giving way increasingly to a corporate economy which generates its own demand. Long-range planning, colossal outlays of capital, and the need for market controls are its dominant characteristics. And these are the very reasons why it has to generate its own demand; it could not long exist otherwise. Man's options in regard to the corporate structure do not include eliminating it—for man himself would lose from such a choice. They do, however, include his need to police the corporate structure constantly so as to curb its power to harm.

## SOCIETY AT THE CROSSROADS

During the laissez faire period, which lasted until almost the end of the nineteenth century, man's faith that the "invisible hand" of economic destiny would lead capitalism to the promised land of plenty proved to be fallacious and naive. As a result, government increasingly intervened—somewhat erratically until the middle 1940s, more systematically thereafter—to eliminate and prevent gross economic abuses, and to reduce the likelihood that periods of depression and inflation would occur. Competing for importance with the intervention by government in the nation's economy has been the transition of the latter from a simplistic consumer-demand commodity-production basis to a corporate-structure basis. The following phenomena characterize the new basis: business and industry owned collectively by affluent and nonaffluent stockholders; the function of business management performed by specialist personnel, these personnel emerging as a dominant economic force; concentration of economic power in a relatively few corporations; and control of market conditioners, by both the private and governmental sectors, as an essential of corporate planning and production.

As the society has moved from an individual marketplace economy to a government-managed corporate economy, the profit motive, while continuing to dominate the life of the nation, has, at least in the opinion of some, undergone a slight modification. That it continues to be a controlling value, only the deranged would question. Evidence of its continuing influence literally leaps from such phenomena as the perpetuation of financial empires, loopholes in income tax and inheritance-tax legislation, the plight of the economically deprived, and the burning desire of most of the unaffluent to become affluent. All of these caution against undue optimism. Penetrating the gloom, however, is a half century of acceptance of welfare legislation by the society, its mounting concern over poverty in the ghettoes and rural

America, its increasing involvement in the problems of minority groups, and its growing recognition of the disparity between what our basic documents say about the human rights of all individuals and what the society actually does about them.

We conclude this chapter with the following quotation written by a Presbyterian theologian. It is a standard that the nation in the last half of the twentieth century could profitably follow as it reassesses its economic values.

> There are universal moral norms by which all [economic] systems should be judged. All should serve justice, not a static justice but a continually transforming justice, humaneness and diversity in society. They should serve the freedom of persons, of persons under all conditions and not only those who have economic advantages. There is needed a conception of the depth and dignity and transcendence of the person that involves a far more inclusive form of freedom than that associated with the stereotyped and dated "Protestant ethic." . . .
>
> [The threat of] the second half of the twentieth century . . . is to the existence of man as a spontaneous, instinctive, . . . spontaneous and mysterious being. . . .[32]

[32] John C. Bennett, "Capitalism, Ethics, and Morality" in *The Future of Capitalism*, op. cit., pp. 169–170.

# Bibliography

Bendix, Reinhart and Seymour M. Lipset (Eds.), *Class Status and Power*. New York: The Free Press, 1966.

Berle, A. A. and Gardner C. Means, *The Modern Corporation and Private Property*. New York: Commerce Clearing House, Inc., 1932.

Dahl, Robert A., *Who Governs?* New Haven: Yale University Press, 1961.

Domhoff, G. William, *Who Rules Commerce?* Englewood Cliffs, New Jersey: Prentice Hall, Inc., 1967.

Friedman, Milton, *Capitalism and Freedom*. Chicago: The University of Chicago Press, 1962.

Galbraith, John Kenneth, *The New Industrial State*. Boston: Houghton Mifflin Company, 1967.

Gruchy, Allan G., *Comparative Economic Systems*. Boston: Houghton Mifflin Company, 1966.

Harrington, Michael, *Toward a Democratic Left*. New York: The Macmillan Company, 1967.

Hayek, F. A., *The Constitution of Liberty*. Chicago: The University of Chicago Press, 1960.

Heilbroner, Robert L., "The Future of Capitalism," *Commentary*, April, 1966, pp. 23–35.

Heilbroner, Robert L., *The Limits of American Capitalism*. New York: Harper and Row, 1967.

Heilbroner, Robert L., *The Making of Economic Society*. Englewood Cliffs, New Jersey: Prentice Hall, Inc., 1968.

Kaysen, Carl, *The Corporation in Modern Society*, edited by Edward S. Mason. Cambridge: Harvard University Press, 1959.

Keynes, John Maynard, *General Theory of Employment, Interest, and Money*. Cambridge: Cambridge University Press, 1936.

McClelland, David C., *The Achieving Society*. Princeton, New Jersey: Van Nostrand, Inc., 1961.

Mills, Charles Wright, *The Power Elite.* New York: Oxford University Press, 1956.

Morris, Robin, *The Economic Theory of Managerial Capitalism.* Glencoe, Illinois: The Free Press of Glencoe, 1964.

Myrdal, Gunnar, *Challenge to Affluence.* New York: Pantheon Books, 1963.

National Industrial Conference Board, Inc., *The Future of Capitalism.* New York: The Macmillan Company, 1967.

Parsons, Talcott, *Structure and Process in Modern Societies.* New York: The Free Press, 1960.

Samuelson, Paul A., *Economics: Introductory Analysis.* New York: McGraw-Hill Book Company (7th edition), 1967.

Stein, Herman D. (Ed.), *Social Theory and Social Invention.* Cleveland: The Press of Case Western Reserve University, 1968.

Tannebaum, Frank, *The Balance of Power in Society and Other Essays.* New York: The Macmillan Company, 1969.

Theobald, Robert (Ed.), *Social Policies for America in the Seventies: Nine Divergent Views.* Garden City, New York: Doubleday and Company, Inc., 1968.

# 4

# Political Values

The political values of any culture constitute an inseparable part of its total value system. They are important for reason of their pervasiveness, affecting, as they do, the lives of all citizens at any given time and the behavior of any single citizen literally countless times throughout his life. Political values are obviously visible in our own country when a citizen, for instance, opts for one political party over another, when the President of the United States makes a State of the Union address, when Congress enacts a bill into law, when the Supreme Court of the land reverses a decision of a lower court, when a state governor and big-city mayor take opposing sides on a controversial civic issue, or when a local justice of the peace fines a motorist for running a stop light. Political values are less visible, however, when a given citizen, conditioned by them, automatically drives on the right side of the road, pays his taxes, places garbage in a can rather than strewing it on the sidewalk, keeps his dog out of the city park, obeys the sign, "Do not pick the flowers," or observes visiting hours in a hospital.

All of these actions reveal the existence of rules of one kind or another which, at some point in our history, had to be made and enforced if people were to live together in reasonable harmony. And the existence of rules implies the prior existence of authority endowed with enough power to bring them into being initially and enforce them subsequently. Thus the value center of this chapter is the arena of government wherein individualism makes concessions to constituted political authority.

To enhance reader understanding, we offer, at this early point in the discussion, definitions of three key concepts: *government, politics,* and *political science.* In respect to the first of the three, government, we submit a definition made by James Madison early in the country's history. Government, said Madison, is "the political and administrative machinery of an organized state." Government used as a noun relates to the institutions and persons who exercise authority in a cultural group. Used as a verb, it relates to the exercise of authority, to the processes of control. If people were angels, no government would be necessary—so said *The Federalist* in 1788. However, because people are not angels but persons—persons, moreover, who often have conflicting interests and desires—some kind of governmental arrangement is a necessity for every civilized group. The arrangement customarily embraces law (or rules of conduct), public officials, and public institutions, all of which vary from culture to culture. And, in the words of the historian, Henry Steel Commager, government is never a static arrangement but always a dynamic one. Or, in the words of Woodrow Wilson, it is an ever living thing.

The second of the three aforementioned concepts, *politics*, relates to the practical aspects of government in action. It embraces such institutions or activities as political parties, the gaining and holding of political office, influencing public opinion, and meeting the many other demands imposed on individuals by the institution of government.

The third concept, *political science*, is, as the term implies, the science of politics. It is one of the several social science disciplines. Its curriculum consists of that systematic body of theory pertaining to government: what government is and does; what the specific institutions of government are; what principles are germane to it; and what types exist in the world.

In the United States, the governmental form is a republic—a type of system in which ultimate power resides in the electorate, and operational power in its representatives. The United States is also a democracy, a word which derives from the Greek words "demos" (meaning people) and "kratein" (meaning to rule). In a democracy, people rule either directly, as in the town meeting of colonial days, or via their elected representatives, as in our existing system. It is this latter—the political system of the United States, that is—that constitutes the theme of the present chapter.

## BASIC DOCUMENTS

Our country is young chronologically but old politically, extending back at least as far as the Magna Carta of 1215. It is also old technologically—in fact, according to one criterion, it may be the oldest. We allude here to Gertrude Stein's interesting bit of logic that the United States is the oldest country in the world because it was the first to enter the twentieth century. Old or young, the United States rests on a base of political documents that brought the nation into being in the first place and that have given it direction since. Some of the more historically significant of these, we reproduce subsequently in part or in toto.

## The Mayflower Compact

One of the earliest was the Mayflower Compact. Antecedent events leading up to it were these. On September 6, 1620, the 180-ton Mayflower set sail from England with approximately 100 passengers, all Pilgrims, aboard. Their goal was to establish a private colony in North America. Landing at Provincetown, Massachusetts on November 11, forty-one of the passengers signed the now historically famous Mayflower Compact. The signatures were made just prior to the departure of a small detail, led by William Bradford, to select a permanent settlement site which, shortly after its discovery, became known as Plymouth, Massachusetts. The Mayflower Compact was one of the first exercises in self government. It represented direct democracy at work. The compact itself reads as follows.

In THE NAME OF GOD, Amen. We, whose names are underwritten, the Loyal Subjects of our dread Sovereign Lord, King James, by the Grace of God, of *Great Britain, France* and *Ireland,* King, *Defender of the Faith,* &,

Having undertaken for the Glory of God, and Advancement of the Christian Faith, and the Honour of our King and Country, a voyage to plant the first colony in the northern Parts of Virginia; do by these Presents, solemnly and mutually in the Presence of God and one of another, covenant and combine ourselves together into a civil Body Politick, for our better Ordering and Preservation, and Furtherance of the Ends aforesaid; And by Virtue hereof to enact, constitute, and frame, such just and equal Laws, Ordinances, Acts, Constitutions and Offices, from time to time, as shall be thought most meet and convenient for the General good of the Colony; unto which we promise all due Submission and Obedience.

In Witness whereof, we have hereunto subscribed our names at *Cape Cod* the eleventh of *November,* in the Reign of our Sovereign Lord, King *James of England, France* and *Ireland,* the eighteenth, and of *Scotland* the fifty-fourth. *Anno Domini,* 1620.

## The Body of Liberties

Yet another legal document of historical significance in the early colonial period was the one promulgated in 1641 by the Massachusetts Bay Colony. Members of the colony, having lived together for several decades without a legal code, had become increasingly apprehensive about the indefinite status of their individual rights and liberties, about the vagueness of legal processes in the colony, and about the possibility of power becoming concentrated disproportionately in too few. Thus they brought into being the so-called Body of Liberties. Containing 98 individual pronouncements, it became the legal code of the fledgling settlement. Rights and liberties of persons, rights of property, and organizational concerns received approximately equal attention; the social responsibilities of citizens received, at best, but cursory attention. Selected of the coded pronouncements consist of the following:

### The Body of Liberties
### (1641)

The free fruition of such liberties immunities and privileges as humanity, civility, and Christianity call for as due to every man in his place and proportion without impeachment and infringement, hath ever been and ever will be the tranquillity and stability of churches and commonwealths. And the denial or deprival thereof, the disturbance if not the ruin of both.

We hold it therefore our duty and safety, whilst we are about the further establishing of this government, to collect and express all such freedoms as for present we foresee may concern us, and our posterity after us, and to ratify them with our solemn consent.

We do therefore this day religiously and unanimously decree and confirm these following rights, liberties, and privileges concerning our churches and civil state, to be respectively impartially and inviolably enjoyed and observed throughout our jurisdiction for ever.

1. No man's life shall be taken away, no man's honor or good name shall be stained, no man's person shall be arrested, restrained, banished, dismembered, nor any ways punished, no man shall be deprived of his wife and children, no man's goods or estate shall be taken away from him, nor any way endamaged under color of law or countenance of authority, unless it be by virtue or equity of some express law of the country warranting the same, established by a General Court and sufficiently published, or in case of the defect of a law in any particular case, by the word of God. And in capital cases, or in cases concerning dismembering or banishment, according to that word to be judged by the General Court.

2. Every person within this jurisdiction, whether inhabitant or foreigner, shall enjoy the same justice and law, that is general for the plantation, which we constitute and execute one toward another without partiality or delay.

· · ·

8. No man's cattle or goods of what kind soever shall be pressed or taken for any public use or service, unless it be by warrant grounded upon some act of the General Court, nor without such reasonable prices and hire as the ordinary rates of the country do afford. And if his cattle and goods shall perish or suffer damage in such service, the owners shall be sufficiently recompensed.

. . .

9. No monopolies shall be granted or allowed amongst us, but of such new inventions that are profitable to the country, and that for a short time.

. . .

12. Every man whether inhabitant or foreigner, free or not free, shall have liberty to come to any public court, council or town meeting, and either by speech or writing to move any lawful, seasonable, and material question, or to present any necessary motion, complaint, petition, bill or information, whereof that meeting hath proper cognizance, so it be done in convenient time, due order, and respective manner.

. . .

17. Every man of or with this jurisdiction shall have free liberty, notwithstanding any civil power, to remove both himself, and his family at their pleasure out of the same, provided there be no legal impediment to the contrary.

. . .

48. Every inhabitant of the country shall have free liberty to search and view any rules, records, or registers of any Court or office except the Council; and to have a transcript of exemplification thereof, written, examined, and signed by the hand of the officer of the office, paying the appointed fees therefor.

. . .

56. If any man shall behave himself offensively at any town meeting, the rest of the freemen then present shall have power to sentence him for his offence. So be it the fine or penalty exceed not twenty shillings.

. . .

59. Civil authority hath power and liberty to deal with any church member in a way of civil justice, notwithstanding any church relation, office, or interest.

. . .

67. It is the constant liberty of the freemen of this plantation to choose yearly at the court of election out of the freemen all the general officers of this jurisdiction. If they please to discharge them at the day of election by way of vote, they may do it without showing cause; but if at any other General Court, we hold it due justice, that the reasons thereof be alleged and proved. By general officers we mean, our governor, deputy governor, assistants, treasurer, general of our wars, and our admiral at sea, and such as are or hereafter may be of the like general nature.

## Declaration of Independence

A third document of historical significance, unprecedented at the time in content and political import, is the Declaration of Independence. An eloquent masterpiece authored by Thomas Jefferson, it consists of three parts. In the first part, the Declaration establishes the principle that under certain circumstances a subgroup of a given culture is justified in breaking political bonds with the primary group. A necessary first step dictated by sound decency is, it says, an explanation of the causes that "impel" separation. In the case of the colonies, Jefferson identified the causes as being humanistic and moral in nature. The central theme of this first part is that the only justifiable purpose of government is to serve the welfare of people; that, when it fails this purpose, the people have the right, even the duty, to overthrow it.

In the second part, the Declaration details the specific causes that made the break with Britain inevitable. This section, a bill of particulars, alleges the following acts by the mother country generally, and King George III specifically: denying the colonies their right to participate in many of the important processes of government, exploitation of the defenseless, arbitrary exercise of police power, false imprisonment, enslavement, and waging war on the colonies.

In the third section, the Declaration pronounces the colonies to be free and independent, "absolved of all allegiance to the British Crown." There were 56 signatories to the Declaration including such famous names as Samuel and John Adams, Benjamin Franklin, Benjamin Harrison, and, of course, Thomas Jefferson.

Any current reader of the Declaration of Independence may well ask whether the principle of political divisibility, defended in it, operates today in regard to our own country as it did two hundred years ago in regard to Great Britain. This issue was germane in the Civil War period. Conceivably it is still germane in respect to the revolutionary movement of some of the radicals of the present day. Parts one and two of the Declaration are presented en toto in the following; part three is an excerpt.

A DECLARATION
By The REPRESENTATIVES of the
UNITED STATES OF AMERICA
In GENERAL CONGRESS Assembled

When in the Course of human Events, it becomes necessary for one People to dissolve the Political Bands which have connected them with another, and to assume among the Powers of the Earth, the separate and equal Station to which the Laws of Nature and of Nature's God entitle them, a decent Respect to the Opinions of Mankind requires that they should declare the causes which impel them to the Separation.

We hold these Truths to be self-evident, that all Men are created equal, that they are endowed by their Creator with certain unalienable Rights, that among these are Life, Liberty, and the Pursuit of Happiness— That to secure these Rights, Governments are instituted among Men, deriving their just Powers from the Consent of the Governed, that whenever any Form of Government becomes destructive of these Ends, it is the Right of the People to alter or to abolish it, and to institute new Government, laying its Foundation on such Principles, and organizing its Powers in such Form, as to them shall seem most likely to effect their Safety and Happiness. Prudence, indeed, will dictate that Governments long established should not be changed for light and transient Causes; and accordingly all Experience hath shewn that Mankind are more disposed to suffer, while Evils are sufferable, than to right themselves by abolishing the Forms to which they are accustomed. But when a long Train of Abuses and Usurpations, pursuing invariably the same Object, evinces a Design to reduce them under absolute Despotism, it is their Right, it is their Duty, to throw off such Government, and to provide new Guards for their future Security. Such has been the patient Sufferance of these Colonies; and such is now the Necessity which constrains them to alter their former Systems of Government. The History of the present king of Great-Britain is a History of repeated Injuries and Usurpations, all having in direct Object the Establishment of an absolute Tyranny over these States. To prove this, let Facts be submitted to a candid World.

· · ·

In every state of these Oppressions we have Petitioned for Redress in the most humble Terms: Our repeated Petitions have been answered only by repeated Injury. A Prince, whose Character is thus marked by every act which may define a Tyrant, is unfit to be the Ruler of a free People.

· · ·

We, therefore, the Representatives of the UNITED STATES OF AMER-ICA, in General Congress, Assembled, appealing to the Supreme Judge of the World for the Rectitude of our Intentions, do, in the Name, and by Authority of the good People of these Colonies, solemnly Publish and Declare, That these United Colonies are, and of Right ought to be, FREE AND INDEPENDENT STATES; that they are absolved from all Allegiance to the British Crown, and that all political Connection be-tween them and the State of Great-Britain is and ought to be totally dis-solved; and that as FREE AND INDEPENDENT STATES, they have full Power to levy War, conclude Peace, contract Alliances, establish Commerce, and to do all other Acts and Things which INDEPENDENT STATES may of right do. And for the support of this Declaration, with a firm Reliance on the Protection of divine Providence, we mutually pledge to each other our Lives, our Fortunes, and our sacred Honor.

Signed by ORDER and in BEHALF of the CONGRESS,
JOHN HANCOCK, PRESIDENT.

## The Constitution of the United States

Of all the political documents conceived by man through the ages, the Constitution of the United States is nonpareil. It is a unique instance of a social group first bringing a constitution into being and then employing it to effect statehood. The Constitution was conceived and ratified not by an existent sovereign power but by the people of thirteen nonsovereign colonies acting through their state conventions. Democracy in Great Britain evolved developmentally—from situation to situation and from statute to statute—through the centuries. Democracy in the United States had direct birth. What the founding fathers actually did was codify into law what constituted the finest of their cultural-political past. The Constitution rests on, and operates out of, the concept of popular sovereignty. It was people, collectively, who conceived it. And it is people through their designated representatives and the established organizational structure of government who can, and do, change it periodically.

The Constitution, a surprisingly brief document, treats only of basic principles of government, including organizational ones, leaving to legisla-tive bodies and courts the tasks of interpreting and implementing them. When adopted by the Constitutional Convention in September 1787 and pronounced the law of the land a year and half later in March 1789, the Constitution consisted of a Preamble and seven basic articles. Today, it consists addi-tionally of twenty-four amendments. The first ten, constituting the so-called Bill of Rights, were ratified December 15, 1791. The twenty-fourth, establishing the illegality of poll taxes as a voting requisite, was ratified as recently as February 4, 1964.

The Preamble is a philosophical introductory statement, highly compact and fundamental, but general:

> We the People of the United States, in order to form a more perfect union, establish justice, insure domestic tranquility, provide for the common defense, promote the general welfare, and secure the blessings of liberty to ourselves and our posterity, do ordain and establish this Constitution for the United States of America.

The seven basic articles of the Constitution deal with the following themes:

Article I:       The legislative authority.
Article II:      The executive authority.
Article III:     The judicial authority.
Article IV:      Relation between states and the federal government.
Article V:       Method of amending the Constitution.
Article VI:      Miscellaneous provisions including confederate debt and supremacy of the Constitution.
Article VII:     Ratification of the Constitution.

The twenty-four amendments deal with the following themes:

1. Rights of religion, speech, press, assembly, and redress.
2. Right of individuals to keep and bear arms.
3. Restrictions on the quartering of troops.
4. Protection against unreasonable searches and seizures.
5. Due process rights.
6. Rights of persons accused of criminal offenses.
7. Rules of common law.
8. Security against unjust punishments.
9. Individual vs. group rights.
10. Rights of states: the "elastic" clause.
11. Restriction of judicial power.
12. Presidential elections.
13. Abolition of slavery.
14. Citizenship rights (particularly those of racial minority members).
15. Voting rights (particularly those of racial minority members).

16. Income taxes.
17. Direct election of senators.
18. Prohibition of intoxicating beverages.
19. Woman suffrage.
20. "Lame Duck" provisions.
21. Repeal of prohibition.
22. Limitation of presidential tenure (two terms).
23. Electors for Washington, D.C.
24. Illegality of poll-taxes.

As stated or implied earlier, the Constitution is a document of broad concepts and principles. It depends on the Congress to implement them with congruent legislation. It depends on the United States Supreme Court to rule on legislation that, when legally contested, gives appearance of being unconstitutional. Thus the Constitution, not at all immutable and final, is a document of progressive interpretation. In 1896, for instance, the Supreme Court, in the case of Plessy v. Ferguson, ruled in favor of the separate-but-equal doctrine of education for Negroes. In 1954, however, the Court, in the case of Brown v. Board of Education of Topeka, reversed that decision, ruling conversely that arbitrary racial separation in education makes for racial inequality. Between 1810 and 1963, the Supreme Court reversed 109 of its previous decisions, thereby providing conclusive proof, if any were needed, that the Constitution is a document not of final pronouncements but one demanding continuous interpretation.

Yet the Constitution is specific enough to have convinced most citizens, legislators, and legal experts for two hundred years that government by the people is not only a majestic concept but a viable scheme. The Constitution is particularly specific in the first ten amendments which leave no doubt that individuals should possess certain personal rights—of religion, of speech, of assembly, and of redress of grievances. These amendments also leave no doubt that individuals possess certain property rights.

The Constitution, however, is notoriously vague or noncommittal about the social responsibilities of citizens. Rugged individualism without social responsibility leads inevitably—and well it should—to its own demise. As stated by William Allen White Sr., the late beloved sage of Topeka, Kansas, "Liberty is one thing you can't have unless you give it to others."[1] The Constitution is also vague or noncommittal about governmental responsibility for the welfare of those who, through no fault of their own, are unable to reap

[1] Louis Heren, *The New American Commonwealth* (New York: Harper and Row, Publishers, 1968), p. 79.

the benefits of freedom. We refer here, for instance, to captives of city ghettoes, the racial poverty stricken, the rural disadvantaged, the mentally handicapped, and the emotionally unstable. The failure of the Constitution to provide for individuals such as these commits the federal and state governments to compensate for the lack. And the traditional response of "alms giving" has long since been found wanting. This value issue will be elaborated in greater detail in the final chapter.

## The Emancipation Proclamation

We include as the final document of this section the Emancipation Proclamation. That its theoretical impact was, until recently, greater than its practical impact, none can deny. Yet even the slowness of the culture to implement it detracts not a bit from its historical importance and social significance. It has an uncontested place of significance in the nation's traditions.

### THE EMANCIPATION PROCLAMATION
### January 1, 1863
### ABRAHAM LINCOLN

By The President of The United States of America: A Proclamation

Whereas, on the twenty-second day of September, in the year of our Lord one thousand eight hundred and sixty-two, a proclamation was issued by the President of the United States, containing, among other things, the following, to wit:

That on the first day of January, in the year of our Lord one thousand eight hundred and sixty-three, all persons held as slaves within any state, or designated part of a state, the people whereof shall then be in rebellion against the United States, shall be then, thenceforward, and forever free; and the Executive government of the United States, including the military and naval authority thereof, will recognize and maintain the freedom of such persons, and will do no act or acts to repress such persons, or any of them, in any efforts they may make for their actual freedom.

That the Executive will, on the first day of January, aforesaid, by proclamation, designate the states and parts of states, if any, in which the people thereof respectively shall then be in rebellion against the United States; and the fact that any state, or the people thereof, shall on that day be in good faith represented in the congress of the United States by members chosen thereto at elections wherein a majority of the qualified voters of such state shall have participated, shall in the absence of strong countervailing testimony be deemed conclusive evidence that such state and the people thereof are not then in rebellion against the United States.

Now, therefore, I, Abraham Lincoln, President of the United States, by virtue of the power in me vested as commander-in-chief of the army and navy of the United States, in time of actual armed rebellion against the authority and government of the United States, and as a fit and necessary war measure for suppressing said rebellion, do, on this first day of January, in the year of our Lord one thousand eight hundred and sixty-three, and in accordance with my purpose so to do, publicly proclaim for the full period of 100 days from the day first above mentioned, order and designate as the states and parts of states wherein the people thereof, respectively, are this day in rebellion against the United States, the following, to wit:

Arkansas, Texas, Louisiana (except the parishes of St. Bernard, Plaquenimes, Jefferson, St. John, St. Charles, St. James, Ascension, Assumption, Terre Bonne, Lafourche, St. Mary, St. Martin, and Orleans, including the city of New Orleans), Mississippi, Alabama, Florida, Georgia, South Carolina, North Carolina, and Virginia (except the forty-eight counties, designated as West Virginia, and also the counties of Berkeley, Accomac, Northampton, Elizabeth City, York, Princess Ann, and Norfolk, including the cities of Norfolk and Portsmouth), and which excepted parts are for the present left precisely as if this proclamation were not issued.

And by virtue of the power and for the purpose aforesaid, I do order and declare that all persons held as slaves within said designated states and parts of states are, and henceforward shall be, free; and that the Executive government of the United States, including the military and naval authorities thereof, will recognize and maintain the freedom of said persons.

And I hereby enjoin upon the people so declared to be free to abstain from all violence, unless in necessary self-defense; and I recommend to them that, in all cases when allowed, they labor faithfully for reasonable wages.

And I further declare and make known that such persons of suitable condition will be received into the armed service of the United States to garrison forts, positions, stations, and other places, and to man vessels of all sorts in said service. And upon this act, sincerely believed to be an act of justice, warranted by the Constitution upon military necessity, I invoke the considerate judgment of mankind and the gracious favor of Almighty God.

## ECHELONS OF GOVERNMENT

At the chapter's beginning, we defined government, in the words of James Madison, as the political and administrative machinery of an organized state. In this section, we propose to identify and briefly analyze the several levels that combine to make up that machinery.

### The People

The people themselves constitute the most basic level of government. Politically speaking, they consist of the electorate, the voting members of the population, that is, who make their voices heard through the processes of representative government, through lobbying, through the communications media, and through person-to-person contacts. The Constitution itself opens with the words "We the people." And the fact that people impose their power indirectly, for the most part, detracts little, if at all, from their fundamental importance as a power source. Who can deny that people collectively—outside as well as inside the frame of representative government—did not in recent times change the course of events in Viet Nam, the nation's posture in regard to racial minorities, or big-city police tactics at the time of civil rights confrontations. Unquestionably, the people are the ultimate source of power in the United States.

### The Several Political Levels

Government in the United States exists and operates at three political levels: national, state, and local. The prevailing concern of the federal government (admittedly not always evidenced) is the welfare of all the people: all 3.9 million who made up the nation's population when the Constitution became law in 1789, and all the more than 200 million who constitute it today. The federal government's political power derives from the combined sources of the Constitution, federal legislation, and Supreme Court rulings. The prevailing concern of each of the fifty states and thousands of local communities is, as logic would indicate, the welfare of the specific social group for which the given state or local community is politically responsible. The states derive their authority from the so-called elastic clause—the 10th amendment of the Constitution: "The powers not delegated to the United States by the Constitution, nor prohibited by it to the States, are reserved to the States, respectively, or to the people." Local communities derive their authority from state constitutions and state legislation. The primary focus of this chapter is not state and local, but national, political concerns—concerns that in one way or another affect the lives of all the country's citizens.

## The Presidency

The three levels of government—national, state, and local—all function through three operational branches: executive, legislative and judicial. It is the executive branch of the federal government in general, and the presidency in particular, that constitute the central theme of this section.

The executive branch of the federal government consists of the President, the Vice President, the Executive Office of the President (created in 1939), the cabinet—whose roots are in tradition but not in the Constitution, and the several million government employees who perform functions too numerous to be detailed here. By popular definition, the function of the executive branch of government is to administer laws and manage the operational affairs of government. This definition, however, oversimplifies the executive function, as the following discussion will reveal.

The chief executive officer is the President of the United States. George Washington became the first one in 1789; Richard Milhouse Nixon became the thirty-seventh one in 1968. The president and the vice president are the only governmental officials elected by all the people of the United States. Apropos of this point, the following colorful statement by John Bright, English political scientist of the nineteenth century, is germane here.

> Every four years there springs from the vote created by the whole people a President over that great nation. I think the whole world offers no finer spectacle than this; it offers no higher dignity; and there is no greater object of ambition on the political stage on which men are permitted to move. . . . to my mind there is nothing more worthy of reverence and obedience, and nothing more sacred, than the authority of the freely chosen magistrate of a great and free people; and if there be on earth and amongst men any divine right to govern, surely it rests with a ruler so chosen and so appointed.

The power and prestige of the presidency, enormous in Bright's time, have increased with the passage of the years. The executive branch, conceived initially as just one of three important echelons of government, has unquestionably, in recent years become the most powerful of the three. And the reason resides in the office of the president itself. Emergency situations—wars, the Great Depression, and the threat of communism, for example—have collectively enhanced the power of the presidency. So too has the mounting complexity of life and thus of the presidency itself. As stated by Professor

Rossiter of Cornell University, "The man who holds this noble office enjoys a measure of authority and prestige that is unique among all chief executives in countries governed on constitutional principles."[2] Another political scientist writes that the bounds of presidential authority "have been extended beyond the most improbable dreams of an early monarch. . . . It is common to assume that he wears a number of hats, and they are certainly more numerous than medieval crowns."[3]

His roles are, indeed, significant and numerous. (1) He heads the Executive Office of the President, created in 1939 to give needed help to the President in performing his ever increasing, complex duties. The Executive Office includes, among others, the following agencies: Bureau of the Budget, Council of Economic Advisers, National Security Council, Central Intelligence Agency, Office of Trade Negotiations, Office of Science and Technology, Office of Emergency Preparedness, National Aeronautics and Space Council, Council for Urban Affairs, Office of Intergovernmental Relations, Council on Marine Resources, and the White House Office which consists of the president's intimate personal staff. (2) He presides over and gives leadership to his Cabinet (12 members). (3) He is Commander-in-Chief of the Army. (4) He is the country's top diplomat. (5) He prepares the budget. (6) He recommends legislation to Congress: the presidency, in fact, is often referred to as the third house of Congress. (7) He exercises the veto power (on occasions) over legislation. (8) He acts to maintain stability in the nation's economy. (9) He is chief executive over the more than two million federal employees. (10) He is the leader of his political party. (11) He exercises leadership over, or at least maintains liaison with, the following important independent agencies of the Executive Department, of which we have listed less than half.

> Atomic Energy Commission
> Civil Aeronautics Board
> Farm Credit Administration
> Federal Communications Commission
> Federal Mediation and Conciliation Service
> Federal Power Commission
> Federal Reserve System
> Federal Trade Commission
> Interstate Commerce Commission
> National Aeronautics and Space Administration
> National Labor Relations Board

[2] Clinton Rossiter, "The Presidency," in Stephen Bailey (Ed.), *American Politics and Government* (New York: Basic Books, Inc., 1965), p. 43.
[3] Louis Heren, *The New American Commonwealth,* op. cit., p. 6.

Securities and Exchange Commission
Selective Service System
Small Business Administration
Tennessee Valley Authority
U.S. Civil Service Commission
U.S. Information Agency
U.S. Tariff Commission
Veterans Administration

Committed to the responsibilities inherent in all these roles, presidents need organizational ability as well as knowledge and insight to perform their executive functions effectively. As stated by the Princeton political scientist, Professor Somers,

> Ultimately the government must speak with a single voice. It is at the president's desk that the vast complex of government problems and their vast considerations, touching many conflicting interests of a large nation and often many other parts of the world, finally converge and must somehow be joined and reconciled.[4]

## The Congress

For a president to execute, a lawmaking body needs to legislate. And it is the Congress that performs this governmental function in the United States. The eighteenth century spawned many revolutionary ideas, but none was more exciting than that people could govern themselves. In the United States, this idea assumed institutional form in the Congress, a bicameral body consisting of the Senate and House of Representatives. From the English philosopher, John Locke, the founding fathers borrowed the concept of majority rule and legislative supremacy. From the French jurist, Montesquieu, they borrowed the concept of the separation of powers. Combining these two concepts, they brought into being the executive, legislative, and judicial branches of government. All have a twofold mission: to perform the technical functions specified or implied for them in the Constitution, and to prevent power from becoming too highly concentrated in either or both of the other two.

In the tradition of Locke, it was intended that Congress should be central among the three—which it was in the early days of the country. In more recent times, however, the executive branch has assumed a position of preeminence.[5] Reasons for this reversal consist of the following. (1) The

[4] Herman M. Somers, "The President's Office" in Stephen K. Bailey (Ed.), *American Politics and Government*, op. cit., p. 68.
[5] James MacGregor Burns in "The United States Congress," Stephen K. Bailey, op. cit., develops this theme in a highly interesting way.

president, as single leader of the executive branch, is able to act with greater dispatch in times of emergency than the Congress which, by its very nature, is more heavy footed. (2) The president acts from a single party base; the Congress, from a multiparty base. (3) The president has a unitary constituency of all the people; the Congress has a divided constituency of sectional interest groups. (4) The president, if at all sagacious and sensitive, is both urban and rural oriented; the Congress customarily is more rural than urban oriented. (5) The president, not a captive of past practices, is able to bring originality to the position of presidency; the Congress, notoriously a slave to tradition, worships at the shrine of established procedure and seniority.

John Gardner writes of this traditionalism in *Time to Act* (September 1970), the first pamphlet published by Common Cause, an organization created to make the American government more workable and credible.

> [The seniority system] awards the chairmanship of each committee to the member from the majority party who has served on that committee for the longest stretch of time. He may be approaching senility, . . . he may not have had a new idea since World War II. But if he has served on the committee one day longer than other members, chairman he will be.

Unquestionably, reform is long overdue in both the Senate and the House. Because these combine to make up the most powerful legislative branch of government in the world, they should keep up with the times. Probably the most that can be said for them is that they are reasonably effective in spite of themselves. They need desperately, however, to get out of old ruts, become streamlined, and reachieve the eminence that was once theirs and, conceivably, could once more be theirs.

## The Supreme Court

The third branch of government basic to this overview is the judicial branch, with the Supreme Court of the United States central to it. Like the other two branches, the judicial branch has sanction in the Constitution: "The judicial power of the United States shall be vested in one supreme court, and in such inferior courts as the Congress may, from time to time, ordain and establish." The Court's functions (Article III) are these: (1) to interpret and relate the Constitution to the changing social needs of each new generation, (2) assess the constitutionality of contested legislation, and (3) defend the rights and freedoms of all citizens. Like the presidency, the Supreme Court is national in scope; thus it is a court of all the people irrespective of personal and regional differences. It is both a trial and an appellate court, acting in either role, however, under specific ground rules laid down in the Constitution.

Throughout the nation's history, the role of the Supreme Court has been nothing if not controversial. Some have viewed it as having a socially neutral role; others, as having a socially interpretative role. In support of the first position, Justice Owen Roberts (on the Court from 1930 to 1945) held that the Court should be neutral in regard to all legislation, neither approving nor condemning any. The Court's only office, said he, is "to ascertain and declare whether . . . legislation is in accordance with, or in contravention of, the provisions of the Constitution." In support of the second position, Justice Felix Frankfurter (on the Court from 1939 to 1962) held that the Court should be socially interpretative. Said he, "Preoccupation by our people with the constitutionality, instead of with the wisdom, of legislation or executive action, is preoccupation with a false whim."

The Supreme Court, irrespective of the position taken by its members on this issue, has served the country best by playing the role of watchdog of government. As stated by James Madison two centuries ago, government has two obligations: to control both the governed and itself. The Supreme Court has, throughout its history, helped the government to do the latter, namely, control itself. The process of judicial review has joined hands with the electoral process, the occasionally exercised impeachment process, the bicameral division of the legislature, the separation-of-power concept along with its implementation, and the due-process-of-law provision of the Constitution to keep the government honest—or, at least, more honest.

In respect to the rights and privileges of individuals, the central concern of the Supreme Court was, until well into the twentieth century, property. The central concern today is civil rights broadly conceived—the ones identified in the Constitution as the inalienable inheritance of all individuals irrespective of their personal and social differences. Thus the Court today is playing only a moderately active role in respect to the economic rights of individuals; an aggressive role in respect to their civil rights. The many recent cases pertaining to race, religion, assembly, and student rights attest to the validity of this statement. The shift of emphasis has been from the more materialistic tangibles to the more idealistic intangibles.

## Private Interest Groups

Because government, almost by its nature, tends to become detached from the people it serves, a bridge between the two is an ever existing need. In the United States, private interest groups constitute one such bridge.[6] Some observers refer to them as the true political parties of the country. Private interest groups are just what the term implies: groups that bring, sometimes

[6] A source on which I leaned heavily in writing this section was Earl Latham, "Interest Groups in the American Political System" in Stephen K. Bailey (Ed.), op. cit., Chapter 11.

impose, their slanted interests on government officials and agencies most likely to support their causes. Their goal is to influence in their favor legislation and other instruments of public policy. Their method is to convince officeholders of the merit—intrinsic or political—of their causes. Extensive in number, they include groups as diversified as the National Education Association (which lobbies for more federal aid to education); oil interests (which lobby, among other reasons, to protect their oil-depletion income-tax shelter); the American Medical Association (which lobbies against anything smacking of socialized medicine); unions (which, conversely, lobby actively for it and other welfare benefits); racial groups (which lobby for stronger civil-rights legislation); and so forth.

Private interest groups operate collectively from the following base: (1) national political conventions, in which they attempt to shape party platforms and choice of candidates, (2) elections, in which they campaign for candidates congenial to their causes, (3) legislative agencies, in which they lobby for favored treatment, (4) government contracting agencies, which they pressure for concessions, and, (5) courts, before which they initiate test cases. Interest groups representing, for instance, the industrial giants operate from all these bases. A group representing, for instance, the humane treatment of animals conceivably would operate from only the third of these.

Interest groups are important forces in the political arena of our country. In the opinion of some, their often employed covert methods make them suspect. In the opinion of others—probably most others—they serve the purpose they are supposed to serve, namely, to bridge the gap between government and the people. These latter individuals thus hold, as do I, that because private interest groups fill a role that needs to be filled, they should be controlled but not condemned.

## POLITICAL ISSUES

To this point in the chapter, we have presented definitions of certain key political terms, reproduced and interpreted the content of some of the more basic of the nation's political documents, and identified and briefly discussed the primary echelons of government. The intent of the overview was to provide perspective for this and the next section which treat, respectively, of political issues and values. And when either of these overlaps the topic of economics, central in Chapter 3, we make no apology, for the political and economic sectors are often inseparable.

### Economics and Office Holding

What kinds of persons in government should represent the over two hundred million people of the United States, is an increasingly perplexing issue of our times. The fact of representative government in the country is an un-debatable issue: Article I of the Constitution and practical politics make it that. However, whether the candidates whom the people elect to political office actually represent—whether, in fact, they are capable of representing—all or even most of the people is anything but an undebatable issue.

The issue, both an economic and political one, is as simple as the question: Can a person of modest economic means be elected to major political office? The general answer, with admitted occasional exception, is "No," the reason being the almost prohibitive cost of campaign electioneering. The two categories of persons who gain political office consist of the affluent and others who, while not affluent themselves, receive support from individuals who are. Domhoff in his controversial book, *Who Rules America?* states categorically that

> members of the American upper class and their employees control the Executive branch of the federal government. That much we will be able to demonstrate with considerable ease, and from it we will argue that they also control the Judicial branch and the regulatory agencies.[7]

He then adds that the power elite control Congress less completely than they do the other two branches of government, but the difference is one of degree only.

John Gardner in *Report from Washington* (December 1970), yet another Common-Cause pamphlet, speaks to the issue of campaign costs as follows:

> The most spectacular feature of the November [1970] elections was the skyrocketing of campaign costs. Million dollar campaigns were a commonplace. The use of loopholes in the campaign spending laws became a national scandal. And we took a long step toward the day when no American will be able to run for office unless he is wealthy or willing to put himself under obligation to sources of wealth

The question now becomes: Can office holders who belong to, or who are obligated to the more favored socio-economic sectors of the population, adequately represent persons who belong to the less favored sectors. A flippant, but not too flippant, response might well be the Biblical question: "Can a camel go through the eye of a needle?" My straight response is a modified "Yes," provided the office holders in question are socially sensitive and dedicated persons.

In financial matters, with income tax legislation a significant case in point, this social dedication has rarely been strikingly evident—and I understate the case. The history of income tax legislation is one of vested economic interests

[7] G. William Domhoff, *Who Rules America?* (Englewood Cliffs, New Jersey: Prentice Hall, Inc., 1967), p. 84.

fighting to preserve themselves. Thus tax laws which should have a broad social base too often have a parochial one. Paul Douglas, senator from Illinois during the period 1950–1968, states flatly that "not more than one of every hundred citizens actively working on a tax bill is trying to represent the general interest."[8] Our tax system, he says, "is riddled with injustices that violate the simple principle, upon which I think that all could agree, [namely], that people with equal incomes should pay equal or approximately equal taxes."[9]

One of the most completely documented indictments of income tax legislation is contained in Philip Stern's *The Great Treasury Raid* (Rev. Ed.), 1964.[10] As a research assistant in the Senate for a number of years, Stern concentrated on tax matters and subsequently published his findings in book form. Selected of his more provocative observations include the following.

1. Tax evasion is a serious legal offense, but tax avoidance via legal loopholes constitutes approved social behavior. As queried by a well known congressman: "Why pay toll with a free bridge near by?"

2. It is not uncommon for millionaires or multimillionaires to pay no taxes whatsoever.

3. If tax loopholes were eliminated, tax payments could be cut in half.

4. Oil corporations pay approximately half the income tax paid by other corporations. Wrote Stern with tongue in cheek, "Lady Luck . . . raised H. L. Hunt (Texas oil man) from a barber-ranch hand-lumberjack to an oil tycoon worth between $2 and $3 billion."

5. "Old loopholes never die. They just get bigger."

If the single instance of tax legislation is at all typical, one may conclude that the interests of the lower socio-economic groups are not adequately represented in government. What they logically need is representation from their own ranks consisting of individuals who will plead their causes directly, individuals capable of pleading them authentically. However, for this outcome to be realized, government would need to subsidize election campaigns, removing them, in the process, from the arena of economic competition. Such a pattern is common in Great Britain, but whether the United States is ready for it is moot. The social revolution of the day is advancing the cause of readiness, however. And the revolution may soon become strong enough to force on the country the outcome of direct representation in government of the nonaffluent masses.

[8] Paul H. Douglas, *In Our Time* (New York: Harcourt, Brace and World, 1968), pp. 24–25.
[9] Op. cit., p. 5.
[10] Philip M. Stern, *The Great Treasury Raid*, revised edition (New York: Random House, 1964).

## Government, Business, and the Military Complex

The increasingly close relationship among the three sectors of government, business, and the military reinforces the need for political representation in government to have a broad socio-economic base. The growing affinity between government and business was elaborated in Chapter 3. The related affinity between the military and business was highlighted by the late President Eisenhower in his waning days in office. His parting advice to the country was to "guard against the acquisition of unwarranted influence, whether sought or unsought, by the military-industrial complex."

The close working relationships of the three sectors is open knowledge. Government unquestionably needs business—particularly in the area of defense. In the mid-sixties, for instance, the United States government was the primary purchaser of Boeing, Ratheon, and Lockheed products. It was the exclusive purchaser of Republican Aviation products.[11] Corporate industry just as surely, as noted in Chapter 3, needs government. Corporations which engage in long-range planning entailing the output of vast sums need government to protect them from the caprices of the supply-and-demand economic market. And the military complex is dependent for survival on both government and industry.

The issue is not whether government, industry, and the military establishment do, or do not, need each other; should, or should not, have a close relationship with each other—because, by their very nature, they cannot avoid having mutual affinity. The issue, rather, is a combined one of (1) whether their relationship exists within a framework of defensible public goals, and (2) whether government can become representative enough, and be responsible enough, to keep the country "radared in" on those same goals. Thus the issue is one of axiology, challenging all to rethink the values they claim to live by. Most persons, in my opinion, are disenchanted with the traditional values of puritanical materialism grounded as they are in inflexible absolutes and unfounded free-will propositions. Yet the search for a replacement has, to date, been frustrating, to say the least. This topic will undergo further development in the book's final chapter.

The second part of the issue points back to the discussion of the previous section. And its message here is that legitimate national goals can be formulated only by a nationally oriented body representative of all the people. And those goals, once formulated, can be implemented and maintained only if all primary socio-economic groups have a strong political voice in the processes of implementation and maintenance. Denied such voice, they will continue to

---

[11] Michael D. Reagan, *Politics, Economics, and the General Welfare* (Chicago: Scott Foresman and Company, 1965), p. 113.

witness in certain parochial groups power possessed and exercised in amounts disproportionate to their numerical importance. These latter will, predictably, consist of the economically affluent, leaders within the military complex, representatives of narrow sectional interests, and headstrong radicals who will seek to destroy without having a program to replace what is destroyed. In the process, the interests of these minority groups will obliterate the interests and rights of the vast majority of the country's citizenry.

The paramount need is for man's values and goals to rise so far above those of the industrial and military systems that, in the words of John Galbraith,

> Aesthetic goals will have pride of place; . . . Intellectual preparation will be for its own sake and not for better service to the industrial system. Men will not be entrapped by the belief that apart from the goals of the industrial system . . . there is nothing important in life. . . .
>
> [Under such an arrangement], the industrial [including the military] system will fall into its place as a detached and autonomous arm of the state, but responsive to the larger purposes of the society.[12]

When the United States entered the twentieth century, it elected to have modern industry, and, barring holocaust, there is no way back—assuming anyone may want to go back. Thus, as stated by the economist Boulding, ethical development must keep pace with industrial, military, and political development.[13] If it does keep pace, the close ties among government, industry, and the defense establishment will benefit more than harm the society. If it does not keep pace, President Eisenhower's warning may well prove to be a self-fulfilling prophecy.

## VALUES PERTAINING TO POLITICS

We end this chapter on the theme of values—in this instance, political values that have shaped and that continue to shape our culture. And the occasional repetition that crops up in this section is, in our opinion, inevitable inasmuch as political values are never distinct from personal, social, and economic values—the central themes of Chapters 2 and 3.

### Individualism

Standing first in the hierarchy of political values is the concept of individualism, which, as noted in Chapter 2, has roots not only in political theory

[12] John Galbraith, *The New Industrial State* (Boston: Houghton Mifflin Company, 1967), p. 399.
[13] Kenneth E. Boulding, *The Meaning of the Twentieth Century* (New York: Harper and Row, Publishers, 1964), pp. 23–24.

and practice but in humanism, Judaism, Christianity, and frontier traditions. The term individualism assumes overtones of liberty and freedom in the political arena; of the importance of all humanity, in the humanistic arena; of the obligations imposed by free will, in the religious arena; and of the rights implied by rugged individualism, in the frontier-cultural arena.

As a political concept, individualism generally projects itself in two ways: as a positive affirmation of the rights and liberties of people, and as a negative protest against the tyranny of abusive political authority. The Declaration of Independence is a case in point. In a positive vein, it "holds these truths to be self-evident, that all Men are created equal, that they are endowed by their Creator with certain inalienable Rights, that among these are Life, Liberty, and the Pursuit of Happiness. . . ." In a negative vein, it protests against the "History of repeated Injuries and Usurpations [of King George III of Britain], all having a direct Object the Establishment of an absolute Tyranny over these States."

The Constitution of the United States is a freedom document second to none, projecting a protective cover over an extensive range of rights and freedoms. These, as noted earlier, include life itself, religion, speech, assembly, press, due process, private property, protection against unwarranted seizures, franchise, unjust punishments, and so forth. As also noted earlier, however, the Constitution is mute about the social responsibilities implied by freedom. Relatedly, the Constitution is silent about the personal and social rights of individuals who, because of biological and environmental deprivation due to no fault of their own, lose their rights by default. In this connection, one of history's many lessons is that any denial of the rights and freedoms to the few inexorably leads to a denial of the rights and freedoms to the many.

To head off such an outcome before it becomes irreversible, the country, in my opinion, should assign top priority to the following political goals:

1. A decent standard of living for all, including subsistence, adequate medical care, decent housing, gainful employment, optimal educational opportunity, and personal dignity.

2. A program of formal education underwritten by the country at large that places greater emphasis on social responsibility and commitment than on rugged individualism. Such a program, without deemphasizing the cognitive component, would reach out to incorporate the emotional and social components.

3. Fiscal legislation to support the first of these two goals, and an attitudinal reform on the part of the nation's leaders to support the second.

I realize that these goals, to many, smack of starry-eyed idealism. Yet what is the Constitution itself but a starry-eyed, idealistic document? What is humanism but an idealized conception of the intrinsic worth of humanity?

And, in a practical vein, investments by the society in the cause of the socio-economic deprived pay dividends to the established in-group as well as to the needy recipients. In our overpopulated world, we live too closely together to escape each other's problems. And having an awareness of them, we have a commitment to work toward their solutions.

## Checks and Balances in Government

The concepts of individualism, freedom, and personal rights, including the right of private ownership of wealth, shine brightly in the political fabric of our country. To insure their perpetuation and, in the process, assure the diffusion of power, our founding fathers fashioned a government out of the principle of checks and balances. The golden-mean concept of the ancient Greeks constituted a philosophical frame both for the human rights that the new government was committed to guarantee and for the new government itself. The goal was avoidance of extremes.

In respect to human rights, the goal was individualism conceived in perspective, freedom for the one but also for the many, private ownership but not monopoly, majority rule but minority rights, and so forth. The intent, imperfectly realized, was individual values in the context of social interests. In respect to government, the outcome was a constellation of paired forces directed at more or less common goals but committed, at the same time, to check the operational activities and products of their paired opposites. These paired forces include the following, among others: government and the people, federalism and statehood, church and state, Senate and House of Representatives, executive power and legislative power, executive power and judicial power, judicial power and legislative power, judicial power and state rights, and so forth.

As a general rule, the nation has prospered to the extent the check-and-balance principle has functioned effectively. It has been able to tolerate, without being permanently scarred by, such temporary dislocations as a sovereign executive branch in time of war or a super-legislative judicial branch during the Great Depression. However, when these dislocations become long-term as they were in the South where states' rights dominated for a century following the Civil War or as they have been in the legislative branch which for almost a half century has been overly resistive to change, the nation suffers.

The social revolution of the day may well be a reflection of the check-and-balance system having gone awry. As indicated earlier, government represents some of the people much more adequately than it does all of the people. And although much of this imbalance is a product of human frailties, too much of it cannot go uncorrected for too long without dire consequences resulting. As another instance, many who are arguing today for states' rights hold individual rights in contempt. Is this not an instance of legislative intent being circumvented with impunity by misdirected police power? And for the legislative branch to be as much a labyrinth of procedural absurdity as a producer of socially defensible legislation is yet another indication of a possible breakdown in the check-and-balance system.

Even if the system is working, this chilling fact remains: Millions in the United States are denied the rights and privileges promised them in the Preamble and Bill of Rights of the Constitution. Until this denial is reversed, the inevitable conclusion is that many of the political values that "we the people" profess to hold sacred stop far short of practical implementation. To deny this conclusion is to be hypocritical. To accept it is to accept a mandate to join well-meaning law-abiding citizens in correcting the conditions that make the conclusion valid. And I hasten to add that I am recommending action inside, not outside, the established political arena. Democracy that is true democracy constantly polices and changes itself for the better. It is this kind of action from within that I am talking about.

Common Cause, referred to several times earlier in the chapter, is a recent example of an organizational attempt to change government from within. Created in the latter part of 1970, its goal is to make government a more viable and responsive democratic institution. John W. Gardner spearheaded its creation. He wrote in his membership-drive letter sent in the Fall of 1970:

> We must end the war. We must bring about a drastic change in national priorities. We must renew our attack on poverty and discrimination. And we must keep at it until we build a new America. . . .
>
> We are going to build a true "citizens' lobby"—concerned *not* with the advancement of special interests but with the well-being of the nation. . . .
>
> We have not behaved like a great people. We are not being the people we set out to be. We have not lived by the values we profess to honor.[14]

Gardner and his staff keep Common Cause members abreast of significant political happenings in the country. Members, in turn, are encouraged to keep Gardner and his staff abreast of issues they regard as important. Members, above all else, are urged to pressure their congressmen to vote in prescribed ways on issues of greatest political significance.

## Efficiency and Integrity in Government

For the past several decades, government at all levels in our country has increasingly become a target of attack. The attackers, a motley conglomera-

---

[14] The address of Common Cause is 2100 M Street, N.W., Washington, D.C. 20037. Annual membership dues are $15.00.

tion, have come selectively from the ranks of the New Left, dissident blacks, pathological rebels against authority, and individuals of diverse orientations in pursuit of social reform. Government has been charged generally with falling far short of its potentials. It has been charged specifically with progressing too slowly toward the goals of avoiding unnecessary wars, eliminating poverty, eradicating racism, controlling the industrial military complex, representing all citizens equitably, and protecting the many diverse rights and freedoms guaranteed citizens in the Constitution.

The most serious charge is the one made against elected public officials, namely, that too many of them lack basic integrity. Politicians, so the accusations go, make campaign promises with no intention of keeping them. Office holders work too much for their self-interests and the causes of those to whom they are politically beholden, too little for the important human concerns of "all the people." Judges do too little to reduce the tremendous backlog of court cases, thereby denying due-process rights to the citizens. Conflict-of-interest cases are widespread. Vested interests receive favored treatment. And at the national level of diplomacy, misrepresentation to "foreign" powers is routine.

Granted that these violations of public trust are almost as old as man himself, they constitute a more serious threat to our nation today than ever before. For one reason, opportunities for corruption in public office are on the increase as a result of government's mounting involvement with business, industry, and the military complex. And because the opportunities for corruption are greater, the possibilities of concealment are comparably greater. A second reason why violations of public trust threaten more ominously today than ever before emanates from the ever present danger of nuclear destruction. Politicians in high places literally hold the fate of the nation, and mankind as a whole, in their hands. Thus integrity and efficiency have the status of high values. The social stakes today are too high for the situation to be otherwise.

# Bibliography

Bailey, Stephen (Ed.), *American Politics and Government*. New York: Basic Books, Inc., 1965.

Bendix, Reinhart and Seymour M. Lipset (Eds.), *Class Status and Power*. Glencoe, Illinois: The Free Press, 1966.

Corwin, Edward S. and Jack W. Peltason, *Understanding the Constitution*, 3rd ed. New York: Holt, Rinehart and Winston, Inc., 1964.

Dahl, Robert A., *Pluralist Democracy in the United States: Conflict and Consent*. Chicago: Rand McNally and Company, 1967.

Deutsch, Karl W., *Nationalism and Its Alternatives*. New York: Alfred A. Knopf, Inc., 1969.

Domhoff, G. William, *Who Rules America?* Englewood Cliffs, New Jersey: Prentice Hall, Inc., 1967.

Douglas, Paul H., *In Our Time*. New York: Harcourt, Brace and World, 1968.

Easton, David, *A Systems Analysis of Political Life*. New York: John Wiley and Sons, 1965.

Harris, Fred R., *Alarms and Hopes, A Personal Journey, A Personal View*. New York: Harper and Row, Publishers, 1968.

Heren, Louis, *The New American Commonwealth*. New York: Harper and Row, Publishers, 1968.

Hitch, Charles, *Decision Making for Defense*. Berkeley: University of California Press, 1965.

Hofstadter, Richard (Ed.), *Ten Major Issues in American Politics*. New York: Oxford University Press, 1968.

Leach, Richard H., *Governing the American Nation*. Boston: Allyn and Bacon, 1967.

Miller, S. M., *Max Weber: Selections from His Works*. New York: Thomas Y. Crowell Company, 1963.

Mills, Charles Wright, *The Power Elite*. New York: Oxford University Press, 1956.

Myrdal, Gunnar, *Challenge to Affluence.* New York: Pantheon Books, Inc., 1963.

Parsons, Talcott, *Structure and Process in Modern Societies.* New York: The Free Press, 1960.

Reagan, Michael D., *Politics, Economics, and the General Welfare.* Chicago: Scott Foresman and Company, 1965.

Rossiter, Clinton, *Parties and Politics in America.* Ithaca, New York: Cornell University Press, 1960.

Sorenson, Theodore C., *Decision Making in the White House.* New York: Columbia University Press, 1963.

Stern, Philip M., *The Great Treasury Raid.* New York: Random House, 1964.

Tannebaum, Frank, *The Balance of Power in Society and Other Essays.* New York: The Macmillan Company, 1969.

# 5

# Values in Science and Technology

Three revolutions have, in large part, made our country what it is today. The American Revolution changed the shape of its political life. The Industrial Revolution changed the shape of its economic life. And the Scientific Revolution is currently changing the totality of its life.

The impact of science is world-wide and multidimensioned. Its purview is research. Its laboratories are universities, industry, and government. Its tools are many and complex: a microscope, a photoelectric cell, a delicate surgical instrument, a sophisticated computer, a mathematical model, or a stratoscope. Its methods are those of reflective thinking experimenters addressing themselves systematically and innovatively to the solving of problems. Its social products are legion: the telephone, airplane, automobile, refrigerator, antitoxins, medical cures, bridges, space vehicles, the vast world of technology, and so forth.

Science literally surrounds man, bestowing on him undreamed of conveniences and bringing to the world a degree of mechanical efficiency never realized before. Despite this inheritance, however, man regards science ambivalently. Although enjoying its benefits, he fears its power to captivate and destroy.

The history of science is actually the history of man himself. Precivilized man was primitive primarily because he lacked scientific knowledge and thus was denied its products. Lacking these, he depended on his immediate environment for survival. His food was indigenous plantlife, fish in a nearby stream, or animals not far distant. His tools were crude implements of nature: a rock, a stick, or a club. His shelter was a cave or maybe a tree.

Man did not become civilized until he learned the arts of agriculture and animal domestication. These he learned in a rudimentary way some eight to ten thousand years ago. His progressive mastery of these made possible the urban revolution which took place around 3000 B.C. Cities depend for their existence on food surpluses that can be transported to them from outlying regions. Thus agricultural development had to precede urban development. In this connection, cities of ancient cultures were never more than a week or two away from starvation.

In addition to the scientific developments connected with agriculture and animal husbandry, innumerable other ones also led man down the road to civilization. Included among these were astronomy of the Babylonians, algebra of the Arabs, geometry of the Greeks, the water wheel, stirrup, horse collar, and printing—the latter a product of the fifteenth century and thus the most recent of the several listed.

It was the next century that witnessed the birth of the Scientific Revolution. The specific event that precipitated it was the pronouncement by Copernicus in 1543 that the earth moves around the sun. By arriving at this conclusion mathematically and inductively, he parted company with the many deductivists of his and earlier times, among them Saint Thomas Aquinas, who held faith to be a more authentic guide to truth than knowledge. Yet even Copernicus could not break completely with his deductivist past, contending that the earth orbited the sun in a perfect circle. His explanation was that nothing less than a perfect geometrical configuration would do justice to God's perfection. Tycho Brahe and Johannes Kepler, astronomists of the late sixteenth and early seventeenth centuries, reduced Copernicus' proposition to mathematical laws describing in detail the eliptical paths of the various planets.

The latter part of the seventeenth century became scientifically noteworthy as a result of a casual observation made by Sir Isaac Newton. Sitting idly at home because Cambridge University had been shut down by the plague, young Newton observed an apple falling from a tree. This event precipitated a chain of thought that led ultimately to his formulation in 1665 of the so-called Law of Gravity. Newton theorized that if the apple and earth were affected by gravity, objects in outer space should be likewise affected. Thus he concluded that gravity holds the moon in orbit.

Such was the birth and early growth period of the Scientific Revolution. And its impact on traditional dogma was shattering, revealing man and the planet earth as only minute parts of a universe of galaxies. And what had happened in astronomy was soon to happen in the other physical sciences, paving the way for the Industrial Revolution several centuries later, and the across-the-board science revolution of the past several decades.

The products of this latter revolution have been awesome. In chemistry, they include, among others, nuclear fission and fusion, solid state electronic devices, plastics and synthetics, the wonder drugs of medicine and psychiatry, advances in man's understanding of viruses and insecticides, surgical wonders, photocopying, hi-fi, and color photography. In physics, they include advanced insights into the behavior of heavy particles and subnuclear particles, sophisticated planetary instruments and space crafts, and computers. In astronomy, they include giant telescopes; in geology, moon rocks; in microbiology, new and penetrating insights into genetic forms and processes; and in oceanography, discoveries of new forms of life and minerals.

The basic and applied sciences indeed have combined to change the lives and life patterns of almost all mankind. And, ironically, it was World War II that gave them their greatest thrust and Russia's Sputnik of 1957 that served as a booster. That the defense and space establishments have been primary recipients of governmental support for research and development in science is an established fact. Whether the scales have been tilted too much in that single direction will be weighed later in the chapter.

At this point, we call attention to a few isolated bits of information that bear on the theme of science and technology. An almost incredible one is that of the world's totality of scientists of all times, 90 percent are alive today. As of 1968, the names of approximately 300,000 United States scientists appeared (another approximately 100,000 names did not) in the National Register of Scientific and Technical Personnel. Of this total, 40 percent were employed in educational institutions, 32 percent in industry and business, 13 percent in government (10 percent federal and 3 percent state and local), 4 percent in nonprofit organizations, and 11 percent in miscellaneous other organizational arrangements.[1] Another statistic of interest is that since 1910 man has extracted mineral deposits from the earth equal to the total amount he extracted before 1910. Yet another is the ability of countries to recover from disaster. Germany and Japan recovered from the destruction of World War II in little more than a decade, whereas it "took Western Europe almost three hundred years to recover from the fall of the Roman Empire . . . and Germany decades to recover from the Thirty Year's War."[2] A last item of some interest is the allegation by the scientist-philosopher, Lord Snow, of Britain that of all basic science activities taking place in the entire world, an estimated 80% are concentrated in the United States.[3]

## DEFINITION OF TERMS

We pause here to define some key terms that should enhance reader understanding. They consist of the following: science, basic science, applied science, the scientific method, and technology.

[1] Neva A. Carlson, *American Education* (April 1970), p. 37.
[2] Kenneth E. Boulding, *The Meaning of the Twentieth Century: The Great Transition* (New York: Harper and Row, Publishers, 1964), p. 8.
[3] James R. Killian, Jr., "Toward a Research Reliant Society: Some Observations on Government and Science," in Harry Woolf (Ed.), *Science as a Cultural Force* (Baltimore: The Johns Hopkins Press, 1964), p. 12.

*Science* is a derivative of the Latin word *scientia,* meaning knowledge. Thus, true to its etymology, it denotes a body of knowledge. Additionally, it denotes a manner of dealing with knowledge which is called the scientific method. Three definitions of the term science follow. The first two feature the basic concepts of knowledge and method. The third channels colorfully into description.

Science is an organized body of knowledge and a method of proceeding to an extension of this knowledge by hypothesis and experiment.[4]

Science is that mode of inquiry which attempts to arrive at knowledge of the world by the method of observation and by the method of confirmed hypothesis based on what is given in observation.[5]

Science is nothing else than the search to discover unity in the wild variety of nature.[6]

*Basic science* is a covering term for theoretical or so-called pure science. It is descriptive of research and investigation engaged in with no immediate social application as a goal.

*Applied science,* in contrast, is scientific endeavor engaged in with immediate or early social application as a goal.

*Technology* is a synonym of applied science. It is scientific knowledge employed for social purposes. It may take the form, for example, of machine-operated industry, pushbutton warfare, electrically controlled gas furnaces, or outer-space rocketry.

*Scientific method* is a method of problem solving. In a formal sense, it designates a more or less predetermined research approach. Chicago University's George W. Beadle reads the following steps into that approach:

recognition of the problem, choosing the right experimental material, making the proper observations, careful analysis, formulation of a reasonable hypothesis, thorough testing of that hypothesis, generalizing from the verified hypothesis, making proper deductions, and presenting the results and interpretation in a report that is a model of directness, clarity, and thoroughness.[7]

The above steps are quite similar to the more familiar ones of John Dewey announced in 1933. We paraphrase them here.

[4] Glenn T. Seaborg, "Chemistry" in Albert Love and James S. Childers, *Listen to Leaders in Science* (Atlanta: Tupper and Love, Inc., 1965), p. 31.
[5] A. Cornelius Benjamin, *Science, Technology, and Human Values* (Columbia: University of Missouri Press, 1965), p. 20.
[6] J. Bronowski, *Science and Human Values* (New York: Julian Messner, Inc., 1956), p. 27.
[7] George W. Beadle, "An Introduction to Science," in Love and Childers, op. cit., p. 6.

A difficulty is felt.

It is intellectualized and defined.

A hypothesis about a possible solution is formulated.

The hypothesis is developed and evaluated.

The hypothesis is implemented and tested.[8]

In an informal sense, the scientific method is an open way of looking at the world. It is a way of free inquiry, investigativeness, thoroughness, skepticism before unsupported data, willingness to be wrong and admit error, patience, and courage to defend truth. The scientific method is inductive and open ended.

## ISSUES

With the goal of science conceived as an authentic understanding of nature along its many dimensions, and with its posture of openness and inquisitiveness before all of life unequivocally espoused, small wonder that controversy has dogged it through the ages. Critics of science tend to fall into the following categories: the uninformed who view science as a pathological thing inimical to the laws of God or nature; the partially informed who, while enjoying the benefits of science, oversimplify the task of eliminating its offensive technological products and by-products; and the thoughtful and informed who support science in a balanced social context while advocating careful controls over its products.

Four basic issues that have been, and that continue to be, germane to science are these: (1) Is science friend or enemy of religion? (2) What controls should be exercised over it and in what way? (3) Who should support it? And (4) What is its relative importance in the total spectrum of the natural sciences, humanities, and social sciences?

### Science and Religion

Whether science is compatible or incompatible with religion depends for answer on how the terms science and religion are conceptualized. Science, as noted earlier, is two faceted: it is a body of knowledge and a way of investigating life. And, in respect to the second of these, most concur that "the way of science" is investigative and open. Religion, unlike science, resists definitive capsuling, susceptible as it is to an extensive range of interpretations. To some, it is a system of beliefs, convictions, and values. To others, it is the worship of a divine power. To still others, it is an organized system of rituals of one kind or another. Irrespective of the specifics of any given religious orientation, science and religion are incompatible for persons who accept

[8] John Dewey, *How We Think* (New York: D.C. Heath and Company, 1933), p. 107.

"truth" as a deductive phenomenon, defending it, in the process, against attempts at rational or empirical investigation. Science is also incompatible for persons who believe knowledge to be changeless—the same yesterday, today, and forever; and for others who wear the hat of religion on days of worship and of science at other times.

Generally speaking, science and religious liberalism in the western world have been fairly congenial; science and religious fundamentalism have usually been alien and often hostile. The following tenets of fundamentalist orthodoxy have historically set it apart from science. (1) There rules over man and the universe a personal noncontingent God who created all things in the manner of Genesis. (2) God generally acts through natural law but stands above it and is capable of by-passing it when he so elects. (3) He reveals himself through the God-man Christ, the *Bible,* and (in Roman Catholicism) through the Virgin Mary and the organized Church. (4) Truth is predetermined and always the same; man's duty is to discover it. (5) When the conclusions of science differ from those of religious dogma, the latter supersedes. Throughout history, religious fundamentalism and science have confronted each other, often jugularly, over issues that include the following: the shape of the earth (whether flat, round, or eliptical); the place of the planet earth in the universe (whether primary or just a small part of a vastly greater ensemble); explanations of holocausts (divine versus natural); explanations about the evolution of man; and explanations of so-called miracles (whether supernatural phenomena or natural phenomena not understood by man at the time of their manifestation).

Religious fundamentalism and science have long been at odds over the status of knowledge in the lives of men. Fundamentalists are notoriously antagonistic toward what they refer to as "too much knowledge." And they cite the good-and-evil allegory of Genesis 2 as a basic reason:

> And the Lord commanded the man, saying, "You may eat freely of every tree of the garden; but of the tree of the knowledge of good and evil you shall not eat, for in the day that you eat of it, you shall die."

Despite the warning, Adam and Eve ate of the tree. The announced punishment was that women forevermore would be subservient to their husbands and suffer pain in childbirth; that men would have to work by the sweat of their brows; and that both men and women would have to "return to the ground" at death.

The Garden of Eden story has a parallel in Greek mythology: Prometheus, the Titan, stole fire from the Gods and gave it to newly created mankind. In so doing, he disturbed the balance of power that existed between man and the gods. Prometheus' punishment was to be bound "forever" on the rocky crag of Caucasas. However, Hercules, circumventing Zeus in some unrevealed way, ultimately freed Prometheus by destroying the captor eagle who preyed on him. The central message of these two allegories is that man infringes on the prerogative of God when he aspires to too much knowledge. The counter of science to religious fundamentalism on this issue is that there is no such thing as too much knowledge provided it is knowledge authenticated carefully, systematically, and thus defensibly.

Religious liberalism, in contrast to religious fundamentalism, is generally compatible with science both in respect to the latter's content and methods. Religious liberals are noncompetitive with science. Although accepting and utilizing the methods of science, they claim the right also to be affective and intuitive in their search for truth. Their position furthermore is that if science exposes error or inconsistency in time-honored dogma, the dogma could not have been very good in the first place. The progressive acceptance by religious liberals of the theory of evolution is a case in point. Thus they are more intrigued than threatened by such phenomena as the possible existence of some form of advanced life on other planets, by the known ability of chemists to create life in primitive form and to manipulate human genes, and by the social challenge of artificial insemination.

Generally speaking, organized religion and science are, with the passage of time, becoming increasingly more compatible as absolutism in both concedes progressively to relativism. Religious fundamentalism is still "fighting the good fight" but at a less feverish pitch and against an opponent that refuses to fight back. And even religious fundamentalism is not quite as fundamental as it used to be.

## Controls over Science

Whether science is partner or competitor of religion, it is, as stated by a well known scientist, "the most dominant force in modern life. . . . the engine that propels modern society."[9] And if this is dominant, it may also have aspects that for the good of man need to be controlled.

Control over basic science should take the form of assuring individual researchers a high degree of independence in their pursuit of scientific truth. Because basic science by its very nature is a highly individualistic phenomenon, it fails its potential, sometimes even falls under its own weight, when forced to function under the heavy hand of external authority. To the question, then, of how much independence basic science should have, the answer is that it should have all the independence possible within the frame of two controls: the values of any given scientist, and those of the discipline or professional group of which the scientist is a member. Price provides the rationale for this position: "The closer the estate is to the end of the spectrum

[9] Jerome B. Wiesner, "Technology and Society" in Harry Woolf (Ed.), op. cit., p. 35.

that is concerned solely with truth, the more it is entitled to freedom and self government."[10]

The alternative to this position is political control from without, which is incompatible with the individual nature of basic science. Such control is, for the following reason, also a practical impossibility: basic science is primarily an adventure of one or more individuals in the world of the unknown, only secondarily an experience in the world of the known. It thus follows that none other than an individual scientist himself can, with efficiency, steer his course into and through the obstacles of the unknown. The value that rises above all others here is that because pure science is a form of capital investment, it should be controlled in a way that will produce the greatest social yield—and this dictates primary control from within, very little from without.

The line that separates pure (or basic) science from applied science is not in all instances distinguishable. That the second cannot exist without the first we know, but whether pure science can exist as a discrete entity is debatable. In my opinion, because basic and applied science share many interests, employ similar or sometimes identical investigative methods, and, in the last analysis, depend on each other for survival, the goal of discreteness is both unrealistic and undesirable. Better, then, that they share

> the revolutionary vision that the history of man and his institutions is a process of unending change; that man, by discovering the underlying processes by which he is controlled, may learn how *within limits* to modify, shape, and plan the course of his creative revolution.[11]

A vision this grandiose can ill afford the luxury of complete separateness within the scientific estate. To the contrary, the greatest possible unity is necessary if science and technology are to achieve their potentials of maximizing man's understanding of his universe and significantly improving his lot in it. Yet this is not to imply that applied science should be controlled in the same way and by the same sources as pure science.

Irrespective of whether science is a single or dual entity, its technological manifestations are almost everywhere evident. Power, size, speed, and efficiency are its trademarks. One writer refers to technology as the new "American theology promising salvation by natural works."[12]

Its promise of salvation, unfortunately, conceals the actual or potential

[10] Don K. Price, *The Scientific Estate* (Cambridge: Harvard University Press, 1965), p. 137.

[11] Avery Leiserson, "Science and Government," in Stephen Bailey (Ed.), *American Politics and Government* (New York: Basic Books, Inc., 1965), p. 254.

[12] Wilbur H. Ferry, "Must We Rewrite the Constitution?" *Saturday Review of Literature* (March 2, 1968), p. 50.

degeneracy of some of its works. Its power, which has doubled every decade for the past three, "is so vast that man can destroy himself and his entire planet."[13] This possibility sobers with its ominous potential without necessarily making a villain out of power—for the latter has the capability for good as well as evil. Yet many of technology's products, as elaborated in an earlier chapter, are socially repellent: for instance, impersonalization, violation of the right of privacy, poisoned air, polluted water, cacophonous noise, defaced natural beauty, idealism made to defer to materialism—these and others. Chekhov, at the turn of the century, speaking through Uncle Vanya rued many of these social affronts at a time when the Industrial Revolution in Russia was not even a dominant force. How much more would he rue them today—at a time when technology is in full force. Wrote Chekhov:

> . . . Man is endowed with intellect and creative powers so that he may multiply what is given him, but up to now he has not created, he has destroyed. Forests are fewer and fewer, rivers dry up, games become extinct, the climate is ruined, and every day the earth gets poorer and uglier. . . . soon there will be no faithfulness, no purity, no capacity for sacrifice left on earth. . . . In all of you sits the demon of destruction.

The terrible awesomeness of technology's power and the notorious offensiveness of many of its products demand control of both it and science, although in different ways. Apropos of the former, the goal needs to be technology in the service of man, not vice versa. If the society ignores or takes this commitment lightly, the evils of laissez faire will have to be relived, only this time in a much more explosive and dangerous world. The need, in the words of Lewis Mumford, is for

> unconditional cooperation [which] is the price of mankind's survival. If we are sluggish in our response to this situation, we may forfeit the immense human blessing that the very danger, a danger on a cosmic scale, carries with it . . . Morality, in the elementary form of accepted inhibitions, is the first step toward the conscious control of the powers man now commands: without this lower form of morality . . . no higher form can be practiced.[14]

Ignoring the necessary distinctions that need, from time to time, to be made between pure and applied science, we choose here to treat the scientific estate as a whole and examine the respective controls that members of the general public, politicians in public office, and scientists themselves exercise over science in its many forms and products.

[13] Bentley Glass, "What Can Man Be?" *National Education Association Journal* (September 1967), p. 11.
[14] Lewis Mumford, *The Human Prospect*, edited by Harry T. Moore and Karl W. Deutsch (Carbondale: Southern Illinois University Press, 1955), pp. 248, 254–255.

The general public as an agent of control appears in many forms and employs many diverse methods. Individuals, for instance, write their congressmen to support increases or decreases in government subsidies for basic science. Groups in the national capitol lobby for or against vested industrial interests. Student activists protest against industrial pollution. University professors upgrade student understanding of science in any one of countless academic settings. And the communications media take a stand, pro or con, a given scientific issue. The rise of the general public as a molder of public opinion has paralleled the rise of television as an all-pervasive communications medium and the emergence of student power as a mounting political force.

The general public as an agent of control poses the controversial question of how "ordinary" citizens possessed of little knowledge and understanding of science can control its shape and direction. The answer is that such citizens are only part, although an important part, of a greater ensemble whose goal it is to interact collectively to the end of making science a mounting force for social good. Admittedly, formal education needs to do a far better job than it has traditionally done to upgrade the scientific sophistication of the general population. Yet the right of the latter to have and voice an opinion in regard to science in its many forms does not have to await such action—Jefferson underwrote this right two centuries ago.

Politicians and government, as would be expected, constitute another important control over the scientific estate. In this connection, the relationship between science and politics is an ambivalent one differing as the two frequently do in interests and goals. The concerns of politics are usually pragmatic and immediate; those of pure science are more often, when not pragmatic, at least long-range. Politicians tend to be suspicious of science, viewing it as a potential competitor for power, even fearful that it may someday become a new governing influence. Furthermore, to the extent science is associated with the military complex, and even more so with Marxism and other brands of materialism, politicians shun it as a political liability. Conversely, science chronically reels under government's uncertain posture toward it, having borne the brunt of government's capriciousness many times. And the ever possible threat of government to scientific freedom can never be completely suppressed.

In my opinion, government should allow, and generally has allowed, basic science the right of near autonomy as it pursues knowledge down diverse paths and in many, including some bizarre, ways. Additionally, in my opinion, government should exercise close supervision over applied science both in industry and the military, particularly the latter. This it has not done very well. In the process, it should not allow the constitutional ideals of life, liberty, and the pursuit of happiness to be eroded in a world dominated by technological things. As stated relatedly by Price,

> If science wishes to continue to guard its freedom and emphasize its purpose of knowledge and understanding for their own sakes, it might well begin to worry about the prospect of a society dominated entirely by technological purpose.[15]

If our society is ultimately dominated by technology and technological purpose, the people and the politicians whom they elect to office will be blameworthy, for such domination will not have been bred in social isolation. They will be especially blameworthy if allowing the military complex to gain undue control. Yet the facts of the case are that the military complex is on the verge of gaining such control. Military spending, for instance, approximates $80 billion annually, which constitutes an eighth of the gross national product. Large corporations such as Lockheed, Boeing, General Dynamics, and Lytton Industries unquestionably have a favored relationship with the Pentagon. And for 2,100 retired military officers with rank of colonel or higher to hold key jobs in defense industries disturbs with its political implications. Add all this to the "documented evidence" alleged by Senator Proxmire of Wisconsin "that the military and defense industries are guilty of inefficient and otherwise questionable business practices"[16] and the country has definite cause for alarm. We say once more that applied science, whether in industry or the military, needs to be controlled. And a major agency of control should be government at all levels—government protecting citizens from the excesses of technology.

Science itself is a third important agent of control—and the shift here is back once more to internal control. In this connection, the motto of the National Science Foundation is "not the government, nor the National Science Foundation, but the scientists themselves make science policy."[17] The term "scientists themselves" embraces both individual scientists and professional scientific societies such as the American Association for the Advancement of Science, National Academy of Sciences, American Meteorological Society, Society of Economic Geologists, American Association of Pathologists and Bacteriologists, and Institute for Medical Research. The rationale for the control of science by scientists goes something like this. (1) The goal of science is truth. (2) None but the scientifically knowledgeable should pass final judgment on individuals engaged in the pursuit of scientific truth.

---

[15] Don K. Price, *The Scientific Estate*, op. cit., p. 101.
[16] William Proxmire, "The Pentagon and Free Enterprise" in *Saturday Review* (January 31, 1970), p. 14.
[17] A. Hunter Dupree, "A New Rationale for Science" in *Saturday Review* (February 7, 1970), p. 56.

(3) The most exacting kind of control is that exercised by one's peers, for to be exposed by them as professionally inadequate is to lose one's professional status and standing.

This rationale applied to pure science is persuasive; applied to technology, considerably less so, if at all. If Price is correct that the greater the proximity of the scientific estate to truth, the greater its right to freedom and self-government, the reverse also has to hold, namely that:

> the closer . . . [the scientific estate] gets to the exercise of power, the less it is permitted to organize itself as a corporate entity, and the more it is required to submit to the test of political responsibility, in the sense of submitting to the ultimate decision of the electorate.[18]

The obvious implication here is that, for instance, even though scientists made nuclear power a possibility, the social order (the electorate through its political representatives, that is) had ultimately to decide if such power would be employed in defense and space ventures. Again, biochemists have achieved the capability of changing the genetic characteristics of man, but any application of their newly acquired knowledge has to await approval from the collective social order. The same principle applied in the past to wiretapping devices when the question arose as to whether or not they could be legitimately employed by law enforcement agencies. The scientists did their job well; the social jury has yet to announce a verdict. The principle will comparably apply in the future any time new creations of science possess the potential to change people in some significant way.

In the opinion of Don Price, science is most effectively controlled when the check-and-balance principle is adhered to by the following four groups: individual scientists, the professions, administrators, and politicians. Scientists exercise internal control; the professions exercise subtle external control by bringing individual research into a context of purpose; administrators exercise overt external control by objectively expediting, without guiding, the work of individual scientists. And politicians exercise naked external control by making social decisions in respect to exactly which products of science are to be developed, and how they are to be controlled and applied.[19]

Each of these groups, says Price, should check the activities of the other three; the four together should combine to prevent or ameliorate technology's excesses. None of the four, to date, has performed its controlling mission very well. All, however, seem to be tightening their belts for more aggressive action in the future.

Germane to the present discussion is the question asked by every generation: Assuming that a given scientist has created, or knows how to create, a

[18] Don K. Price, *The Scientific Estate,* op. cit., p. 137.
[19] Op. cit., pp. 132–135.

product that can be seriously harmful to man, should he conceal or destroy it? For him to do so would presuppose an espousal of certain a priori propositions that he could defend. And each of these would lead him back to other more remote a priori propositions until ultimately he might arrive at a bedrock principle that would support a final decision. In philosophical terms, the process of infinite regression would have led him ultimately to his decision.

In this connection, the Renaissance man of many parts, Leonardo da Vinci, allegedly destroyed plans for the submarine for fear that man would employ it for destructive purposes. In the same tradition, as recently as 1969, Dr. James Shapiro, a molecular biologist and member of a Harvard Medical School committee that had recently isolated "the first pure gene" deserted science for political activism. He feared, so he said, that his research "would be used for anti-social purposes by government and corporation officials."[20] On the other hand, the Nobel prize winning chemist, Harold Urey, in the 1930s, presented to the world a formula for heavy hydrogen that led ultimately to the Hiroshima and Nagasaki holocausts. Each man made his decision as a value-oriented person in a troubled society at a given time in history. To generalize from any of the three acts would constitute false stereotyping. Each scientist made his decision as a man first and as a scientist second. The point I make here is that there is no such thing as value-free science because there is no such thing as value-free scientists.

## Support for Science

If science needs to be controlled, it also needs to be supported. Nor does support come cheap. In 1964, the country spent $20 billion on research and development, which constituted approximately 3 percent of the Gross National Product,[21] and more than the total federal budget before Pearl Harbor. Today, we spend somewhat less than 2.5 percent, which still represents a staggering amount. Research is costly for a number of reasons. The tremendous amount engaged in is one reason. The increasing reliance of research on expensive computers is another. And the growing prevalence of interdisciplinary team research is still another. The high cost of producing Ph.D.'s in physics and chemistry dramatically reveals, as the following projection attests, the price that the country pays to maintain its scientific estate.

[20] Week in Review, "Rejection of Science Worries American Scientists," *New York Times* (Sunday, April 5, 1970), p. 6.
[21] James R. Killian, Jr., "Toward a Research-Reliant Society: Some Observations on Government and Science" in Harry Woolf (Ed.), *Science as a Cultural Force* (Baltimore: The Johns Hopkins Press, 1964), p. 9.

| | |
|---|---:|
| Elementary particle physics | $910,000 |
| Astrophysics, solar systems, physics, cosmic rays | 500,000 |
| Nuclear physics | 234,000 |
| Plasma physics | 230,000 |
| Solid state and condensed matter | 160,000 |
| Atomic and molecular physics | 93,000 |
| Chemistry | 39,000[22] |

With the scientific estate this demanding of financial support, the federal government alone is capable of providing it. Industry and the universities are junior partners in the enterprise, but they, like many individual researchers, rely heavily on government support to get the job done. For the past several decades, a major issue in universities throughout the country has been whether they have been selling too much of themselves to government. The answer of a growing number is that they had no other choice: the scientific revolution moved the private and public sectors so closely together that they became inseparable.

Granted that government should underwrite science with extensive financial support, it needs to do so within the frame of defensible policy and procedural guidelines. The following, announced in the 1930s, and paraphrased here, are the historically memorable ones of Vannevar Bush, Franklin Delano Roosevelt's scientific adviser:

1. Pure and applied science should constitute related parts of a unified whole.
2. Research should be a function not of a single government agency or complex of agencies, but of many private agencies.
3. Control should be not by dictation but by coordination.
4. Science should be integrated into national policy.

Other guidelines of more recent vintage include the following: support to be balanced between basic and applied science; a significant body of research support, with no political strings attached, to be spread among many universities rather than among the larger ones (contrary to existing practice); a significant weighting of research for peaceful purposes; and support to be granted according to the following criteria:

1. Collective judgment of a given discipline.
2. Social usefulness.

[22] Harvey Brooks "The Future Growth of Academic Research" in Harold Orlans (Ed.), *Science Policy and the University* (Washington, D.C.: The Brookings Institution, 1968), p. 74.

3. Promise of significant results.

4. Novelty.

5. Likely influence on other research.

6. Relationship to national goals.[23]

## The Sciences, Humanities, and Social Sciences

The relative importance of science in the total spectrum of the natural sciences, the social sciences, and the humanities is one of the most fundamental, as well as controversial, issues of the day. And it has been fundamental and controversial for a long time. The humanities reigned supreme from the time of the Golden Age of Greece until the beginning of the modern era. The queen of the humanities was philosophy, and deduction was her sceptre. With the upsurge of science in the sixteenth and seventeenth centuries, philosophy and deduction began to give ground selectively, as well as grudgingly, to science and induction. These latter ushered in the Industrial Revolution and the electronic age, which, as has been established in other contexts, created as many social problems as they solved. Thus science indirectly sired certain of the social sciences, sociology and anthropology in particular, and contributed to the ever mounting complexity of economics, political science, social psychology, and law.

The question of whether any one of the three categories of knowledge—the natural sciences, the social sciences, or the humanities—is more important than either of the other two may be approached in terms of practical-value or theoretical-value considerations. In respect to the first, science was eminent from World War II until the late 1960's, during which it revolutionized the military, transformed industry, and changed man's environment and style of living in ways too numerous to mention. Its promise to man was a better way of life, and, in some respects, it made good its promise. But man paid for its benefits with depersonalization, pollution, vocational upset, and loss of natural beauty. The result was that science in the late 1960's began to decline—slowly but inexorably. The prestige of the military sank to a new low. Government subsidies to science decreased. Students in universities protested against secret research and technological abuses. Scientist-heroes lost some of their luster. And defections in the ranks of scientists increased. These changes, in my opinion, were reactions to an excess of domination by science in the society; conversely, they were symptomatic of a mounting desire by the culture to ameliorate the personal and social problems of people, presaging a period of increasing social action. Indications indeed are strong that the society is moving toward the goal of a more even balance among the natural sciences, the social sciences, and the humanities.

[23] Harvey Brooks, op. cit., pp. 70–72.

Theoretical as well as practical considerations lend support to such a movement. After all, if man is what life is all about, he must be central, not contingent. If he is central, the society has to discover his basic needs, then find ways to meet them. Science is one of these ways. But so too is social engineering that insures adequate living space, clean air, unpolluted water, quiet, and open spaces. So too are the belle arts that make and keep man human. So too, relatedly, is a vision of what man can be: a vision that drives individual man to realize his potential and to help others to realize theirs.

The issue, recently highlighted by C. P. Snow,[24] of science pitted against the humanities and, by implication, the social sciences will, hopefully, soon be laid to rest. With the three complementary, not antagonistic, this is a logical resolution. Man as a social philosopher, viewing life broadly, has to identify and establish his social needs and priorities—to be freeman or slave, tolerant or intolerant, committed or uncommitted, altruistic or self centered, man or animal—then enlist science to help him realize these predetermined outcomes. Under such an arrangement, science plays the role not of Frankenstein monster but of social instrument for good. And if, as stated by Pope, "The proper study of mankind is man," the natural sciences, the social sciences, and the humanities will have to close ranks for the study to be authentic and meaningful. That they actually are closing ranks—in university departments, government, and industry—is a highly encouraging phenomenon of the times. Indeed, a social scientist who is oblivious to the content of the physical sciences, a natural scientist who remains detached from social causes and consequences, and a humanist whose feet never touch ground stand as liabilities to themselves, their colleagues, and collective mankind. Discrete separateness among the three divisions of knowledge is a luxury too dangerous for the social order to tolerate. What is needed, instead, is distinctiveness that finds perspective in unity and breadth.

## VALUES

In this section, I bring together in compressed form those values that, at least in the opinion of many, characterize science in its many manifestations. The coverage is brief in deference to the appearance of at least some of them in other contexts throughout the chapter. They are presented here in the format of a descriptive list. Specifically, they include the following:

1. Openness before knowledge irrespective of source, and inquisitive probing into its meaning.
2. Belief that change characterizes all matter, thus that knowledge is never complete.

[24] C. P. Snow, *The Two Cultures and the Scientific Revolution* (New York: Cambridge University Press, 1959).

3. Belief in the superiority of the inductive method over the deductive method, with a built-in dedication to expose deductive falsity wherever found.

4. Explanation of nature's phenomena in terms of defensible theories and established laws.

5. Thus, rejection of animism, superstition, magic, and religious fanaticism.

6. In the area of basic science, operational autonomy in a personal-social context; in the area of applied science (or technology), social and political accountability.

7. Disavowal of any need to implement divine purpose, deductively conceived.

8. Knowledge conceived as neither good nor bad apart from social implementation.

9. Justification of a broad base of professional and financial support for basic science inasmuch as the latter's purview is the universe and all mankind, the ultimate goal being an international brotherhood of scientists.

10. Espousal of the scientific method of openness, careful hypothesis, data gathering and collation, implementation, and final assessment.

## A POINT OF VIEW

Mankind has to decide whether science will, in the future, be a force for good or ill. On the positive side of the ledger, it has brought him healing drugs, computerized brains, fertile land, sophisticated communications media, rapid transportation, household conveniences ad infinitum, and shorter work weeks. It has enabled him to "conquer" the moon. But it has not, as yet, helped him to conquer the earth. Rather, it has contributed significantly to its disintegration—by a nuclear explosion over Hiroshima, by allowing 80,000,000 automobiles and 400,000 factories in the United States alone to pollute the environment, by mutilating nature's beauty, and by offending man's aural and olfactory sensibilities.

Yet man, not science, is responsible for these social indecencies, for his is the power to deter and control. During the past several decades, he has awakened to the monstrousness of his scientific offenses against himself and his world. What he needs now is to develop enough social consciousness to rectify, whenever possible, his more serious past offenses, and to avoid comparable ones in the future. And, as feelingly expressed by the modern

Cassandra, Lewis Mumford, who has prophesied to a deaf world these many years,

> there is no part of our modern world that we must not be ready to scrap, if the need to scrap it is the price of mankind's safety and continued development.

> The age of atomic disintegration cannot tolerate absolutism in any form: even in the form that regards scientific knowledge as an absolute. . . . Nothing is sacred but human life.[25]

[25] Lewis Mumford, *The Human Prospect*, edited by Harry T. Moore and Carl W. Deutsch (Carbondale: Southern Illinois University Press, 1955), pp. 229–230.

# Bibliography

American Association for the Advancement of Science, *Science*. Washington, D.C.: AAAS, any weekly issue.

Benjamin, A. Cornelius, *Science, Technology and Human Values*. Columbia: University of Missouri Press, 1965.

Boulding, Kenneth E., *The Meaning of the Twentieth Century*. New York: Harper and Row, Publishers, 1964.

Commoner, Barry, *Science and Survival*. New York: The Viking Press, Inc., 1966.

Ferkiss, Victor C., *Technological Man: The Myth and the Reality*. New York: George Brazieler, Inc., 1969.

Glass, Bentley, *Science and Liberal Education*. Baton Rouge: Louisiana State University Press, 1959.

Hitch, Charles, *Decision Making for Defense*. Berkeley: University of California Press, 1965.

Keenan, Boyd R. (Ed.), *Science and the University*. New York: Columbia University Press, 1966.

Lapp, Ralph E., *The New Priesthood*. New York: Harper and Row, Publishers, 1965.

Lear, John, "The Frontier Beyond the Moon," *Saturday Review* (January 18, 1969).

Love, Albert and James S. Childers, *Listen to Leaders in Science*. Atlanta: Tupper and Love, Inc., 1965.

Mumford, Lewis, *The Human Prospect*, edited by Harry T. Moore and Karl W. Deutsch. Carbondale: Southern Illinois University Press, 1955.

Myrdal, Gunnar, *Challenge to Affluence*. New York: Pantheon Books, 1963.

National Academy of Sciences, *Science, Government, and the Universities*. Seattle: University of Washington Press, 1966.

Orlans, Harold (Ed.), *Science Policy and the University*. Washington, D.C.: The Brookings Institution, 1968.

Price, Don K., *The Scientific Estate*. Cambridge: Harvard University Press, 1965.

Prior, Moody E., *Science and the Humanities*. Evanston: Northwestern University Press, 1962.

Proxmire, William, "The Pentagon and Free Enterprise," *Saturday Review* (January 31, 1970).

Silberman, Charles and the editors of Fortune, *The Myths of Automation*. New York: Harper and Row, Publishers, 1966.

Snow, C. P., *The Two Cultures*. New York: Cambridge University Press, 1959.

Toffler, Alvin, *Future Shock*. New York: Random House, 1970.

Vallance, Theodore R., "Classified Research and Related Issues in Science Communication," *AAUP Bulletin* (September, 1969).

Woolf, Harry (Ed.), *Science as a Cultural Force*. Baltimore: The Johns Hopkins Press, 1964.

# 6

# Philosophical Values

Philosophy, the central theme of this chapter, has traditionally been regarded as a storehouse of, or avenue to, truth. Antedating organized science by several thousand years, philosophy has a vintage rivaled only by religion. Philosophy achieved provincial status in the ancient world through the writings of such early savants as Anaximander of Miletus (c. 611–546 B.C.), Confucius of Shantung (c. 551–479 B.C.), Heraclitus of Ephesus (c. 540–480 B.C.), and Anaxagoras of Athens (c. 500–428 B.C.). It achieved worldwide status somewhat later through the writings of Plato (427–347 B.C.) and Aristotle (384–322 B.C.). For two thousand years after Plato's time, philosophy was the unquestioned queen of the scholarly disciplines. In the seventeenth century, however, science emerged as a serious threat to it, a threat that in the nineteenth and twentieth centuries endangered its very existence. Many during this latter period were, in fact, writing philosophy's epitaph. However, by redefining and redirecting its concerns, as will be elaborated subsequently in the chapter, philosophy survived the onslaught of science. As a result, it is very much alive and healthy today.

## WHAT IS PHILOSOPHY

The question, What is philosophy? generally elicits a wide variety of responses from a wide variety of responders. To Socrates, as related in Plato's *Republic*, philosophy is "the spectator of all time and all existence." To William James, it was no less embracing, dealing, so he said,

with the principles of explanation that underlie all things without exception, the elements common to Gods and men and animals and stones, the first whence and the last whither of the whole cosmic procession, the conditions of all knowing, and the most general rules of human conduct.[1]

These two definitions reflect the speculative orientation of Socrates and James that, until recently, imposed on philosophy the task of explaining the totality of life and the universe.

The next definition—that of the Quaker philosopher David Elton Trueblood —attempts to satisfy the demands of both speculative and critical philosophy. The domain of the former is all-embracing including God, man, and the universe. The domain of the latter is more modest including only those understandings that can be validated empirically, semantically, or intuitively. Now for Trueblood's definition.

> The chief function of a philosopher is to try to perform the extremely difficult but manifestly important task of logical reasoning. In the nature of the case, the task must always be twofold. The philosopher must not only reason about the world; he must reason about reasoning itself.[2]

Trueblood goes on to suggest that the essential characteristics of a valid philosophy should consist of the following: (1) beneficent skepticism (that compels man to be critical before all naive assumptions and judgments), (2) catholicity (that elevates wisdom to a plane higher than that of any single sect, system, or generation), and (3) practicality (that elevates philosophy above the status of verbal parlor game and projects it into the mainstream of life).[3]

Critical philosophy shows through more clearly in the writings of Charlie D. Broad, a leading British philosopher at midcentury, as he identifies the tasks of philosophy which are, he says, (1) to determine the precise meaning of concepts and the extent of their relatedness, (2) to criticize all fundamental beliefs that one holds no matter how intimate or deeply rooted they are, and (3) to test one's fundamental beliefs by "resolutely and honestly exposing them to every objection that one can think of . . . [or can] find in the writings of others."[4]

The linguistic branch of critical philosophy would subscribe to the simple definition that philosophy is no more or no less than the critical study of language and its meanings.

Building on this introductory background, we shall, in the remainder of

[1] William James, *Some Problems of Philosophy* (New York: Longmans, Green and Company, Inc., 1911), p. 5.
[2] David Elton Trueblood, *General Philosophy* (New York: Harper and Row, Publishers, 1963), p. 1.
[3] Trueblood, op. cit., pp. 12–17.
[4] Charlie D. Broad, "The Relation of Philosophy to the Sciences" in Melvin Rader (Ed.), *The Enduring Questions* (New York: Holt, Rinehart and Winston, 1956), pp. 10–12.

the chapter, attempt two tasks: first, to identify and briefly describe the concerns that philosophical systems have dealt with through the ages; second, to present in condensed form the major conceptualizations of five philosophical systems: rationalism, empiricism, pragmatism, linguistic analysis, and existentialism.

## PHILOSOPHY'S CONCERNS

The ingredients of philosophy, strictly speaking, are never discrete. Rather they are projections of any given philosopher and the particular philosophical concerns that he espouses. If they are the concerns of speculative philosophy, they generally include, in part or in toto, such complex concepts as mind and body, God and man, goodness and badness, truth and untruth, the beautiful and the ugly—in fact, the universe and all that it embraces. As stated once more by Broad, speculative philosophy takes

> over the results of the various sciences, . . . [adds] to them the results of the religious and ethical experiences of mankind, and then . . . [reflects] upon the whole. The hope is that, by this means, we may be able to reach some general conclusions as to the nature of the Universe and as to our position and prospects in it.[5]

Critical philosophy, in contrast, has as its domain the language and workability of beliefs. Its ultimate is the lucid articulation and practical application of propositions. These latter, at least as articulated by some, are of three types: *analytical statements* that can be verified semantically, *empirical statements* that can be verified through the senses, and *non-sense statements* that cannot be verified. Each of these will be developed in greater detail subsequently in the chapter.

The divisions of speculative philosophy along with their specialized concerns consist of the following.

1. *Metaphysics.* This branch of philosophy subdivides into *ontology* (whose province is the nature of being: man, God, subhuman forms, and inanimate life) ; and *cosmology* (whose province is the origin and structure of the world). Metaphysics poses and attempts to answer such fundamental questions, or conundrums, as these: What is man? Does he have a soul? What is the nature of mind? What is the nature of body? Does man have freedom of choice in life or is he a victim of some kind of determinism? Is his nature intrinsically good or bad? Does reality exist apart from, or is it an extension of, the knower? Is life purposeful

[5] Broad, op. cit., p. 13.

or whimsical? Is there a God, and, if so, what is "He" like? Do man and subhuman forms differ qualitatively or only quantitatively? Does the universe function in response to natural law? And these are just some of the many.

2. *Epistemology.* This branch of philosophy has as its purview knowledge: its origin, nature, limits, and methods. Like metaphysics, epistemology poses and attempts to answer many fundamental questions, among which are these. What are the legitimate sources of knowledge: reason, empiricism, or divine revelation? What is the relation of mind to body or to soul? Does man ever know anything for a certainty or does he know only approximately? What is truth and how is it verified? And can knowledge be taught?

3. *Ethics.* This branch of philosophy has as its purview morality—the standards, that is, that motivate man toward the good and dissuade him from the bad. It also poses and attempts to answer a number of difficult but fundamental questions. For example, what rules of conduct should govern the behavior of human beings? Is the Golden Rule or existentialism's imperative that individual man should act as if he were acting for all mankind a valid principle? Is virtue innate, environmentally engendered, or rationally conceived? Is morality the same for all men at all times, in all situations, and at all places?

4. *Esthetics.* This fourth branch of philosophy has as its purview beauty— one of the five qualities that the mathematician-philosopher, Alfred Lord Whitehead, said should be a product of every civilized society. The other four he identified as truth, adventure, art, and peace.[6] Esthetics is a search for perfection of form in persons and things. Its standards reside both subjectively in the viewer and objectively in external values. Primarily a component of the affective domain, the field of esthetics impinges also on the mental and ethical domains. It finds expression in music, art, literature, costuming, the theatre, and the dance, as well as in nature and people. Speculative philosophers through the ages have, not surprisingly, been considerably less convincing when writing about esthetics than when writing about metaphysics, epistemology, and even ethics. The unquestioned subjectivity of the topic constitutes the reason.

5. *Logic.* This last branch of philosophy has as its purview the assessment of truth. Classical philosophers employed the syllogism as one of its major methods: for example,

---

[6] Alfred Lord Whitehead, *Adventure of Ideas* (New York: The Macmillan Company, 1933), p. 353.

All philosophers are people;
Americans are philosophers;
Therefore Americans are people.

The syllogism unfolds algebraically: If X equals Y, and Z equals X, then Z equals Y.

Socrates employed as his stock-in-trade method the dialogue, which consisted of the following sequential parts:

1. A position on a given issue is adopted. (All men are totally depraved.)

2. An analysis is made of the implications of the issue adopted. (There is no goodness or righteousness in any form in any man.)

3. The analysis reveals falsity. (Some men have demonstrated beyond the shadow of doubt the quality of goodness or righteousness.)

4. Then the original position is false. (All men are *not* totally depraved.)

Logic to modern man includes more than syllogism and the dialectic Socratic dialogue. It includes, also, the scientific method and critical thinking along many lines. It is in this area of logic, or search for proof, that linguistic philosophers have made their greatest contribution. As will be developed in more detail later, their method is to expose to careful analysis all language. They definitely would have applied this method to the syllogism or dialogue excerpt cited above. Through it, they distinguish among conclusions capable of being validated semantically, those capable of being validated empirically, and others incapable of being validated.

## RATIONALISM

Although this section could well have been divided into separate treatments of rationalism and idealism, I chose, because of their interrelatedness, to treat them as a single system. Historically, idealism has been ide*a*ism; thus its kinship to rationalism is a close one. From here on, the term idealism will not be used.

The metaphysics (study of being or reality) of rationalism is clear cut. It rests on the fundamental postulate that mind and all that it implies—reason, ideas, thinking, contemplating, intuiting, inferring, and concluding—are the basic essence of life. Secularists within the rational tradition have generally depicted reason as being noncontingent and discrete. Religionists within the tradition have depicted it as being either a direct part of, or a human extension of, divine mind.

To Plato, as expounded in *Phaedo, Phaedrus*, and others of his dialogues, universal forms or external ideas are endowed with absolute status and thus exist apart from any given knower. These include, for example, justice, fortitude, goodness, beauty, morality, and sensitivity—all essences with independent existence. The task of mortal man in respect to these forms or ideas was, as advanced by Plato, to perceive them authentically—as authentically, that is, as human mind was capable of doing.

To René Descartes (1596–1650), French philosopher and mathematician, the faculty of reason and the ideas it engenders, are primary; the material things that set them in motion are secondary. His oft-quoted deductive statement from *Meditations*, "I think; therefore I am," leaves no doubt that reason was central in his metaphysical position. In the same philosophical treatise, he relatedly wrote: "I am not more than a thing which thinks, that is to say a mind or a soul, or an understanding, or a reason . . . ." Hegel (1770–1831) German idealist philosopher, was just as categorical as Descartes in depicting reason as the fundamental essence of being. "The rational," said he, "is the real and the real the rational." Mind and mind content were categorically central in his position. To the Irish idealist philosopher, Berkeley (1685–1753) they were no less central. According to him, ideas, not sensations, were paramount; to him, perception alone brought material objects into being.

The epistemology of rationalism also resides in the province of reason. Mind, the sole or dominant substance of reality, thus finds expression in the reasoning processes. The method of Socrates was to search his mind and that of his associates to discover the essence of man and goodness. The method of Descartes was to employ the two rational processes of *intuition*—defined by him as "the undoubting conception of an unclouded and attentive mind . . . [that] springs from reason alone"; and *deduction*, defined as "the process of inferring from other facts."[7] The method of Kant (1724–1804), as described in the *Critique of Practical Reason*, was to start with the "given" —those beliefs and postulates that almost everyone would agree to, and ask what else must be true if those are.

The ethical and esthetic systems of rationalism also look to reason for standards. Morality is thus what rational minds deem reasonable. And beauty is adjudged by rational as well as affective processes.

Rationalism, at least in its more extreme form, is highly vulnerable because of its downgrading of the significance of the external world and sense experience. It is one thing for an individual to be rationally contemplative; it is another thing for him to deny the importance of material and sensory phenomena that lie outside himself. Sensitive to this and other issues intrinsic in pure rationalism, few serious thinkers today subscribe to it in unadulterated form. Rather, they subscribe to neorationalism. In so doing, they are able to

[7] Rene Descartes, *Discourse on Method, Part I*, in Elizabeth S. Haldane and G. R. T. Gross (Translators), *The Philosophical Works of Descartes* (Cambridge: Cambridge University Press, 1931), pp. 7–8.

reject metaphysical monism (a position that, in pure rationalism, posits mind to be the one and only component of being); and epistemological monism (a position that posits reason to be the only avenue to knowledge). As neorationalists, they are able to accord mind and reason primary, but not absolute, status.

## EMPIRICISM

The tradition of empiricism parallels, in great part, that of science. Whether it started, as many allege, with Aristotle's espousal of induction, is debatable. That it achieved stature in the time, and through the efforts, of Francis Bacon (1561–1626), is not debatable.

The position of pure empiricism is that man receives information about the world through his sense organs and that he is able to draw valid conclusions from information gained in this way. David Hume (1711–1776) and Immanuel Kant (1724–1804), staunch advocates of pure empiricism, contended that only knowledge gained through the senses is authentic and concretely real; that knowledge gained in any other way is unauthentic. To the critics of empiricism, this narrow view leaves its proponents vulnerable. An alternative is rational empiricism, which does not limit experience to that gained through the senses; rather, it broadens the base to include experience acquired cognitively, semantically, and even, perhaps, intuitively.

Empiricism is a limited philosophical system. Its answers to epistemological and esthetic questions are reasonably persuasive if not necessarily convincing. Its answers to metaphysical questions are consistently less persuasive being most often only inferential. For one to say, for instance, that man is only what he senses from the outside world tells little about what he is psychologically or about what the intangibles of his personality are. Nor does it tell much more about ethics unless, as in the case of Charles D. Peirce (1839–1914) who was a pragmatic empiricist, it holds that all ethical systems need to be validated pragmatically—in the arena of social action, that is. In the last analysis, empiricism is comfortable primarily in the area of epistemology.

## PRAGMATISM

Pragmatism like empiricism is also not, in a classical sense, a complete philosophy. Rather, it is, at one and the same time, a theory about truth and a method of verifying beliefs and values in a social arena. That it only touches lightly on or avoids metaphysical issues is patently obvious. That it elects to touch lightly on or avoid them is, as will be developed subsequently, intrinsic to the system itself.

Three proponents of pragmatism tower above all others: Charles Sanders

Peirce (1839–1914), William James (1842–1910), and John Dewey (1859–1952). Peirce as early as 1878 introduced the term pragmatism in a university lecture but did not, until 1902, use it in any of his writings. These three giants of pragmatism were opposed to all philosophical systems, particularly rationalism, that held truth to be certain and fixed, that espoused rigid a priori positions, and that downgraded the importance of social context as a legitimate arena for validating truth.

Two questions are central in pragmatism: (1) How can ideas be made clear and understandable? And (2) How can truth be verified or corroborated? Peirce in addressing himself to the first of the two questions accepts the conclusion of traditional logicians that clarity of ideas is a function of careful definition worded in language understandable to any would-be perceiver. But, continues Peirce, the clarification of ideas is not a function of abstract symbols alone; concretions also are needed. In other words, the acid test of meaning is language expressed in action that is understandable to observers. Meaning to Peirce, thus, was an objective, not a subjective, phenomenon. It existed, so he opined, when ideas and reality that rose above subjective opinion and bias were in conformity. And only those observers who were critically objective should, he said, have the task of assessing reality.

The issue of assessment takes us to the second question: How can truth be verified or corroborated? Pragmatism's answer, generally, is that truth is verifiable through its consequences. As stated by William James in *Pragmatism: A New Name for Same Old Ways of Thinking*, "The pragmatic method . . . [assesses] each notion by tracing its respective social consequences." It is "The attitude of looking away from first things, principles, 'categories,' supposed necessities; and of looking toward last things, fruits, consequences, facts."

If the test of truth is the analysis of consequences in action, what criterion should man employ in distinguishing between good and bad consequences? To James, consequences were good if they gave emotional satisfaction to observers; bad if they did not. He develops this theme of emotional gratification in *Principles of Psychology*:

> The dog singles out of any situation its smells, and the horse its sounds, because they may reveal facts of practical moment, and are instinctively exciting to these several creatures. The infant notices the candle flame or the window, and ignores the rest of the room, because those objects give him a vivid pleasure. So, the country boy dissociates the blackberry, the chestnut, and the wintergreen from the vague mass of other shrubs and trees, for their practical uses.[8]

[8] William James, *Principles of Psychology* (New York: Henry Holt and Company, 1893), p. 363.

Dewey, like James, also held that for beliefs to be valid, they had to have valid consequences. The term pragmatic, he averred "means only the rule of referring all thinking, all reflective considerations, to *consequences* for final meaning and test."[9] But what makes a consequence valid or invalid? To James, a consequence was valid if it gave pleasure or satisfied a need. To Dewey, it was valid if, in the arena of social action, it verified an idea or hypothesis. It was valid if it passed the test of critical analysis. It was valid if it led not only to the understanding, but to the changing, of experience; if it solved the problem that precipitated the consequence in the first place.

Yet despite my attempt here, and that of the many proponents of pragmatism in the past, to formulate a valid criterion for distinguishing between good and bad social consequences, the results are far from satisfying. All pragmatists are more sure-footed when asserting that beliefs are valid if they "work" than when articulating and expounding a criterion of workability. Both Peirce and Dewey labored mightily to explain the concepts, consequences and workability, but, in my opinion, they were no more successful than the many others who have failed in the same attempt.

Yet pragmatism should be more lauded for its positive contributions to philosophy than faulted for its shortcomings. Apropos of the former, it moved philosophy off the dead center of contemplative thought, projecting it into the arena of social action. Relatedly, it assumed a posture of skepticism toward man's quest for certainty, positing that change is life's only certainty. Just as fundamentally, it joined hands with science as a valuable ally in the pursuit of knowledge.

Pragmatism is most vulnerable, at least in the opinion of its arch critics, on the following points. First, as covered two paragraphs back, the criterion for distinguishing between good and bad consequences of a belief or ethical principle is never easy to ascertain, and, when identified, is never entirely convincing. Second, pragmatism is too futuristically oriented to be entirely palatable. Illustrative in this connection is Dewey's assertive conclusion that

> anticipation is . . . more primary than recollection; projection than summoning of the past; the prospective than the retrospective . . . . Imaginative recovery of the bygone is indispensable to successful invasion of the future, but its status is that of instrument.[10]

Talking to this point, Rader comments:

> How poor and stunted life would be without the heritage of the past. If you cut away the past the present collapses, quite as much as if you

[9] John Dewey, *Essays in Experimental Logic* (Chicago: University of Chicago Press, 1916), p. 330.
[10] John Dewey, *Creative Intelligence* (New York: Henry Holt and Company, 1917), pp. 12, 14.

cut away the future. Most of the spiritual depth and inwardness of life depends upon mental rehearsal and interpretation of our acts, which otherwise would be merely outward and mechanical; and until we look back on the acts, we have no adequate basis for interpreting them.[11]

Pragmatism is vulnerable, although not necessarily blameworthy, for a third reason, namely, for its rejection of all absolutes. Are there not some truths that are absolute, not relative? Is it an absolute, or only a relative, truth that I have a copy of Bertrand Russell's *The Will to Doubt* in my library? Or that mankind does exist in some way? Or that the concept workability is interpreted differently by different individuals?

Finally, pragmatism conceivably is vulnerable because of its one-sided practicalism. As asked by Rader: Cannot a person think just because he likes to do so, because it is fun, rather than because he needs to do so for purely practical reasons? And, relatedly: Does everything have to be socially useful to be good?[12]

## LINGUISTIC ANALYSIS

The barrier that separates pragmatism and speculative philosophy is formidable; the one that separates linguistic analysis and speculative philosophy is just as much so, maybe more so. Linguistic analysis is a hybrid product of late nineteenth century and twentieth century life and thought. It was propelled into being by the following forces: derailment of the eternal quest for certainty, disenchantment with speculative philosophy's tendency to overstate, the mounting influence of science and mathematics, and growth of the linguistic movement.

The British philosopher, G. E. Moore, was a pioneer in the linguistic movement. As a student at Cambridge University, beginning in 1892, he early took exception to philosophical propositions that, lacking clear meaning or consistency, were unsupportable except on illogical grounds. One of his mentors, for instance, espoused the theory that reality is spiritual. Moore reportedly countered with the question: Are chairs and tables, then, spiritual in the same sense that people are? Moore was an early leader in the struggle of a new breed of philosophers to "clean up" the logic and language of philosophy.

Bertrand Russell was another pioneer in the ranks of this new breed. He called himself a logical atomist, averring that truth comes in small particles. His contention was that concepts need to be reduced to their lowest common

---

[11] Melvin Rader (Ed.), *The Enduring Questions* (New York: Holt, Rinehart and Winston, Inc., 1956), p. 155.
[12] Melvin Rader, op. cit., pp. 154–155.

denominators for any conclusions about them to be valid. Russell, a perceptive logician, mathematician, and intellectual genius in his own right, laid the groundwork for the soon-to-evolve movement of logical positivism and the later-to-evolve movement of linguistic analysis.

Logical positivism, a covering label for the so-called Vienna Circle of philosophers, had as its axial theme the principle of *verification*. A. J. Ayer and others of the circle held that for any proposition to be valid it had to be verified via empirical observation or sense experience. They made an exception of mathematical propositions which they conceded were true for reason of their internal logic. The targets of logical positivism, not unlike those of Moore and Russell, were metaphysics, theology, and ethics, none of which was capable of passing the test of empirical verification. Yet the attack on these was less actual than linguistic. The position taken was that the special term *statement* should be reserved for propositions that are verifiable. Conversely, that some other appellation needed to be reserved for utterances of a speculative kind.

The opponents of logical positivism advanced these counterarguments: logical positivism overemphasizes the importance of sense experience, downgrading, in the process, other important kinds of experience; the principle of verification, because present-oriented, renders experiences of the past nonverifiable and thus not very important; and logical positivism makes linguistic distinctions without effecting any actual differences in traditionally held meanings.

By midcentury, logical positivism had eased into the more contemporary system of linguistic analysis. Both look with disfavor on metaphysics and both approach philosophy via the avenue of language. Linguistic analysis, however, addresses itself to language in a more systematic way. Deliberately undoctrinaire, it is a technique of analyzing language: its uses and misuses, meanings, and implications for philosophy.

From the time of its classical advent to the present, philosophy has confused as much as it has clarified the thinking of man. It has confused, in part, because of the complex nature of its subject matter: God, man, knowledge, and the universe. It has confused, also in part, because of its linguistic shortcomings—shortcomings, that is, in the rhetoric of its explanations and pronouncements.

Professor Israel Scheffler, the Harvard University analyst, suggests that there are three conditions for *knowing that*: "the *belief* condition, the *evidence* condition, and the *truth* condition." A belief, unsupported in any way, has a low order of credibility; a statement supported by defensible evidence has greater credibility; a truth that cannot be contested has proper claim to credibility. In respect to the three, it is essential that language content conform to the level of knowing conveyed by each. In the opinion of analysts, speculative philosophy failed to make this needed distinction. Descarte's assertion, "I think; therefore I am," is, for instance, vulnerable if detached from the evidence condition. So is Plato's "God is pure form" or Hegel's "The real is the rational and the rational the real."

Linguistic analysts, like their logical positivist predecessors, generally divide statements, as indicated previously, into three categories: analytical, empirical, and non-sense. These differ on the criterion of verification. Analytical statements are verifiable in the meanings of the symbols they contain or the principles on which they rest. Illustrative is the mathematical statement that $2 + 2 = 4$, or the hypothesis in chemistry that energy is never either created or destroyed. Empirical statements are verifiable in sense experience or laboratory investigation. Illustrative are these two statements: man has lateral as well as frontal vision, and the motor of the automobile is running. Non-sense statements are, to linguistic analysts, ones that are verifiable neither in analysis nor empiricism. The label non-sense connotes that such statements are not demonstrably true or demonstrably false. Illustrative are such familiar assertions of Christianity as "God is love," and "The man who sinneth shall surely die."

The basic premise of linguistic analysis is that, contrary to traditional belief and practice, philosophy is not a fact-producing but a language-clarification system. As stated by one of its early members, "The language game is the primary thing." Yet for any system, either by direct word or implication, to accord language priority status over the "stuff" of life and thought that it represents is to overstate the case. However, linguistic analysis may well have deliberately overstated its case to counteract the hyperbole that metaphysics and religion had been guilty of for several thousand years.

## EXISTENTIALISM

Existentialism, the last philosophical system to be treated in this chapter, shares the modern day philosophical spotlight with pragmatism and linguistic analysis. Rejecting the deductive hypotheses of traditional metaphysical systems and the objective detachment of the natural sciences, existentialism proclaims that existence itself holds the key to man's essence. Its rallying cry is existence before essence. Man lives and by living he becomes. Thus, unlike humanism and theology which depict man as noble for reason of his being human, existentialism commits him to live through to the outcome of nobility.

Existentialism goes back at least as far as Soren Kierkegaard (1813–1855), Danish theologian and philosopher. Left cold by the mechanistic impersonalization of Hegelian rationalism and intensely desirous of discovering meaning in his own tormented life, he gave form and substance to what soon was to bear the label existentialism. Although Kierkegaard was existentialist and

Protestant, existentialism has not, consistently since its inception, remained exclusively Protestant. Among current existentialist writers, Gabriel Marcel and Karl Jaspers, for instance, are Roman Catholic; Martin Heidegger and Jean Paul Sartre, for instance, are atheists; Paul Tillich, like Kierkegaard, is Protestant; Martin Buber is Jewish.

Existentialism is an accrual of tenets that, although not subscribed to by all proponents of the system, are becoming increasingly accepted as intrinsic to it. Three of the more basic we highlight here.

1. *Existence precedes essence.* As already noted, this is a cornerstone of existentialism. It implies a rejection of all a priori conceptualizations about man and the universe. Man does not come into the world a value-oriented entity. Rather, he creates value (or essence) in the process of living. Nor is the universe necessarily good or bad. Rather it is one or the other only in response to any individual's contributions to it and assessment of it. This tenet of existence before essence rules out all deductively conceived universals. Furthermore, it depicts man as an ever emerging entity, always becoming, never having become. As stated by Kierkegaard, man "strives infinitely, is constantly in the process of becoming."[13]

2. *Existence is a subjective phenomenon.* In the process of becoming, man plays the role of an independent agent searching for subjective meaning in life. And in the search, the subject (the searcher himself) is primary; the objects (things, ideas, events) of the search are secondary. In the words of Professor Morris of the University of Illinois (Circle Campus), existentialism "asks us to ask ourselves what significance we can attach to our presence in the world. . . . We are chained to this puzzle, the meaning of our own existing."[14]

Does this commission to man to discover his own existence imply an endorsement of egocentricity? Existentialists say definitely not. And Martin Buber's "I and Thou" and "I and It" concepts constitute one explanation for the answer. Jean Paul Sartre's concept of individual man choosing for the entire human race—to be developed subsequently—constitutes another answer. Buber's thesis is that the truly evolving individual has two kinds of relationships. The first is an altruistic one with "Thou" figures who project him away from himself toward others. This relationship is one of commitment that might even reach as high as an eternal "Thou." Stated somewhat mystically but provocatively by Buber:

[13] Soren Kierkegaard, *The Concept of Dread*, trans. by Lowrie (Princeton, New Jersey: Princeton University Press, 1957), p. 84.
[14] Van Cleve Morris (Ed.), *Modern Movements in Educational Philosophy* (Boston: Houghton Mifflin Company, 1969), p. 286.

The primary word *I—Thou* [italics mine] can be spoken only with the whole being. Concentration and fusion into the whole being can never take place through my agency, nor can it ever take place without me. I become through my relation to the Thou; as I become I, I say Thou.

All real living is meeting.[15]

The second relationship of an individual is with "It" figures that, because detached from an individual in time or space, make no demands on him. Once again in the words of Buber:

The I of the primary word *I—It* [italics mine] . . . has no present, only the past. Put it another way, in so far as man rests satisfied with the things that he experiences and uses, he lives in the past, and his moment has no present content. He has nothing but objects. But objects subsist in time that has been.[16]

Thus the emergent individual defines himself by turning outward as well as inward. He creates himself by relating to others. But whether he does either of these is his choice to make.

3. *Freedom commits man to choose.* It is man's choice either to choose or not to choose freedom because existentialism, by definition, imposes the obligations of freedom on man. The most demanding single one of these is the obligation to make all important life choices that intimately involve him. Nor can he shift this responsibility to institutions (such as the state or a religious group) or to other individuals. The responsibility is his alone. And it becomes all the more agonizing when, as opined by Sartre, the emerging man has to make all important choices in life as if he were making them for the entire human race.

And when we say that a man is responsible for himself . . . [we say] that he is responsible for all men. . . . In fact, in creating the man that we want to be, there is not a single one of our acts which does not at the same time create an image of man as we think he ought to be . . . The man who involves himself and who realizes that he is not only the person he chooses to be, but also a lawmaker who is, at the same time, choosing all mankind as well as himself, can not escape the feeling of his total and deep responsibility.[17]

The existentialist view, then, is that man is responsible for everything he does. Because existentialism is almost completely antideterministic, it pooh-

[15] Martin Buber, "I and Thou," in Thomas O. Buford, *Toward a Philosophy of Education* (New York: Holt, Rinehart, and Winston, 1969), p. 211.
[16] Buber, op. cit., p. 212.
[17] Jean Paul Sartre, *Existentialism*, in Buford, op. cit., p. 123.

poohs the psychic determinism of Freud and the historical determinism of Marx. In lieu, it says to individual man: Like it or not, you are in the world condemned to be free. Define yourself because no one else can or will define you. And in the process of definition, choose not only for yourself but for all mankind. Thus the individual is central in existentialism but not egocentrically so. No individual can be egocentric when employing the human race as a behavior standard.

## PHILOSOPHY AND VALUES

In this last section of the chapter, we return to the central theme of the book by asking: What influence, if any, has philosophy had, or does it currently have, on man's values? A different answer, in my opinion, has to be given in respect to the speculative philosophies of the prescientific period than to the critical philosophies of the present day.

Speculative philosophies of the past, we remind the reader, purported to explain issues as complex as reality, being, knowledge, ethics, esthetics, and logic. Speculative philosophers from both secular and sectarian ranks thought profoundly about these, ultimately proclaiming answers that were logical to some, specious to others. If their answers were not always satisfactory, they were generally more so than those that preceded them. Plato's concept, for instance, of universals subsisting apart from the things that embodied them was a vastly superior explanation of ultimate values than the conceptualization of warring gods and goddesses capriciously pronouncing what mankind's values should be. And if the Biblical explanation of sin is not satisfactory to some, it is a better explanation than that made by animists of an earlier time.

Speculative philosophy has always been a venture into the unknown: an attempt, as it were, to explain the otherwise unexplainable mysteries of life. Unfortunately, the tools of speculative philosophers, consisting primarily of reason and empiricism, each backed up by limited knowledge of life processes, have never been adequate, with the result that their pronouncements have consistently created as many problems as they purported to solve.

The scientific revolution of the past three centuries has dealt speculative philosophy a telling blow. It has diverted man's pursuit of truth from a path of absolutism to one of relativism. It has revealed empirical knowledge to be rarely more than approximately "real" or "true." It has cast doubt on the infallibility of man's rational powers. And it has cautioned man against a dependence on divine revelation that goes counter to natural law.

Religion has also dealt speculative philosophy a telling blow. We support this admittedly sweeping generalization with the following specifics.

1. The concept of the Bible as a verbally inspired and thus literally

authentic document, true in every detail, is receiving increasingly less support with the passage of time. The fact that there are many Bibles which differ in content, that scholars differ in their interpretations of any single version, and that every one contains internal inconsistencies —all these lend credence to our allegation.

2. The Roman Catholic Church has lost its traditionally assumed status as *the* infallible organizational voice of divine authority. The Second Vatican Council of 1962–1963 is support enough for this statement. And this loss of status has made Catholics the world over increasingly skeptical of the pronouncements made by the Church authority.

3. The religious shift in the western world from theological to social concerns has set speculative philosophy back yet another pace. "Civil religion" is the basic faith of Western man—so wrote Will Herberg in *Protestant-Catholic-Jew*, 1955. And the social upheavals of the present day confirm his thesis. In the words of a Professor of Church History of Yale University, the present generation seems to be moving toward

(1) a growing attachment to a naturalism or "secularism" that makes people suspicious of doctrines that imply anything supernatural or which seem to involve magic, superstition, or divine interventions in the natural order; (2) a creeping (or galloping) awareness of vast contradictions in American life between profession and performance, the ideal and the actual; and (3) increasing doubt concerning the capacity of present-day ecclesiastical, political, social, and educational institutions to rectify these contradictions.[18]

The critical philosophies of pragmatism, linguistic analysis, and existentialism have, during the past century, moved in to fill the value gaps left by the receding speculative philosophies. The three, although differing widely in their substantive content, have these characteristics in common: they scorn deduction, they eschew metaphysics, they are oriented in the present or they thrust toward the future, and they operate as bases for changing values.

Of the three, existentialism is probably the most widespread and influential today. Its emphasis on individualism at a time when political and technological institutions are deemphasizing it has great appeal. So too does its advocacy of the individual as his own decision maker, his own value creator.

However, many today exploit existentialism, employing it as a smoke screen for activities that the system itself would condemn. The hippie, for instance, who "does his own thing" without regard for the personalities of others acts

[18] Sydney E. Ahlstrom, "The Radical Turn in Theology and Ethics: Why It Occurred in the 1960's," *The Annals of the American Academy of Political and Social Science* 387 (January 1970), pp. 7–8.

selfishly and not for all mankind. And the radical revolutionary who callously destroys and maims conceivably does so more to fulfill a neurotic need for power than to create a better self or a better world. Existentialism is not a system of license but of discipline and self control. While espousing individualism it also espouses social consciousness.

I conclude here with the thought that speculative philosophies of the past went beyond the abilities of individual philosophers to penetrate and interpret the world of the unknowable. Critical philosophies of the present confine their spectrums to the abilities of individual thinkers to ponder the world of the knowable. While not discouraging speculation about the unknowable, they suggest that the language of its pronouncements should be appropriate and the pronouncements themselves should be unassertive.

# Bibliography

Ayer, Alfred J., *The Foundation of Empirical Knowledge*. New York: St. Martin's Press, 1961.

Barrett, William and Henry D. Aiken (Eds.), *Philosophy in the Twentieth Century*. New York: Random House, Inc., 1962.

Barzun, Jacques, *The House of Intellect*. New York: Harper & Row, Publishers, Inc., 1959.

Black, Max, *Philosophy in America*. Ithaca: Cornell University Press, 1965.

Blackham, H. J., *Reality, Man, and Existence: Essential Works of Existentialism*. New York: Bantam Books, Inc., 1965.

Blanshard, Brand, *The Nature of Thought*. New York: The Macmillan Company, 1940.

Broudy, Harry S., *Building a Philosophy of Education*. Englewood, New Jersey: Prentice-Hall, Inc., 1954.

Chomsky, Noam and M. Halle, *Sound Patterns of English*. New York: Harper and Row, Publishers, 1968.

Dewey, John, *How We Think*. New York: D.C. Heath and Company, 1933.

Feigl, Herbert and Wilfred Sellars, *Readings in Philosophical Analysis*. New York: Appleton-Century-Crofts, Inc., 1949.

Greene, Maxine, *Existential Encounters for Teachers*. New York: Random House, Inc., 1967.

Hook, Sidney (Ed.), *Language and Philosophy*. New York: New York University Press, 1969.

Hutchins, Robert M., *The Conflict in Education in a Democratic Society*. New York: Harper and Row, Publishers, Inc., 1953.

James, William, *Pragmatism*. New York: Longmans, Green and Co., 1910.

Kahn, Steven M. (Ed.), *The Philosophical Foundations of Education*. New York: Harper and Row, Publishers, 1970.

Lovejoy, Arthur O., *Reflections on Human Nature*. New York: The Johns Hopkins Press, 1961.

Maritain, Jacques (Ed.), *The Education of Man*. Notre Dame: University of Notre Dame Press, 1967.

Morris, Van Cleve, *Existentialism in Education*. New York: Harper and Row, Publishers, 1966.

Olson, Robert G., *An Introduction to Existentialism*. New York: Dover Publications, 1962.

Park, Joe (Ed.), Selected Readings in the Philosophy of Education, 3rd edition. New York: The Macmillan Company, 1968.

Reck, Andrew J., *The New American Philosophers*. Baton Rouge: Louisiana State University Press, 1968.

Russell, Bertrand, *Mysticism and Logic*. New York: Doubleday and Company, Inc., 1957.

Russell, Bertrand, *The Autobiography of Bertrand Russell*. New York: Simon and Schuster, 1969.

Sartre, Jean Paul, *Existentialism and Human Emotions* (translated by Frechtman and Barnes). New York: Philosophical Library, Inc., 1957.

Scheffler, Israel, *Conditions of Knowledge*. Chicago: Scott, Foresman and Company, 1965.

Temple, William, *Nature, Man and God*. New York: The Macmillan Company, 1956.

Trueblood, David Elton, *General Philosophy*. New York: Harper and Row, Publishers, 1963.

Waismann, Friedrich, *The Principles of Linguistic Philosophy* (Ed. by R. Harre). New York: St. Martin's Press, 1965.

Whitehead, Alfred N., *The Function of Reason*. New York: The Beacon Press, 1958.

# 7

## Values of the New Left

*The New Left*, a term coined in 1960, is descriptive of an increasingly active and important segment of today's society. Just what the term connotes, however, differs from user to user. To the publishers of the *Random House Dictionary of the English Language*, 1968, it applies to "a group of liberals, esp. young intellectuals, that has advocated complete racial equality, disarmament, nonintervention in foreign affairs, and radical changes in the political and economic system." To Professor Howard Zinn of Boston University, it is descriptive of "that loose amalgam of civil rights activists, Black Power advocates, ghetto organizers, student rebels [and] Vietnam protesters."[1] To me, the New Left is descriptive of activists, primarily from the ranks of current and recent student bodies, secondarily from the ranks of black revolutionaries who, claiming disillusionment with the social order, seek to effect significant change in it.

Politically, the New Left ranges from forces that are ultraliberal to others that are aggressively radical. Tactically, it ranges from nonviolent dialogue to overt violence. Numerically, its membership can only be approximated. A 1968 Fortune Magazine poll of college and university students revealed the following data:

Youth, 18–24 years of age, who in 1968 were attending
or had attended some institution of higher learning.                8,000,000

Of this total,

    1.  Practical-minded youth whose primary goal
        was change in themselves, not in the society.    4,800,000

    2.  Socially concerned youth whose primary goal
        was change in the social order.    3,200,000

[1] Howard Zinn, "Marxism and the New Left" in Priscilla Long (Ed.), *The New Left* (Boston: Porter Sargent Publisher, 1969), p. 56.

3. Of the socially concerned youth, those who had participated actively in one or more protest movements.                                    640,000

4. Of the socially concerned youth, those who were militant radicals.[2]                        13,000 (ca)

The poll reported the more practical-minded 4.8 million as stating: "For me, college is mainly a practical matter. With a college education, I can earn more money, have a more interesting career, and enjoy a better position in society." In contrast, it reported the more socially concerned 3.2 million as stating:

> I'm not really concerned with the practical benefits of college. I suppose I take them for granted. College for me means something more intangible, perhaps the opportunity to change things rather than make out well within the existing system.[3]

Leadership of the New Left has been as varied as its philosophy, tactics, and members. The socialist G. Wright Mills, until his death in the early 1960's, helped to give direction to and formulate its philosophy. Staunton Lynd, Christopher Lasch, and Charles Hamilton are three of its more contemporary doctrinaire scholars. Among its other leaders have been, or are, Alan Haber, President of Students for a Democratic Society from 1960 to 1962; Carl Oglesby, president of the same organization in the mid-1960's and editor of a 1969 book on the New Left; Peter Irons who, on ideational grounds, chose jail over military service; John McDermott, traveler, field secretary of the New University Conference and editor of *Viet Report*; Stokely Carmichael, Black Power advocate and Prime Minister of the Black Panther Party from 1968 to 1969; Eldridge Cleaver, an avowed black revolutionary and author of a 1969 social-protest book, *Soul on Ice,* who, at outs with the law in 1968, was granted exile first in Cuba and more recently in Algeria; Huey Newton, Minister of Defense of the Black Panther Party and its cocreator in 1967; and Bobby Seale, the second cocreator, who, as one of the so-called Chicago 7 in 1970, was first gagged and later jailed by Judge Julius Hoffman for contempt of court. And these are only a few of the many leaders and spokesmen of the New Left who might have been named.

[2] Time-Life, Inc., *Youth in Turmoil* (New York: Time-Life Books, 1969), p. 17. The statistics above and the two quotations come from the 1968 Fortune poll conducted on 718 statistically sampled youth.
[3] Op. cit., p. 32.

## EVOLUTION OF THE NEW LEFT

The student-activist movement did not, despite surface appearances to the contrary, experience instantaneous birth. It was, rather, like all significant social groups and movements, an evolutionary product. Uncritically viewed, it is no more nor less than the most recent of a long tradition of younger generations rebelling against an older one. A few of today's "oldsters" viewing it in this way suggest that the current crop of youthful protesters, while employing different tactics, have motives no different from those that characterized the jazz generation of their own day. This conclusion is more wishful than valid.

The New Left movement, realistically viewed, is a product of social disillusionment that has been mounting in our culture for a half century—roughly since World War I. This first great holocaust of the twentieth century tarnished or shattered the idealism of many thinking people, particularly in regard to democracy as a sure-fire political form, and humanism as an attainable social form. A surface reaction to the disillusionment of the twenties was feminine rejection and masculine escape: women flattened their breasts and men escaped into bathtub gin. Racoon coats, flapper attire, and the eating of live goldfish were other manifestations of the reaction.

Then, in the thirties, came the Great Depression and with it a generation of disenchanted youth whom Gertrude Stein labeled the Lost Generation. It was foreshadowed in Hemingway's *Sun Also Rises,* 1926, whose characters, while railing against life's futility, covered up with a veneer of Jazz-Age-like behavior. They searched in vain for meaning in life, they traveled endlessly and aimlessly, they were convinced that God was either capricious or dead, they drank incessantly, and they felt psychologically castrated. Theirs was a search for purpose that was not to be found. What little satisfaction they realized from life was gained by losing themselves in its futility.

Next came the post–World-War-II forties and fifties, and with them the so-called Beat Generation. This latter was one that shunned such major responsibilities as marriage, child care, and work—responsibilities that normal youth of every generation have traditionally been expected to assume. The Beat Generation escaped into the physical aspects of life, in the manner more or less of Walt Whitman, refusing, however, to assume the social responsibilities associated therewith. If Hemingway's *Sun Also Rises* was the literary classic of the Lost Generation, Jack Kerouac's *On the Road,* 1957, was its counterpart of the Beat Generation. And Allen Ginsberg was its poet.

A contemporary sequel to the Beat Generation is the Love or Flower Generation (or Hippie culture) of today which, rejecting the materialism and customs of the conventional culture, escapes into a way of life in which each individual "does his own thing" without regard for conventional middle-class mores or standards. Hippies are mainline society dropouts but, unlike their Lost or Beat Generation counterparts, they are dropouts with a purpose, namely, to "drop into" some alternate and more satisfying nonmaterialistic, communal way of life. Hippies are not part of the New Student Left for a number of reasons, the primary one being that they seek to withdraw from, not to effect change in, the dominant culture.

## PROFILE OF THE NEW STUDENT LEFT

The disillusionment precipitated by World War I and acerbated first by the Great Depression, later by World War II, and finally by the period of materialism and affluence that the war engendered proved to be fertile ground for youth activism. What manner of activism was bred on that ground? Or, asked differently, what constitutes a reasonably valid profile of the 600 to 700 thousand student activists whose goal is to remake the existing social order? The profile includes some, if not most, of the following characteristics.

Student activists *are affluent*.[4] The typical one (admittedly a statistical, not an actual, entity) owns a car, has money in his pocket, and thus, because economically secure—or, at least, more secure than most—has time to engage in social activism. His affluence also lessens the apprehension that he conceivably would otherwise have over the possibilities of substandard academic performance or failure in college, a record of objectionable behavior retained in the files of college or civil authorities, and possible loss of institutional aid. His nonaffluent counterpart, in contrast, even if inclined to social activism, generally has only limited opportunity to engage in it, more dependent as he is on his own resources for a livelihood. Furthermore, the possibilities of academic failure or of a court record that might plague him for life or of a financial setback are very real to him. These tend to delimit the extent of his activism.

Student activists *support civil rights* avidly, according them high priority among their social goals. This is an area where both whites and blacks, collectively concerned about the social injustices to which blacks have long been, and continue to be, subjected, are particularly diligent. Nor is their struggle aimed exclusively at the plight of blacks; it is waged, additionally, in behalf of Puerto Ricans, American Indians, and all other socially and politically wronged ethnic groups. As stated by one writer, the commitment of student activists is

> to the principle that individuals must contribute actively to the attainment of a more generous and decent world. . . . [to] the ethic of indi-

[4] Op. cit., p. 14.

vidual freedom in the existential present. . . . the vigorous pursuit of these social goals makes possible the experience of meaningfulness and freedom that is the touchstone of the moral life.[5]

Student activists *are nonpatriotic in the conventional meaning of the term,* and the concept of chauvinism has to them absolutely no respectability at all. Actually, it is a whipping boy. Activists are least patriotic in respect to war in general and the Indo-China war in particular. In the *Fortune* magazine survey, 67 percent indicated that the United States made a mistake in sending troops to Viet Nam; 69 percent identified themselves as doves; and only 22 percent indicated any deep concern about the possibility of the United States losing its position of power in the world.[6] Patriotism also leaves little or no imprint on activists in situations where international communism is the issue. Generally speaking, they regard communism as no more than a bogy man kept alive by political connivers desirous of maintaining continued support for the military-industrial complex.

Student activists *have little faith in the past,* a recurrent theme of theirs being "Who needs history?" Richard L. Tobin speaks to this question in a recent editorial of the *Saturday Review.*

> Everywhere we look, the extremist minority is convinced that the present moment, however exciting or ridiculous, is the thing that matters and that deliberate rejection of the past is the only way to look upon a future where all men are brothers in a peaceful world. . . . Who needs history? President Garfield called history the unrolled scroll of prophecy, and it is said that those who do not heed it are condemned to relive it.[7]

Formal education admittedly tends, at times, to bury students in the past— so much so that the present is often no more to some than the hurly-burly of a lived-in ghetto; no more to others than a subdued existence in an affluent suburb. Yet the past does not have to compete with the present; rather, it should complement it. Shakespeare's aphorism, "What's past is prologue" (*Tempest*), is still valid even if trite. Nor is Carlyle's, "The present is the living sum-total of the past" (*Characteristics*), any less valid. The serious concern that student activists have for social justice, individualism, and commitment is indeed praiseworthy. But their tendency to downgrade the past by denying its relevance to the present is an irrational one. After all, as

[5] Edward J. Shoben, Jr., "Thoughts on the Decay of Morals," in G. Kerry Smith, *Stress and Campus Response* (San Francisco: Jossey-Bass, Inc., Publishers, 1968), p. 134.
[6] Time-Life, Inc., *Youth in Turmoil,* op. cit., pp. 34–35.
[7] Richard T. Tobin, "Who Needs History," *Saturday Review* (September 6, 1969), p. 22.

opined by Will Durant, "Our ancestors were not all fools." Nor did the present generation create the values of compassion and commitment.

Student activists *challenge constituted authority.* Their challenge, ideational for the most part, sometimes becomes physical when their points of view or activities are severely counterchallenged. Taking the establishment to task for its hypocrisy, they accuse it of practicing racism while proclaiming equality, of waging war while espousing peace, of being elitist while espousing egalitarianism, of paying lip service to morality while demonstrating immorality in public pronouncements and political acts; in general, of reciting democratic platitudes while engaging in undemocratic behavior.

Unfortunately, our social order is vulnerable in regard to each of these accusations. It is unquestionably racist, although whether as racist as Harold Taylor suggests in the following, is debatable.

> White, middle-class, racist America does exist. It *is* in control of American politics and American society. It does work its will through the full integration of its attitudes, values, and power within the economic system linked to government, the military, business, technology, the mass media, and education. It is a system. It does try to cover over the real problems of America by rhetoric, entertainment, social rewards, patriotism, and appeals to self interest.[8]

The United States, at least relatively, is not only racist but also warlike, elitist, immoral, and hypocritical—an allegation that lends itself to easy documentation. But even when it is documented, should we then conclude that the present youth generation has the necessary antidotes to make the country unracist, peaceful, egalitarian, moral, and intellectually honest? Those who answer "No" to this question are grist for the student-activist mill, generally regarded as reactionaries or do-nothing liberals who, irrespective of exact orientation, support the status quo by resisting those who would bring about change in it. Yet to answer "Yes" to the question is to assume that today's youth are unique almost to a point of being superbeings. This they are not. They are not alone in identifying the shortcomings of the country's way of life. Nor are they alone in their desire to correct them. Their tactics, however, are admittedly different.

In my opinion, student activists oversimplify the cures that they imply are in their power to effect. Their assumption that sincerity, self-integrity, and self-service will, in themselves, effect cures underestimates the influence of traditional institutions and behavior patterns and downgrades the complexity of decision making. Nor, as indicated by Professor Schwab of the University

[8] Harold Taylor, *Students Without Teachers: The Crisis in the University* (New York: McGraw-Hill Book Company, 1969), p. 69.

of Chicago, are ideals and practical problems simply matched; rather they are brought together by compromise—a term which need not imply deviousness.[9] Students, however, eschew compromise; they want capitulation. Thus many adults who otherwise laud student activists for challenging authority and questioning every possible aspect of the social or political status quo take umbrage at their rigidity. Emotional fervor has its place, but when allowed to operate too long outside the context of intellectualism, it easily converts to oversimplification and, at times, to self-righteousness. Student activists lay claim today to moral integrity, and some regard it almost as an exclusive possession. If they have it, may they never lose it. But unduly immodest claims about it raises doubt about its authenticity.

Student activists *hold the entire social order, including its political and social institutions, suspect.* The more moderate activists challenge the social order; the more radical ones reject it. Both groups accuse the society of being crassly materialistic and inhumane. Money and size, they say, give the lie to claims of social purpose and concern. Products are designed, produced, and marketed not to satisfy social needs but to make a profit for the already economically favored. And while this goes on, a large part of the population lives in poverty. The attack of the activists zeros in on capitalism as the country's economic system, war as a servant of capitalism, representative democracy as not functioning equitably, Puritanism as an outmoded ethical system, and the courts and police authority either as inept or degenerate governmental agencies. And, once again, the objects of the attack are vulnerable. However, to attack is one thing: to come up with viable alternatives, as will be developed in a later section, is another.

## THE STUDENT RADICALS

Within the ranks of the 600 to 700 thousand student crusaders for change in the country's institutions and practices, a militant body of radicals constitutes a hard core. It is a core, however, that lacks unity, fragmented as it is among many groups competing in many places. Students for a Democratic Society, SDS, occupies a central place in it. This student organization had an evolutionary birth. It was a spin-off of the Student League for Industrial Democracy which, in turn, was a spin-off of the League for Industrial Democracy which came into being in 1905. SDS, belying its widespread visibility, is a small organizational entity consisting of approximately 6000 dues-paying members affiliated with 300 to 400 decentralized chapters throughout the country.[10]

[9] Joseph J. Schwab, *College Curriculum and Student Protest* (Chicago: University of Chicago Press, 1969), pp. 36–41.
[10] Time-Life, Inc., *Youth in Turmoil*, op. cit., p. 134.

In 1962, the promulgation of a manifesto of 52 pages, the so-called Port Huron statement, gave SDS national visibility. In it, a prototype of the then New Left was depicted. It was to possess "real intellectual skills," was to be "committed to deliberateness," was to consist of "younger people who matured in the post-war world," was to "start controversy across the land . . . [in an effort to] transform modern complexities into issues that can be understood and felt close-up by every human being." Its operational centers were to be colleges and universities, and its program was to be action, not theory, oriented. The manifesto declared:

> To turn these possibilities into realities will involve national efforts at university reform by an alliance of students and faculty. They must wrest control of the educational process from the administrative bureaucracy. They must make fraternal and functional contact with allies in labor, civil rights, and other liberal forces outside the campus. They must import major public issues into the curriculum . . . They must make debate and controversy, not dull pedantic cant, the common style for educational life. They must consciously build a base for their assault upon the loci of power.[11]

The manifesto, in general, was an idealistically liberal, even though somewhat inflammatory, document. Within four or five years after its promulgation, however, its status was little more than historical. By then, SDS had become a radical, revolutionary organization determined not to work for social change within the existing establishment but to seek the latter's destruction. The record written by The Weathermen in 1970, one of ravaging and killing, gives credence to this allegation. The new radicals include not only SDS but the following groups as well:

*The Resistance:* an antidraft student organization.

*Resist:* a peace, antidraft group of professional social critics including, for instance, Noam Chomsky and Paul Goodman.

*New University Conference:* a university protest group consisting primarily of teachers and graduate students.

*Young Socialist Alliance:* a Trotskyite student organization.

*National Mobilization to End the War in Vietnam.* MOBI: The title is self-explanatory.

*Progressive Labor:* a Peking-oriented group.

[11] Mitchell Cohen and Dennis Hale (Eds.), *The New Student Left: An Anthology* (Boston: The Beacon Press, 1966), p. 223.

*W.E.B. DuBois Clubs:* an assorted group of campus organizations, communist oriented.

*Black Panther Party:* a black self-styled revolutionary group, organized in 1967, that justifies violence as a counter to the social injustices that, it alleges, are endemic in the white community.

The Black Panther Party, as indicated above, had its advent in 1967. The founders were Bobby Seale and Huey Newton: the place was Oakland, California. The overall goal of the party, as stated by Eldridge Cleaver in the September 1969 edition of *Ramparts*, is to

> get on with the business of building the type of revolutionary machinery that we need in the United States in order to unite all the revolutionary forces in the country to overthrow the systems of Capitalism, Imperialism, and Racism.

Taking the law into their own hands, the Black Panthers, says Cleaver, will "shoot anyone [including law enforcement officers] who uses a gun, or causes others to use guns, to defend the system of oppression, racism, and exploitation."

Black Panthers make the following claims: (1) the country's social-political system is corrupt; (2) blacks have to struggle for the rights that they should have had in 1776; (3) thus they are justified in opposing "the establishment," by force of arms, if necessary.

The party is currently hewing a trail of vengeance and bloodshed. And law-enforcement agencies are countering with what, at least in the opinion of many, may be overreaction. Thus the situation may well get worse before it gets better, for polarization, fear, and violence are unlikely harbingers of an early peace.

## PROGRAM OF THE NEW LEFT

From the foregoing, it is evident that the New Left differs extensively from group to group. It also differs extensively from individual to individual. Some groups and individuals are activist but not radical; others are both activist and radical. Whatever their orientations, however, they mutually crusade for social change on the following platform which, in overview, is both negatively antiestablishment and assertively doctrinaire. Its negativism is projected against what the New Left regards as inadequacies in the existing social order. And the latter, at least in the opinion of many intellectuals, breeds such negativism. As stated by Lipset in regard to students, one should not be surprised at

138        *Values in Transition*

... a sharp increase in student activism in a society where, for a variety of reasons, accepted political and social values are being questioned. . . . And . . . in societies where rapid change, instability, or weak legitimacy of political institutions is endemic, there is what looks like almost constant turmoil among students.[12]

In the words of Harold Taylor, "the prestige of the negative is at its height" in today's world.[13] In keeping with this phenomenon, the New Left has incorporated into its platform the following negative positions.

*It is Antirational.* The New Student Left goes to Herbert Marcuse, its doctrinaire philosopher, to support this stand. Marcuse's thesis is that our highly complex society holds people captive by making them excessively dependent on its institutions and services. The society, he says, equates reason and conformity. And, he protests, "to impose Reason upon an entire society is a paradoxical and scandalous idea."[14] The New Student Left is antirational in the sense of being opposed to the rationalism of social authority, to rationalism that prevents full expression of individualism. It is also antirational in the sense of relying more on feeling and passion than on logic as guides to behavior. In the words of one activist, "political hysteria" is preferable to "cool reasonableness."[15] The New Left assumes, or at least seems to assume, that reason and logic operate consistently at the expense of human warmth and sensitivity.

*It is Anticonformist.* The New Student Left, because antiestablishment, is also anticonformist. Each individual is to "do his own thing" in his own way irrespective of mores and standards. This anticonformist theme will be developed in greater detail in the treatment of the tactics of protest.

*It is Antimaterialistic.* The society, so say the student activists, worships at the shrine of materialistic values: of products and production, money, competition, profit, markets, job prestige, gross national product, and so forth. The recommended alternative, once more as proposed by Marcuse, is a social order that meets the basic needs of all its people without making them captives on the treadmill of its own selfish ends. A social order which consistently "manufactures" needs in an artificial manner sacrifices humanistic values in the process—so the thesis goes.

*It is Antielitist.* The socialist views of C. Wright Mills had, from its

[12] Seymour M. Lipset, "Student Activism," *Current Affairs Bulletin*, XLII (July 15, 1968), 52–53.
[13] Harold Taylor, *Students Without Teachers: The Crisis in the University*, op. cit., p. 46.
[14] Herbert Marcuse, *One Dimensional Man* (Boston: The Beacon Press, 1964), p. 11.
[15] Quoted by Walter Goodman in "The Liberal Establishment Faces the Blacks, the Young, the New Left," *New York Times Magazine* (December 29, 1968), p. 30.

earliest beginnings, a marked influence on the New Student Left. Mill's central thesis, as developed in Chapter 2, was that the elite, with economic and political power constituting the criteria, are the dominant power-wielders in the country. They own and give direction to industry; they are king makers in government and thus they control the country. His counter thesis was that economic and political power should be populist, not elitist. And although his views stopped short of recommending tactics for social change, he laid a theoretical groundwork on which the New Student Left found it convenient to build. His death in the early 1960's diminished his ideational influence but little.

*It is Antiliberal.* To student activists, the typical liberal is one whose words may carry a stirring message but whose actions customarily get lost in inertia. Furthermore, so they aver, he is tied so firmly to the philosophy of the governing establishment that the pragmatic testing of nonestablishment ideas constitutes an impossibility. In contrast,

> To be radical . . . is to judge the quality of life and society by its reality as perceived in experience, not to accept anything that is said about reality by accredited authorities, inside or outside the university. It means to judge the quality of an act or an idea by its consequences in the lives of persons, not by its relation to an ideology of liberal democracy, democratic socialism, or the varieties of contemporary communism.[16]

Also in a negative vein, student activists are *antiwar, antidraft, anti-imperialist, anti–en loco parentis* in college and university living, *antipollution, antiracist, antipoverty, antihypocrisy,* and *antipolice-brutality.* And, if they are militant radicals, they are nihilistic in their tactics. The social conditions to which the New Student Left is opposed are, it is to be noted, not necessarily different from those to which some or many of the nation's remaining population are opposed.

The positive side of the question, for what causes is the New Student Left crusading, elicits, selectively, the following responses from some or all of its members.

*Change in the social order.* This is a canopied response to which all student activists would subscribe.

*Social justice.* The position taken on this issue is that justice in the country has traditionally meant justice for the privileged affluent but not for the deprived unaffluent. It is justice more in respect to property than people. As stated by one spokesman of radical orientation,

---

[16] Harold Taylor, op. cit., p. 72.

Our spiritual, educational, and political leaders celebrate "freedom" but they too often mean "bend your knee to power and consensus." They proclaim "democracy;" but they too often mean submission to the existing structure of corporate power. They call for "honesty, truth, and morality;" but they too often practice deception, hypocrisy, and ruthless violation of the rights of others in "patriotic" pursuit of policy aims "vital to the national interest."[17]

The brand of justice verbally espoused by the New Student Left is justice that is honest and fair, that is consistently enforced, that is antiracial, that promises peace abroad as well as here at home, that is administered by just people.

*Populist power.* The goal in regard to this issue of justice is to take power from the elite and place it in the hands of the populist masses. The contrasting groups, it should be noted, are the elitists and nonelitists, not the bourgeoise and proletariat as espoused by Karl Marx.

*Greater role in decision making.* At the civic level, the New Student Left crusaded successfully for the right to vote at age eighteen. Their logic was that if an individual could drive at sixteen and kill at eighteen, he should be able to vote before he was twenty-one. At the college and university level, the New Student Left has demanded a more active decision-making role in such matters as curriculum, faculty hiring, discipline, and living arrangements.

*Autonomy in personal lives.* The position taken in respect to this issue is that young people should have greater autonomy, at an earlier age, in regard to dress, grooming, sex, right of assembly, parietal hours in college residences, and speech. One college educator, himself very much a moderate, writes:

> Whether or not a student burns a draft card, participates in a civil rights march, engages in premarital or extramural sexual activity, becomes pregnant, attends church, sleeps all day, drinks all night is not really the concern of a collegiate institution as an educational institution.[18]

*Immediate cures.* Rebelling against the traditional slowness of social change, student activists want change *now*. They treat explanations as rationalizations, they turn away from compromise, and they resist promises of future action. It is their contention that if the "time is out of joint"—as they

[17] Arnold S. Kaufman, *The Radical Liberal: New Man in American Politics* (New York: Atherton Press, 1968), p. 26.
[18] Lewis B. Mayhew, "A Rendering of Accounts" in G. Kerry Smith (Ed.), *Stress and Campus Response*, op. cit., p. 154.

believe, or pretend to believe, it is—the immediate present is the time to set it right.

## TACTICS OF THE NEW STUDENT LEFT

As stated previously, the program of the New Student Left, except for its antirational and occasional nihilistic aspects, is one which most liberals and moderates, irrespective of age, could generally support. In the process of implementation, however, the program tends to become suspect inasmuch as the tactics often belie the tenets. The tactics divide into those employed by the nonviolent activists and those employed by the militant radicals.

The tactics of the nonviolent activists include the following.

*Extensive employment of rhetoric.* This, for instance, includes the sweeping assertion, the trite admonition, or the oversimplified conclusion. Illustrative are such long-time hackneyed expressions as "The establishment is totally corrupt and decadent," "Do your own thing," "If you are not for (whatever I am for), you are my enemy," "Go to where the action is," and "If there are dragons to be slain, slay them." Furthermore, the rhetoric of activists is replete with overused words such as irrelevant, illegitimate, decadent, insensitive, racist, integrity (or lack of it), degeneracy, despair, alienation, hypocrisy, and commitment; as well as such technical argot as hip, trip, pot, acid, strait, turn on, cop out, bag, rap, chick, and fuzz.

*Appeal to the emotions.* In the words of Raywid, "the heart of the new reformism is just that: heart. . . . a preoccupation with feeling." Relatedly, as has already been established, the appeal is to antirationalism. The liberal has traditionally distrusted the emotions; the activist, today, distrusts reason. In the future, opines Raywid, "Hopefully we can arrive at some proper 'mix' of reason and emotion . . . ."[19]

The problem of the emotional appeal is twofold. First, it quite easily leads to a mob-kind of situation wherein people are swept along by high-sounding rhetoric, by the persuasiveness of a convincing voice, or by the sheer weight of a clamoring peer group. Second, the emotional appeal tends to muzzle those who might wish to counter a given cause celebre on grounds of reason. And emotional reactions to situations are often forerunners of physical violence.

During the week-long Peace Strike at Northwestern University in May of 1970 (one that was milder than most others in the country at the time), I personally saw the warped effects of a movement that started out in a fairly

[19] Mary Anne Raywid, "Irrationalism and the New Reformism," *Educational Leadership*, 26 (May 1969), 744–745.

rational way but soon became pathological. It was initially conceived as a peaceful but forceful reaction to our country's then recent involvement in Cambodia. Its base soon expanded, however, to include protest against the My Lai murders in Vietnam, against police brutality that had taken place two years previously in Chicago during the Democratic Convention, against the killing of certain Black Panthers, against Vice President Agnew, and against the "irrelevant" curriculum of the university which, it was alleged, should concede to the curriculum of a "New University"—these among many others. The base of the protest ultimately expanded to include protest against all within the university—students, faculty, administrators, and trustees—who would not support the student protest. "If you are not for me, you are against me." The protest, contentious and strident, muted the voices of moderation. Mass hysteria unquestionably reigned.

Most students, fortunately, "kept their cool" thereby curbing the possible excesses of the more radical and militant. Many of the more concerned students campaigned tirelessly and conscientiously for peace. The more militant, unfortunately, set up and "policed" a roadblock on a crowded thoroughfare, stormed the university building that housed the R.O.T.C. unit, and vandalized to a lesser extent in other ways.

The student protesters, beyond question, won many over to their cause with their emotional appeal. But were their methods legitimate and defensible? Were the converts truly knowledgeable about the complexities of the cause or were they swept by emotionalism? Was the university the proper place for the attack? And did the strike do more long-term harm than short-term good? These are questions that the future alone can answer.

*Attack the opposition's weak spots.* A familiar tactic of the New Student Left is to lay bare the shortcomings or failures of the opposition, assess blame, and clamor for immediate and total rectification. The shortcomings of the so-called establishment are, as previously developed, disturbing and obvious. They include racism, elitism, hunger amid affluence, an industrial-military complex that verges on the totalitarian, pollution, court delays, uneven enforcement of civil rights, traffic in drugs, and the shame of ghettos —these and many more. However, as previously stated, to attack is one thing; to rectify is another. Few would deny that an attack is needed. The real issue is whether the attack should take place inside or outside the establishment. And until the New Student Left emerges with a platform that is more than merely anti-establishment at its best, or nihilistic at its worst, its motives as viewed by the established in-group will be as suspect as the motives of the in-group give appearance of being to the New Left.

*Polarize alternatives.* Another tactic of student activists—which is an old propaganda technique—is to polarize alternatives into black and white opposites and insist on a choice between them. The choices might, for example, be revolution or oppression, reform or decadence, honesty or hypocrisy, shared decision making or tyranny, social justice or police brutality, to be for "the cause" or against it, to act now or never. Invariably, of course, morality is on the side of "the cause"; immorality, on the side of the opposition. "And come the apocalypse," morality will ultimately win out.

*Make unnegotiable demands.* Another propaganda technique employed by the New Student Left—specifically a popular technique of the blacks as well—is to make impossible demands on established authority and then retaliate or threaten retaliation when they are not met. In colleges and universities, the demands might, for instance, include the following. Cancel all government contracts because the government is in the business of war. Give students veto power over the hiring of all faculty members. Guarantee amnesty to those of "our number" who, provoked by injustice, lose control of themselves and commit acts of violence. The underlying rational for this tactic of making unnegotiable demands is that "our cause" will be colored with moral justification when the establishment, faced with "viable" alternatives, makes choices unfavorable to "our" cause.

*Provoke overreaction.* The tactics of rhetorical eloquence, appeal to the emotions, attack on weaknesses of authority, proposal of polarized alternatives, and submission of unnegotiable demands, all are aimed, in part, at provoking established authority to overreact. When the methods are successful, authority loses face, fringe moderates become activists or radicals, and counterreaction by radicals requires less justification.

Other tactics of the nonradical activists include *teach-ins, marches, picketing, assemblies, political campaigning,* and person-to-person *proselytizing.*

The tactics of the militant radicals are, as would be expected, more violent. They include occupation of buildings, sit-ins, formation of roadblocks, rock throwing at law officers and buildings, obscenities directed at law officers, sniper fire, riots and the inciting of riots, training of neophytes in revolutionary tactics, disruption of assemblies, and advocacy of violent overthrow of the established order. The purposes of such tactics are to publicize the cause of a given moment or of the revolutionary cause in general, to provide training in revolutionary tactics, to make converts, to invite counterreaction and, hopefully, overreaction, and to implant fears in the general public.

Thus what started out as peaceful protest in the early 1960's has become, in a mounting number of instances today, violent protest. The program of the New Student Left, viewed substantively, is basically moral; in fact, few outside the ranks of hard-core reactionaries and conservatives would systematically oppose it. But as the New Student Left has progressively moved from dissent to resistance, particularly to violent resistance, the movement has become increasingly suspect—suspect of immorality, as viewed by some, of downright anarchy, as viewed by others. As stated by Shoben, the shift has been

> from a vigorous competition among moral ideas and ethical models to a clash in which raw might is the only determiner of the outcome. . . . When contending parties attempt to settle their differences by weapons alone, one side always considers the other to be illegitimate, unredeemable in its villainy, and inaccessible to either reason or moral suasion.[20]

If the confrontations between the New Student Left and constituted authority continue to mount in intensity, the nation will soon face two alternatives, both of which are repulsive: general anarchy or violent repression. In either event, the stage might easily be set for the rise of a charismatic dictator. Charles de Gaulle exploited this kind of climate. Much worse, so did Adolph Hitler.

My position in regard to protest, even violent protest, is that it does, under certain circumstances, have legitimacy; history convincingly supports this point of view. But, in my opinion, it has legitimacy only when meeting the following specifications:

1. When social conditions are so corrupt and inhumane that radical correction is absolutely essential.

2. When support for this conclusion is pragmatically sanctioned—that is, when a majority (preferably a top-heavy majority) of the population is convinced that the social conditions in question are in a state this deplorable.

3. When correction is not possible under the established order.

4. When the means of correction will not unduly harm the innocent.

5. When social disobedience is based on principles imbued with high moral quality—principles that can be clearly articulated and that will inspire its followers to accept punishment in defense of them. This tenet rejects the now popular concept of amnesty.

6. When social disobedience gives substantial promise of achieving immediate or long-term success.[21]

Conceivably what the New Student Left needs is, as suggested by Kaufman who himself is generally to the left of liberal,

> a new breed of indefatigable radicals, passionately moral, yes—but also calculating and unfailingly energetic in pursuit of liberal goals . . .

[20] Edward J. Shoben, Jr., op. cit., pp. 138–139.
[21] Edward S. Shoben, op. cit., pp. 139–140.

[who] realize that they are destined to despair . . . unless they acquire disciplines of reason in the same measure that they already possess moral concern.[22]

## DILEMMA OF COLLEGES AND UNIVERSITIES

Political foment has, in recent years, unquestionably reached endemic proportions in colleges and universities. What apparently started out as a single episode at Berkeley in 1964 has since become almost a way of life in institutions of higher education throughout the country. The Berkeley affair, indeed, precipitated a chain of events that has literally revolutionized campus life. What happened at Berkeley in 1964 had related counterparts subsequently at the University of Chicago in 1966, at Columbia University in the same year, at the University of Wisconsin and Harvard University in 1969, and at Ohio State University in 1970—and these are merely a selected few of the several hundred that might have been named. An irony of the confrontations is that the names of the young radicals who led them—for instance, Mark Rudd, Mario Savio, Tom Hayden, and Jerry Rubin—are, in most households, better known than those of all but a few college or university presidents.

The uprising at Berkeley came as a surprise; yet the social climate was ripe for it. Traditionally—in fact, until World War II—our institutions of higher learning were classically oriented. Their curriculums were perennialist in nature, thus highly theoretical, consisting in great part of the liberal-arts disciplines. Their implicit goal was to educate the intelligentsia, although generally only the more affluent and socially favored of this group would, in all likelihood, later become leaders in business, industry, politics, and the professions.

World War II, in many ways the most grandiose populist venture of all times, changed the character of higher education. First, thanks to the "G.I. Bills" it changed the nature of the college population by feeding into it students of diverse interests, ages, and social backgrounds. The country needed trained manpower and subsidized all servicemen who could qualify. In the process, elitism conceded to populism. Second, the curriculums of institutions of higher education became progressively less classical and conversely more practical. Returning G.I.'s desired, for instance, to learn about contemporary political affairs more than about metaphysical concerns, more about Keynesian economics than about Middle-Age mercantilism, more about modern medical theories than about Galen's humors and bloodletting.

[22] Arnold S. Kaufman, op. cit., p. 55.

The foremost explicit goal of colleges and universities has always been to educate students liberally: to free minds of ignorance, superstitions, and prejudice; to encourage internal and external examination and criticism; to cultivate powers of reason; and to expedite the process of value building. A secondary explicit goal of colleges and universities has generally been public service which takes the form of research and consultation. A tertiary explicit goal has been the perpetuation and advancement of knowledge.

The classical goals of higher education, traditionally conceived, led into the practical goals of post–World War II days which, in turn, led into broad social goals of the 1960's and early 1970's. These latter were pursued nonmilitantly until 1964; progressively more militantly after that.

What brought on the change? Why the increased aggressiveness at and after the Berkeley uprising? The following constitute the more credible reasons.

1. *Colleges and universities entered the war game.* Victory in World War II was achieved as much in the science laboratories of institutions of higher education throughout the country as on distant battlefields. Nor did university research conducted for the defence establishment end with the termination of hostilities. On the contrary, it continued unabated into the period of the Cold War. Thus when students engage in confrontations with colleges and universities, they point the finger of blame at the latter's military involvements. Campus protests against war-tinged symbols such as recruitment by the much maligned Dow Chemical Company, the existence and activities of a campus-based R.O.T.C. unit, or stock owned by a college or university in a war-related industry—all are part of the syndrome.

2. *Relatedly, colleges and universities have lost their status of academic neutrality.* The classical trappings of an earlier period generally set colleges and universities apart from life's mainstream, protecting them, in the process, from its turbulence. Today, involved as they are in industry and the military, they are wide open to criticism. Mark Rudd, SDS leader during the Columbia University confrontation, described the situation as follows.

We see the university as a factory whose goal is to produce: (1) trained personnel for corporations, government and more universities, and (2) knowledge of the uses of business and government to perpetuate the present system.[23]

[23] Quoted from *The Saturday Evening Post* (September 21, 1968) by Jerome Skolnick, "Student Protest," *AAUP Bulletin* (September, 1969), p. 317.

3. *They have become politicized.* That higher education has lost its neutrality by engaging in political activity is common knowledge. However, the specifics of the process require explanation. Higher education has become political to a greater or lesser degree in the following ways. First, as indicated two sections back, it has aligned itself with the war game, entering into and fulfilling literally thousands of contracts for military research. This, by any standard, constitutes political activity. Second, it regularly enters into and fulfills contracts for research in business and industry. Whether this kind of activity is political or merely practically academic is debatable. Third, higher education, because governed by trustees (in private institutions) and regents (in public ones), who themselves are primarily conservative, tends, so far as these individuals are influential, to support conservative points of view and enterprises. Institutions of higher education receive the lion's share of private-sector support from affluent, conservative alumni and big-business and corporate donors. Furthermore, their financial holdings are in conservative financial enterprises. Thus, insofar as the trustees (or regents) are more influential than the faculty in policy matters, they tend to align themselves with conservative political causes.

Yet granted that colleges and universities support conservative political causes, a distinction needs to be made between those causes which the institutions *as institutions* support and those which faculty members *as individuals* support. For an institution of higher learning to take a stand, or be asked by the Student Left to take a stand, pro or con, on a political issue such as the war in Cambodia, legitimacy of the draft, campus recruitment by Dow Chemical Company, the pill, freedom of individual females to abort, or the socialist party, implies that all, or at least a majority of, faculty members in the institution support that stand. And even in the instance of majority support, the institution has no clear-cut mandate to take a stand. Does a faculty-administration vote of 500 for a given cause to 400 against justify a public announcement that XYZ University believes thus and so? Scarcely! The point I make here is that a college or university, although legally a corporate agency, is professionally a community of single individuals who are hired because of their professional expertise, not because of their political viewpoints. Thus, faculties have the right, even the duty, to resist institutional efforts of any kind to mute their political opinions by collectivizing them.

Holding this point of view, a number of us at Northwestern University signed the following statement of May 11, 1970.

While it is the prerogative—even the duty—of every member of the University community, be he student, faculty, or administration to express his political views in such legal manner as he may deem appropriate, we the undersigned believe it is highly improper for the University itself to enter into the political arena. Not only is this unsuitable for a University, but it infringes on the individual rights of those in the Community who hold opposing views.

While we recognize the need for special University action to meet unusual situations, such as the threat of violence, these actions must conform with the maintenance of academic standards.

We wish to express these opinions to the University Administration, and to our representatives in Washington.[24]

4. *Students are becoming increasingly concerned over the distance that separates ideals from their social implementation.* As students, on one hand, become increasingly better informed about what the society declares its social goals to be while, on the other hand, perceiving that the society falls short—sometimes hopelessly short—of implementing them, their militancy increases. Cases in point are "justice" delayed three to four years in trial courts, gross differences in educational opportunities for varying ethnic groups, bail arrangements that penalize the indigent, free speech permitted more for in-groups than for out-groups, a university that ignores community blights, a professor who consistently stifles dissent, or income tax legislation that serves vested interests. Students unquestionably are better informed today about social injustices than they were a generation or two ago, but, unfortunately, social practices are little, if any, more ethical. Thus, with the difference between the "what might be" and the "what is" standing out all the more starkly, the results understandably are an increased concern and thus more aggressiveness on the part of the younger generation.

5. *What is done on campus can make a difference.* Students at Berkeley, the scene of the first full-blown student confrontation, were undoubtedly surprised—in fact, even downright amazed—at the reaction their confrontation elicited not only at the University of California itself but throughout the nation. However, once the dynamics of the situation were analyzed and understood, the amazement soon faded. The analysis revealed the college or university to be as much a status symbol of elitism as an academic institution. Thus to attack the university was to

[24] This was initiated by a coterie of individual faculty members of Northwestern University acting as individuals, not as university representatives.

attack the establishment. Furthermore, it was early discovered that colleges and universities were relatively safe targets for social attack. Most professors were generally no worse than neutral toward, and some were supportive of, student activism; administrators, conscious of past inconsistencies if not actual hypocrisies, generally reacted hesitantly and uncertainly; fellow students tended, at worse, to fade to the sidelines; campus police were generally powerless; and civil authorities rarely acted except on invitation from campus authorities. Thus college and university campuses proved to be both meaningful social symbols and relatively safe places for students to create confrontations.

6. *The student population has changed.* As indicated previously, college and university populations have changed significantly in recent years with World War II constituting the greatest single cause. Through the media of the Serviceman's Readjustment Act of 1944 and its sequel later in the same year (for wounded veterans), the federal government subsidized college education for returning servicemen on the basis of, more or less, one month of college education for every month spent by them in any branch of the armed services. These acts applied irrespective of the social status, race, religion, politics, or age of the servicemen; and irrespective of all other factors except those applying to admissions policies of colleges and universities. The G.I. Bills coupled with the Black Power movement of the 1960's resulted in college populations becoming more socially heterogeneous. Campus struggles for liberal causes thus gained support from certain nonelitist individuals and groups that were not present on college campuses—at least not in the same number or proportion—before World War II.

7. *College and university faculties have changed.* The changing nature of college and university student bodies has a parallel in college and university faculties. The latter, in fact, are inheritors of the heterogeneity that began to characterize student bodies of the post–World War II period. Contrary to the traditional stereotype of college professor as academic scholar detached from the society, today's professor, no less a scholar, cannot escape social problems on or off campus. The latter are generally too pervasive and demanding to allow him this luxury.

In connection with student confrontations per se, a hard core of young faculty radicals are customarily active in such movements. Professor Staunton Lynd, formerly of Yale University and more recently of Roosevelt University of Chicago, is a well publicized case in point. At a less scholarly level, so too are Marlene Dixon, recently of the University of Chicago, and Angela Davis, recently of the University of

California at Los Angeles. And to the extent these individuals are respected political leaders as well as academic scholars, they are forces
of power. Only Lynd, of the three mentioned above, meets both of these
specifications.

In student confrontations, faculty radicals generally feel that they
have an a priori mandate to align themselves with the student cause.
Thus their decision is easy. Faculty liberals, however, are generally
pulled apart, torn as they usually are between two loyalties: the institution they serve and the social cause the students claim to espouse. If
typical, they support the process of methodical negotiation, of student
amnesty from criminal prosecution when property rights of the university have been violated, and of force to be applied only as a last
resort.

Most faculty conservatives, as well as some moderates, with S. I.
Hayakawa a case in point, are generally law-and-order people. Assuming student radicals to be anarchists, they resort early to the use of
punishment by civil and university authorities.

8. *Grants compromise colleges and universities.* As developed a few
pages back, colleges and universities are allies with government and
industry in research and development. This makes them vulnerable in
two ways. It makes them vulnerable on financial grounds in that grants
are notoriously unreliable: they may be secured for the asking today
and be impossible to secure tomorrow. Thus any institution that builds
a major part of its program on this soft-money base is asking for
trouble. The alliance also, in certain instances, makes colleges and
universities vulnerable on moral grounds. All projects contracted for
that cannot be defended ethically stamp colleges and universities as
unethical via the process of association. Thus a "war" contract casts
them in the position of being in favor of war, and so forth.

## SOME POSSIBLE ANSWERS

Because the dilemma of colleges and universities, and the society itself, is
many faceted and pervasive, antidotes to it frustrate with their elusiveness and
inadequacy. In regard to student confrontations that are endemic in the
country, the antidote of surrender is inconceivable, and of harsh repression,
intolerable. This leaves the antidote of reasonable compromise which embraces the following essentials, each of which, admittedly, lends itself more
readily to verbal defense than to practical implementation. Our remarks are
aimed directly at colleges and universities, only indirectly at the greater
society.

*Colleges and Universities Need Clarity of Purpose.* In working through to this clarity, they need, first of all, to resist the lure of doing the same old things merely because they are comfortable. This posture of resistance to the status quo forces decision makers in institutions of higher learning to assess traditional programs and practices, leading ultimately to the retention of some and the discarding of others. An even more significant outcome—if the process of assessment is realistic—conceivably might be the reformulation of purposes that are to guide the institution into the future. If a primary purpose is instruction of students, programming to get the job done adequately constitutes an imperative. If another purpose is service, it should not stop short of meaningful implementation.

If the goal is research, the situation almost automatically becomes complicated. The questions, how much, of what kind, by whom, who will pay the bills, and what strings will be attached, will ultimately demand answers. Inevitably the issue of research for military purposes will arise. And when it does, decision makers have no choice but to take one of the following stands, or a related one.

1. Enter contracts for military research, irrespective (or almost irrespective) of its nature, on the premise that values and activities that are legitimate in the greater society can, without apology, be supported in colleges and universities.

2. Refuse contracts that dramatically increase man's potential to maim or destroy himself or others. The atomic research conducted at the University of Chicago during World War II could have been a case in point. Research on napalm or poison gas are cases in point today.

3. Enter contracts only for those government projects that have peaceful purposes. Yet the dividing line between projects that are for peaceful purposes and others that are for purposes of violence is not always easy to locate. For instance, research in lunar gravity, fissionable materials, petroleum chemistry, and stress tolerance can have either purpose. And, relatedly, they can have one purpose today and the opposite one tomorrow.

4. Get out of government contracts altogether in the hope that a collective movement in this direction will ultimately force the government to do its own research in its own institutions. But would this improve the situation? And would colleges and universities lose a significant number of quality researchers as a result?

Each of the four options is defensible in certain respects and indefensible in others. At the time of this writing, I favor options 3 and 4 in that order. My preference for 3 is tempered by the difficulty involved in deciding which projects are for the cause of peace and which other ones are not. My preference for 4 is for the following reasons. First, detached governmental research conducted by colleges and universities frequently runs counter to the humanistic values that institutions of higher education generally claim to espouse. A second reason is that the research usually has strings attached to it, thus tending to weaken the power structure of the university. A third reason is that the research, if secret or restricted in any way, makes untenable the traditionally proclaimed position that all research sponsored by colleges and universities can be openly debated and publicized. Finally, government research tends to establish a barrier between faculty members, and to divide the allegiance of any single one engaged in it.

The chief argument against option 4 is that many institutions today would have to close their doors or curtail their programs significantly if government support were withdrawn. This argument is convincing in terms of the practicalities of the moment. It is less convincing in terms of what is most desirable for the future. If humanistic values are to be the criterion, the moral issue has to take priority over the strictly economic one.

Whether a given college or university takes a stand for option 1, 2, 3, or 4 is undeniably important. Of only slightly less importance is the need for it to make a forthright announcement of the stand taken, avoiding hypocrisy in the process. Any college or university literally invites confrontation when it is so evasive about what it believes that it cannot convincingly sanction what it does.

*Organization for Decision Making Needs to be Improved.*  Traditionally colleges and universities have functioned under a line and staff organizational arrangement. Under it, trustees or regents have filled the role of a board of directors, contributing their business expertise to the institution. Administrators have performed budgetary, maintenance, and governance functions. Faculties have controlled the curriculum and their own membership. And students have, although with exceptions, followed orders that others have made.

Increasingly, this rather rigid line-and-staff pattern has revealed operational weaknesses. Trustees and regents have exposed themselves as being ultra-conservative politically, more interested in economic than in academic or student-personnel concerns, and as verging on the anachronistic. Administrators have revealed themselves as being too authoritarian toward students and also, although somewhat less so, toward faculty members, and of being too elitist oriented. Faculties have revealed themselves as being more interested in research and professional prestige than in students and instruction. And students, understandably, have fought back often aggressively at institutional authority.

The situation is ripe for the following antidotes. Trustees and regents need to prove their worth by becoming involved in important campus affairs—or die on an anachronistic vine. Administrators need to become more involved in important student and faculty concerns and less in business and student-discipline concerns. In respect to the latter, the traditional role of *en loco parentis* is no longer theirs because they are not parents, pastors, clinicians, or judges.

The overall need is for trustees, administrators, faculties, and students to share more problems together, deliberate more together, and differ, if necessary, more together. Each will have vested interests and organizational autonomy in certain areas but none should employ these to shut off dialog. The latter, indeed, is capable of preventing otherwise manageable problems from becoming unmanageable issues. Whenever possible, authoritarianism should concede to shared decision making.

*Curriculums Need to be Revised.*   Any college or university engaged in clarifying its purpose and making organizational adjustments in response to it can not avoid the process of curriculum revision. The specifics of the latter I leave for others to develop.

The overall product of curriculum revision, however, I wish personally to conjecture about here. It would be a product, I predict, that would have a better balance between theory and practice than most curriculums have today. The traditional vogue has been the classical extreme: a curriculum centered in lectures, textbooks, and libraries; oriented in history; and almost contemptuous of the problems of the pulsating world. The current student-activist curriculum model is, in contrast, a utilitarian product centered in inner cities, minority groups, ecology, provincial economics, and pragmatic values of the here and now; a product that ignores history.

The curriculum that is needed for the future is one that is oriented both in theory and practice, in the past and the present, that is systematic yet flexible, that breeds civility without breeding elitism. College and university curriculums of the past several decades have, unquestionably, placed too much emphasis on science, mathematics, and technology. Their counterparts today are, conceivably, placing too much emphasis on the social sciences, particularly sociology. The humanities have been neglected under both schemes. The uncontested need is for balance in college and university curriculums. It will not work social miracles, but without it social change will be that much more difficult to bring about.

*Reasonableness is Needed.*   It is not at all melodramatic to state that the problems currently besetting the social order threaten its very existence. They pertain broadly to honesty in government, world peace, racial justice, economic morality, a decent environment, and survival itself. The commitment of today's youth to solve these problems has no parallel in history. But they do not march alone. In fact, millions of the over-thirty generation march with, or near, them down the concourse of human decency and justice. And the march did not begin yesterday; it began with the advent of civilization.

There is a critical need for all, of whatever age, who march down this concourse to be exemplars of reason—not of reason detached from the emotions but of reason authenticated by the emotions. And the latter, if they are to perform well the task of cognitive cleansing agent, need to be healthy, not pathological. Neither reason alone nor feeling alone is enough. A balance of the two is what is needed. Admitting to projecting an ideal here, I am willing to settle for approximations.

# Bibliography

Bell, Daniel, "Columbia and the New Left," *The Public Interest* (Fall 1968).

Cohen, Mitchell and Dennis Hale (Eds.), *The New Student Left*. Boston: The Beacon Press, 1966.

Douglas, William O., *Points of Rebellion*. New York: Vintage Books, Inc., 1969.

Draper, Hal, *Berkeley: The New Student Revolt*. New York: Grove Press, Inc., 1965.

Earisman, Delbert L., *Hippies in our Midst*. Philadelphia: Fortress Press, 1968.

Fact-Finding Commission, *Crisis at Columbia*. New York: Vintage Books, Inc., 1968.

Fortas, Abe, *Concerning Dissent and Civil Disobedience*. New York: The New American Library, 1968.

Friedman, Robert (Ed.), *Up Against the Ivy Wall, a History of the Columbia Crisis*. New York: Atheneum Publishers, 1968.

Harrington, Michael, *Toward a Democratic Left*. New York: The Macmillan Company, 1967.

Hartnett, Rodney T., *College and University Trustees: Their Backgrounds, Roles, and Educational Attitudes*. Princeton, New Jersey: Educational Testing Service, 1969.

Jacobs, Paul and Saul Landau, *The New Radicals*. New York: Vintage Books, Inc., 1966.

Katz, Joseph, *The Student Activist*. Washington, D.C.: United States Office of Education, 1967.

Kaufman, Arnold S., *The Radical Liberal: New Man in American Politics*. New York: Atherton Press, 1968.

Keniston, Kenneth, *Young Radicals: Notes on Committed Youth*. New York: Harcourt, Brace and World, 1968.

Kerouac, John, *On the Road*. New York: The Viking Press, Inc., 1957.

Lasch, Christopher, *The Agony of the American Left*. New York: Alfred A. Knopf, Inc., 1969.

Lipset, Seymour M. (Ed.), *Student Politics*. New York: Basic Books, Inc., 1967.

Luce, Phillip A., *The New Left*. New York: David McKay Co., Inc., 1966.

Mailer, Norman, *The Armies of the Night*. New York: The New American Library, Inc., 1968.

Marcuse, Herbert, *One Dimensional Man*. Boston: The Beacon Press, 1964.

Oppenheimer, Martin, *The Urban Guerilla*. Chicago: Quadrangle Books, Inc., 1969.

Rubin, Jerry, *Do It: A Revolutionary Manifesto*. New York: Simon and Schuster, Inc., 1970.

Rubin, Jerry, *Do It: Scenarios of the Revolution*. New York: Simon and Schuster, Inc., 1970.

Rudolph, Frederich, *The American College and University*. New York: Vintage Books, Inc., 1965.

Schwab, Joseph J., *College Curriculum and Student Protest*. Chicago: University of Chicago Press, 1969.

Skolnick, Jerome, "Student Protest," *American Association of University Professors Bulletin* (September 1969), 309–326.

Smith, G. Kerry, *Agony and Promise*. San Francisco: Jossey-Bass, Inc., 1969.

Smith, G. Kerry, *Stress and Campus Response*. San Francisco: Jossey-Bass, Inc., 1968.

Spender, Steven, *The Year of the Young Radical*. New York: Random House, Inc., 1968.

Students for a Democratic Society, *New Left Notes*, any issue.

Taylor, Harold, *Students Without Teachers: The Crisis in the University*. New York: McGraw-Hill Book Company, 1969.

Time Incorporated, *Youth in Turmoil*. New York: Time-Life Books, 1969.

Walker, Daniel, *Rights in Conflict*. New York: E.P. Dutton and Co., Inc., 1968.

Wolf, Leonard, *Voices from the Love Generation*. Boston: Little, Brown and Co., 1968.

Yablonsky, Lewis, *The Hippie Trip*. New York: Western Publishing Co., Inc., 1968.

# 8

# Values of the Black Community

As has been established several times previously in other contexts, the primary targets of today's social revolution are economic inequity, the population explosion, war, environmental abuse, and racism. The last of these leads into the theme of the present chapter, namely, the search of American Negroes for a satisfactory value system. This search they participate in with all mankind because it is no respecter of human differences. However, the methods that characterize it and the values that culminate from it differ, some or much, from culture to culture. Thus Negroes or blacks (we shall employ these terms interchangeably) are in the process of reshaping their values under circumstances unique to them.

At this early point in the discussion, the question, just who is the American Negro, is germane. Unfortunately, the question is more easily asked than answered. To say, as several dictionaries do, that his ancestors were members of the dominant black race of Africa sheds some light on the issue. To describe his skin as black, his hair as kinky, his nose as broader and his lips as thicker than those of the "typical" white person, although generally accurate, overgeneralizes the differences. Perhaps the pragmatic answer recently given by the editors of *Ebony* is as satisfactory as any:

> There is no general legal definition of the term "Negro" in the United States. . . . The concept of race as used by the Bureau of the Census is derived from that which is commonly accepted by the general American public.[1]

To this public, the Negro has historically been many things: slave or freeman, animal or human being, unintelligent or intelligent, a thing to be despised or a creature of God to be respected and loved. For almost two and a

[1] Editors of *Ebony*, The Negro Handbook (Chicago: The Johnson Publishing Company, Inc., 1966), p. 3.

half centuries—from Jamestown in 1619 to the Emancipation Proclamation in 1863—he was a slave. Throughout this period, and for a century thereafter, the white race defined him; today, he is in the process of defining himself.

From the vantage point of today's enlightenment, the institution of slavery throughout its entire existence gave the lie to man's basic humanity. From the vantage point of history, the institution can be at least understood if not condoned. Man evolved socially from the clan, to the tribe, to the feudal state, and more recently to the nation. And during the course of his social evolution, outsiders were enemies—and to be an enemy was to be brutalized and maybe enslaved. Yet slaves of an earlier day were, as often as not, ultimately absorbed, rescued, or freed. Slaves in the United States generally remained slaves for life. And once slavery became institutionalized, its victims lost their status as human beings and became chattels or things.

Those white slave-owners who had qualms about the morality of their roles conveniently found in the *Bible* expiation for their guilt. Genesis 9:22–26 gave them a comfortable "out."

> And Ham, the father of Canaan, saw the nakedness of his father [Noah], and told his two brothers outside. Then Shem and Japheth took a garment, laid it upon both their shoulders, and walked backward and covered the nakedness of their father; their faces were turned away, and they did not see their father's nakedness. When Noah awoke from his wine, and knew what his youngest son had done to him, he said, "Cursed be Canaan; a slave of slaves shall be he to his brothers." He also said, "Blessed by the Lord my God be Shem; and let Canaan be his slave."

They received additional moral support from the first part of Ephesians 6:5–9 wherein Paul exhorts slaves to be obedient to their masters "in fear and trembling." However, many took the last part of the exhortation less seriously, namely, for masters to be kind to their slaves. They also played down the message of 1 Corinthians 12:13 that "slaves and free" are all part of one spiritual body "made to drink of one Spirit"; and the related message of Acts 17:26 that "God made from one every nation of men to live on all the face of the earth." Rationalizing these latter passages and others of an uncomfortable nature, most slave-owners went through life avowing that God himself sanctioned the institution of slavery; thus that it could not possibly be wrong.

The extremists of the proslavery element offered explanations about the origins of the Negro that were as pathological as they were bizarre. The Reverend G. C. H. Hasskarl, at the turn of the present century, argued in *The Missing Link: Has the Negro a Soul?* that the black man was not a descendant of Adam and Eve but a beast which Noah took into the Ark. And

Charles Carroll reached a similar conclusion in *The Negro a Beast; or, In the Image of God?*

Historical instances of the white community's rationalization of slavery and of its current suppression of the civil rights of Negroes are almost legion. As stated by a highly articulate Negro writer in 1909,

> Every system of oppression seeks to justify itself. The institution of slavery ransacked science, history, literature, and religion in quest of fact and argument to uphold the iniquitous system. There is almost an exact parallel between the methods employed in support of human slavery and those that are now being resorted to in justification of "social equality."[2]

## BACKGROUND INFORMATION

Black-white racial problems in the country today are evolutionary products of history. Their roots reach as far back as 1442 when a Portuguese shipowner presented Prince Henry with a gift of ten African slaves. Other nations soon entered the black-flesh market, with Spain, England, and France being particularly active. White Europeans also rationalized slavery on Christian grounds. After all, were not slave traders doing the Lord's work by rescuing potential Christians from heathen savagery? Christianity was again avoided, however, when early slave traders debated the relative merits of "tight packing" versus "loose packing." The tight packers herded in more black humanity but also lost more in transit because of the unlivable conditions that tight packing often created. The loose packers herded in less black humanity and also lost less in transit. Tight packing, however, usually carried the day.

Slavery came to the United States colonies in 1619 when "twenty African laborers were brought into . . . port and sold by a captain of a Dutch ship."[3] Slavery achieved legal status for the first time in the colonies when Virginia, in 1661, accorded it statutory recognition. The original 20 slaves increased to 12,000 in 1708, to 120,000 in 1756[4] and to more than 300,000 by the end of the eighteenth century.[5]

[2] Kelly Miller, *Race Adjustment: Essays on the Negro in America*, third edition (New York: Neale Publishing Co., 1909), p. 15.

[3] Katz, William Loren, *Eyewitness: The Negro in American History* (New York: Pitman Publishing Corporation, 1967), p. 20.

[4] Davis, John P., *The American Negro Reference Book* (Englewood Cliffs, New Jersey: Prentice-Hall, Inc., 1969), p. 7.

[5] Muse, Benjamin, *The American Negro Revolution: from Nonviolence to Black Power* (Bloomington: Indiana University Press, 1969), p. 8.

As of 1969, the population of the United States divided among the races as follows:

|  |  |
|---|---|
| White | 178,400,000 |
| Negro | 22,600,000 |
| Nonwhite, Non-Negro | 2,200,000 |
| Total | 203,200,000[6] |

In the same year, the median age of the nonwhite population was 21.2 years; of the white population, 27.8 years. The 22,344,000 Negroes in the United States in 1968 constituted 11.1 percent of the total population.[7] Of that number, 68 percent lived in or on the fringes of cities; 32 percent lived in towns or rural areas.[8] For nonwhites, the infant death rate per 1,000 live births in 1967 was 35.9; for whites, 19.7.[9] For nonwhites, the life expectancy at birth in 1967 was 64.6 years; for whites, 71.3 years.[10]

The following important social-political landmarks paved the way for the civil-rights movement of the present day.

1863:  *The Emancipation Proclamation.* It went into effect on January 1 of that year.

1865:  *Thirteenth Amendment.* This elevated the Emancipation Proclamation to the status of constitutional law.

1868:  *Fourteenth Amendment.* This extended the rights of due process to Negroes.

1865–1876:  *The so-called Reconstruction Period.* The North left 25,000 troops in the Southern States to facilitate social and political changes necessitated by the abolition of slavery. Fourteen Negro Congressmen held office during the period 1870–1876. Generally speaking, however, Jim Crow practices prevailed during the Reconstruction Period. Negroes made progress, but it was slow.

1876:  *Army troops were removed from the Confederate States,* thus bringing social and political progress for Negroes almost to a standstill.

1877:  *Henry O. Flipper became the first Negro to be graduated from West Point.*

1895:  *Booker T. Washington, Negro statesman-scholar, articulated his*

[6] U.S. Bureau of the Census, *Statistical Abstract of the United States* 1969 (Washington, D.C.: Government Printing Office, 1970), p. xiii.

[7] Op. cit., p. 10.

[8] Op. cit., p. 20.

[9] Op. cit., p. 57.

[10] Op. cit., p. 53.

"*Atlanta Compromise*," which constituted an appeasement to the white society. In it, he admonished Negroes to reject, at least temporarily, the goal of social equality while educating themselves realistically for a vocational role in the then existing social order.

1896: *Plessy v. Ferguson case.* In this, the Supreme Court enunciated the separate-but-equal doctrine, thus legalizing racial segregation on public carriers, in schools, and in public institutional accommodations of almost all kinds.

1900: *By the turn of the century, Negroes had lost practically all of the social-political rights they had gained since the Emancipation Proclamation.*

1915: *Birth of a Nation.* This movie, based on Thomas Dixon, Jr.'s *The Clansman* of 1905, depicted Negroes as debauched animals and Klu Klux Klan members as righteous saviors. The movie, pathological to the core but socially persuasive, set racial progress back a long way.

## MOODS OF NEGROES

Negroes have run the gamut of the emotions during their three and a half centuries of slavery and suppression in the United States. They have experienced frustration and despair at one end of the emotional continuum and hope at the other end. During the current period of the civil rights renaissance, they are developing pride in their race and are evidencing a formidable determination to wrest justice from the social order. The subsequent quotations—most of them poignant—capture the spirit of these moods.

### Mood of Frustration and Despair

For all who came to these shores, America was a land of freedom, hope, and opportunity. For all except the Negro. He came in chains and for hundreds of years had to fight just to be free. With few friends, and against almost hopeless odds, the black men and women struggled to stay alive, to obtain their freedom, and to share in the American dream of human dignity and justice for all.[11]

### We Wear the Mask

We wear the mask that grins and lies,
It hides our cheeks and shades our eyes,
This debt we pay to human guile
With torn and bleeding hearts we smile,
And mouth with myriad subtleties.

[11] Katz, *Eyewitness*, op. cit., p. 3.

Why should the world be over-wise,
In counting all our tears and sighs?
Nay, let them only see us, while
    We wear the mask.

We smile, but, O great Christ, our cries
To thee from tortured souls arise.
We sing, but oh the clay is vile
Beneath our feet, and long the mile;
But let the world dream otherwise,
    We wear the mask![12]

During the 1950's and early 1960's, an often heard sardonic quip among blacks was: "Dogs have television shows. Negroes don't."

## Mood of Hope

We do not believe that things will always continue the same. The time must come when the Declaration of Independence will be felt in the heart, as well as uttered in the mouth, and when the rights of all shall be properly acknowledged and appreciated. God hasten that time. This is our home, and this is our country. Beneath its sod lies the bones of our fathers; for it, some of them fought, bled, and died. Here we were born and here we will die.[13]

I have a dream that my four little children will one day live in a nation where they will not be judged by the color of their skin but by the content of their character.[14]

## Mood of Determination

The Negro must now be aware that no fundamental change in his status can come about through deference to or patronage from whites.[15]

We know through painful experience that freedom is never voluntarily given by the oppressor; it must be demanded by the oppressed . . . .[16]

[12] By permission. Paul Laurence Dunbar, *The Complete Poems of Paul Laurence Dunbar* (New York: Dodd, Mead and Company, 1916), p. 71.
[13] An 1831 anonymous quotation which appears in the flyleaf of Katz, *Eyewitness*, op. cit.
[14] From a speech by Dr. Martin Luther King made to the hordes that marched on Washington, D.C. in August of 1963.
[15] Parsons, Talcott and Kenneth B. Clark, *The Negro American* (Boston: Houghton Mifflin Company, 1965), p. xvii.
[16] From an 8,000 word paper written by Dr. Martin Luther King in April of 1963 in a Birmingham jail. He had been imprisoned for leading a protest march against the brutal slaying of two black youths.

We return from fighting. We return fighting. Make way for democracy. We saved it in France, and by the Great Jehovah, we shall save it in the U.S.A. or know the reason why.[17]

For CORE, nonviolence . . . ended on a balmy night, September 1, 1963, in a sleepy town in Mississippi, when a uniformed mob screamed for my [James Farmer's] blood. The casketless hearse in which I escaped became for CORE a symbol of the burial of peace.[18]

## GOALS OF NEGROES

The moods of blacks at any given point in time mirror how successful they have been in attaining their goals. When not successful, frustration and despair were their legacy. When highly successful, negative emotions understandably conceded to hope and determination.

To the question, just what are their major goals, we identify the following irreducible four: (1) social ideals to become reality, (2) self-acceptance and definition of blacks by blacks, (3) acceptance of blacks by the white community, and (4) economic and political power.

The first of these, social ideals to become reality, is basic to the other three. Its imperative to the social order is as simple, albeit as complex, as this: Convert into practice the ideals that permeate your basic documents. Specifically, translate into action the ringing words of the Declaration of Independence.

We hold these Truths to be self-evident, that all men are created equal, that they are endowed by their Creator with certain inalienable Rights, that among these are Life, Liberty, and the Pursuit of Happiness.

Promote "the general welfare" as called for in the Preamble to the Constitution of the United States. Give us the "right to be secure in . . . [our] persons, houses, papers, and effects" as guaranteed in the Fourth Amendment. Do not deprive us of "life, liberty, or property, without due process of law." When you do, you violate the Fifth and the Fourteenth Amendments. Take seriously the affirmation of the Fifteenth Amendment: "The right of citizens to vote shall not be denied or abridged by the United States or by any State on account of race, color or previous condition of servitude." Make good the promise of the Emancipation Proclamation that we shall be truly free.

[17] Written by the editor of *Crisis* (a Negro magazine) in 1919. See Parsons and Clark, op. cit., p. 61.
[18] James Farmer, in Inge Powell Bell, *CORE and the Strategy of Non-Violence* (New York: Random House, Inc., 1968), Foreword.

The hiatus between legal pronouncements and social implementation is a major cause of frustration for Negroes. The following instances are illustrative. Restricted covenants went by the board in 1948 and open housing became the law in 1968, but housing for Negroes is not yet truly open. The Civil Rights Act of 1957 and the Voting Rights Act of 1965 "insured" Negroes the right to register and vote, but the voting hurdle for many is still formidable. The Brown v. Topeka case of 1954 gave them equal educational opportunity, but as of the school year 1966–1967, only 15.9 percent of Negroes in the eleven former confederate states were in desegregated schools.[19] Negroes have won the legal battle for equal vocational opportunity and the right to use public accommodations, but total victory in either category is far from having been won.

The struggle by Negroes to narrow the gap between social ideals and reality has a parallel in their relentless crusade to define and accept themselves. Their search is for identity, for a conviction of personal worth, for self-acceptance, and for a place in history. Until recently, because defined primarily by the white culture, anonymity was their lot. As slaves, they were relegated to the status of nonbeings, more or less. They rarely got into official records or history books; and when they did, they were identified, as often as not, as Nigger Joe or Black Jim. As free men, they played until recently the role of second-class citizens in a white man's world. Small wonder, then, that their self-images failed most tests of adequacy.

Blacks today, looking not to whites but to themselves for acceptance, are forging identities such as never before. They are increasingly discovering and giving visibility to their past and present contributions to mankind and to their place in history. Racial pride is becoming increasingly theirs and, with it, individual pride. That they frequently overplay their roles today is evident even to many within their own ranks. With the passage of time, however, the emotions that need priming today should become increasingly more authentic and spontaneous.

Black separatism is the current vogue of the day. Its message to the white community is essentially this: You freed us from slavery but you rejected us as human beings by denying us our rights as citizens. We now return the favor, in part, by socially rejecting you. I am convinced, however, that this rejection is temporary, dependent as the black community is on the white one for economic power. Thus I contend that a long-term goal of blacks, even though currently concealed for understandable political reasons, is to have a place of importance not outside the dominant social order but one of equality within it.

The black community needs both political and economic power to achieve

---

[19] Muse, *The American Negro Revolution*, op. cit., p. 285.

social equity. Thus I hold that a better guarantee of equity is when Negroes and whites engage in common causes than when they compete from positions of separatism. The latter as a base of power is, at best, a limited, short-term expedient. Integration—true integration, that is—constitutes the only stable base.

## NEGRO LEADERS

The long and relentless struggle of Negroes for freedom has, as would be expected, produced many noteworthy leaders, a selected few of whom we weave into the treatment here. The ones included meet the criteria of historical significance, personal magnetism, distinctiveness of points of view, and size of following.

*Frederick Douglass* (1817?–1895) is the pioneer of the group. Born a slave in Baltimore, he learned early, despite the surveillance of his master, to read and write. When a young man, he escaped to the North and spent the remainder of his life crusading against slavery in all its guises. He spoke widely, published his own newspaper, traveled abroad, supervised an underground railroad, and, in the postwar period, held several important posts in government, one being minister to Haiti. He was a credit to his own race and to all humanity.

*Booker T. Washington* (1856–1915), an advocate of social accommodation, guided his race through the troubled times of the post-Reconstruction period into the twentieth century. He urged Negroes to prepare themselves "realistically" for the society that awaited them. At the Tuskegee Institute that he founded in 1881, he trained students in both manual and academic skills. His approach, although dictated by the period in which he lived, "constituted status quoism purely and simply . . . [and] was so far out of line with the country's traditions and values that understandably it was short lived."[20]

*W. E. B. DuBois* (1868–1963), rejecting the social-accommodation approach of Booker T. Washington, challenged Negroes to rise above the white culture. DuBois, the first Negro to receive a Ph.D. degree from Harvard, was an intriguing mixture of realism and idealism, depending on which racial group he was describing at any given time. In treating of whites, he exposed racism for what it was and assaulted it relentlessly. In treating of blacks, he was incredibly idealistic, depicting them customarily as saintly and Christ-like. In his later years, he expanded the Christ-like stereotype to include the entire proletariat.

Washington's goal was Negro adjustment to the culture. DuBois' goal was

[20] Gail M. Inlow, *The Emergent in Curriculum* (New York: Wiley and Sons, Inc., 1966), pp. 200–201.

Negro nobility: ". . . we black men," he wrote in 1903, "seem to be the sole oasis of simple faith and reverence in the dusty desert of dollars and smartness."[21] Certain of his writings feature a black Christ, a black madonna, a black God—but a white devil. Thus, although DuBois preached the doctrine of brotherhood, he was unable to rise above racial hatred.

DuBois appealed to the intellectuals; Garvey, to the multitudes. A Jamaican gist, sociologist, Negro apologist. And he *did* many things: edited *Crisis* (the organ of NAACP), spoke widely, wrote widely, and influenced countless numbers of both blacks and whites. His place in history is equaled by few of his race. Yet in the 1930's, he had to transfer the mantle of Negro leadership to a rising group of young black intellectuals who were soon to be leaders of the New Renaissance. Rejecting DuBois' idealization of blacks as being too mystical, they built their platform on the realism of racial equality. Their position was that if all races in America are equal, all races then should have equal rights.

*Marcus Garvey* (1887–1940)—a different breed of reformer from Douglass, Washington, and DuBois—literally burst on to the American stage around 1916, preaching the doctrine of African nationalism. He urged Negroes to migrate en masse back to Africa:

> The Negro must have a country, and a nation of his own. . . .

> Let the Negroes have a government of their own. Don't encourage them to believe that they will become social equals and leaders of the whites in America, without first on their own account proving to the world that they are capable of evolving a civilization of their own.[22]

DuBois appealed to the intellectuals; Garvey to the multitudes. A Jamaican Negro—moon-faced, squatty, verbal, and volatile—Garvey campaigned as "The Provisional President of Africa" and was founder of the Universal Mutual Improvement Association. He was very much at home in a decade that spawned Amie Semple McPherson (a white Pentecostal divine healer), Father Coughlin (a Catholic reactionary), and Father Divine (the self-assumed Black Christ).

Garvey ran afoul of the law in 1925 and, when pardoned in 1927, was deported to his native country. His black migration to Africa never did take place. Yet he aroused the pride of millions of Negroes, stirring them such as few demigods had been able to stir them before.

*Elijah Muhammed* (1903?–        ), a black leader of today is, like Marcus

[21] W. E. B. DuBois, *The Souls of Black Folk: Essays and Sketches* (London: Archibald Constable and Co., 1903), pp. 11–12.

[22] Marcus Garvey, *An Appeal to the Soul of White America* (Baltimore: Soper Library, Morgan State University, 1923), n.p.

Garvey before him, an advocate of Black Nationalism. To Muhammed, however, its locale is to be not Africa but a geographical area, never specifically identified, here in the United States. Muhammed (a Georgian christened Elijah Poole) purports to be the chosen "Messenger of Allah." In this role, he is leader of the Black Muslims whose doctrinal cornerstones are separation of blacks, hatred of whites, rejection of Christianity, and espousal of a hybrid form of Mohammedanism. The Muslims point forward to an apocalypse in which the black race, after destroying the white one, will rule supreme on earth. In a positive vein, Black Muslims preach the virtues of personal hygiene, sexual morality, and industry.

A schism opened in the ranks of the Black Muslims in 1963 when Malcolm X, the charismatic "second-in-command," started a splinter movement that gave initial promise of dwarfing the parent one. His assassination in 1965, however, constituted a fatal blow to its chances. Probably the best known Black Muslim alive today is Muhammed Ali, born Cassius Clay. The Muslim organization probably reached its zenith in the mid-1960's. Since that time it has, in my opinion, been on a progressive decline.

*Martin Luther King* (1929–1968), generally conceded to be most influential social activist Negro of all times, ushered in the civil rights movement of the present day. Son of a Baptist minister, he himself became a Baptist minister, completing the requirements at Morehouse College in Atlanta. Subsequently, he earned the Doctor of Philosophy degree at Boston University.

King, an adequate but not an eminent scholar, internalized the ideas of others, ultimately converting them into a design for social action. He drew most heavily on the theologians Karl Barth, Reinhold Neibuhr, and Martin Buber (an existentialist); on the idealist philosopher, Hegel; on Quaker theology in general; on George D. Kelsey, the professor who reportedly influenced him most at Morehouse College; and on Mahatma Gandhi. In composite, King's message was essentially this: man is fundamentally good, the white man is not immoral but sick when he oppresses his black brothers, Negroes need to pursue the Christ idea, and resistance to be moral and effective must take the form of nonviolence. Typical is the following passage:

> We will match your capacity to inflict suffering with our capacity to endure suffering. We will meet your physical force with soul force. We will not hate you, but we cannot in all good conscience obey your unjust laws. . . . Bomb our homes and threaten our children; send your hooded perpetrators of violence into our communities and drag us out on some wayside road, beating us and leaving us half dead, and we will still love you. But we will still wear you down by our capacity to suffer.[23]

[23] Martin Luther King, *Stride Toward Freedom: The Montgomery Story* (New York: Harper and Row, Publishers, 1958), p. 217.

King catapulted to prominence in 1956 as leader of the historically famous bus boycott in Montgomery, Alabama. Racial segregation was the target. The boycott was a success story, with the Supreme Court ruling in November of 1956 that segregation on buses violated the Constitution of the United States.

The march on Birmingham, in 1963, further enhanced King's image as a civil rights leader par excellence. The targets in this instance were school segregation, a host of unsolved murders and bombings, and civil rights injustices in other forms. Birmingham allegedly had even banned a school book which showed black and white rabbits playing together. Birmingham's response to the march assumed various forms: the mass arrest of thousands, a number of reprisal bombings, beatings administered to arrested blacks, jet streams from fire hoses hurling them back, and Bull Conner's police dogs attacking or threatening them. This naked display of force so repelled the nation that a revised Civil Rights Bill, in the hands of a committee at that time, was assured passage. It became law in 1964.

King's life was a saga of love, nonviolent protest, courage, and sacrifice. It earned him the Nobel Prize for Peace in 1964, only the second time that this accolade had been awarded to a Negro. It also brought him an assassin's bullet that cost him his life on April 4, 1968.

*Stokely Carmichael* (1941–      ), generally credited with popularizing, if not actually originating, the term black power, is the last Negro leader to be treated of here. He is a prototype of the black radicals who rose to positions of power in the last part of the last decade. As will be developed in the next section, he assumed leadership of the Student Nonviolent Coordinating Committee, SNCC, in 1966, at a time when the organization was changing from a platform of nonviolence to violence. Like other black nationalists, he rejects integration as a weak substitute for power, calling it "an insidious subterfuge for white supremacy." An admitted anarchist, Carmichael preaches and urges violence. Commenting on the riots that plagued the country's large cities in the last decade, he wrote:

> I do not call them riots. I call them rebellions. It is not for me to endorse, condone, or condemn them. It seems to me that the people of a community have to decide how to overcome their own oppression, and if a rebellion is the way, then that is the way and it is all right with me.[24]

Carmichael attracted a hard-core coterie with his excesses but repelled most blacks, the result being that his own power noticeably waned in the late 1960's. Keeping ahead of the law ultimately became his most pressing pastime.

[24] The Los Angeles Times " 'Black Power' Advocate Seeks Chicago Backing," (July 29, 1966), p. 6.

## NEGRO ORGANIZATIONS

As would be expected, the crusade by Negroes for equality in the American social order has had the support of many organizational groups. The treatment in this section concentrates on the so-called Big Five of the 1960's.

### National Association for the Advancement of Colored People

The longest lived and unquestionably the most prestigious of all Negro organizations is the National Association for the Advancement of Colored People, better known as NAACP.[25] Founded in 1909, it has a membership of well over a half million persons. Basically a conservative, middle-class organization, it works tirelessly and forthrightly within the existing social order to upgrade the status of Negroes along all lines.

NAACP's impact has been strongly felt in the areas of legal defense, housing, employment, voting rights, and education. In the legal areas of 1963, its staff of 16 attorneys and 102 cooperating lawyers across the country

> defended 10,487 citizens arrested during civil-rights demonstrations, represented Negroes in 30 cases carried to the Supreme Court, and fought 168 separate groups of legal actions in 15 states, involving integration of schools, medical services, public facilities, recreation, employment and housing. The Fund's [Legal Defense and Education Fund, that is] had multiplied five times in ten years; in 1964, it reached $1,460,965.[26]

NAACP's most memorable and significant accomplishment was the Brown v. Topeka Supreme Court decision of 1954, influenced in large part by the persuasiveness of Thurgood Marshall—who himself later became an associate justice.

### National Urban League

George Edmund Haynes, Fisk Professor and later Director of the Division of Negro Economics, Department of Labor, spearheaded the founding of the National Urban League in 1910. It was created to help Negro migrants make the transition from rural to urban living. In the context of this broad purpose, its continuing goal has been to facilitate the vocational adjustment of transitional migrants. Basically a civic and nonpolitical organization for a half century, it has recently entered, although nonmilitantly, the political arena

25 I credit Muse, op. cit., pp. 18–23, for much of the content of this section.
26 Muse, op. cit., p. 20.

of the modern-day civil rights movement. Until his death in 1971, Whitney Young was the Executive Director of the National Urban League. Intellectual, suave, and moderate, he worked within the frame of the existing establishment to upgrade the status of Negroes. And in that establishment, his political star shone brightly for years.

### Congress of Racial Equality

A third member of the Big Five is the Congress of Racial Equality, CORE. Founded by James Farmer in Chicago in 1942, it became a national entity the following year, its members consisting of both blacks and whites. Until well into the 1960's, its approach was to identify a given area or instance of social abuse and proceed to attack it aggressively but nonmilitantly. Employing this approach, CORE desegregated a Chicago restaurant in 1943, engaged in a freedom ride in 1947 to test the legality of segregation in buses engaged in interstate traffic, and desegregated a New Jersey swimming pool in 1947–1948. Later, in 1959, it carried out voter-registration sit-ins in Marion, South Carolina, and in Miami, Florida. "With the freedom-rides of the Summer of 1961, CORE shot into national prominence as a major force in the new civil-rights movement."[27]

As of 1964, convinced by the urban race riots that it was out of contact with the lower class Negroes of ghettos, CORE gave up its role of peaceful fire fighter and adopted a new one of militant (or at least semimilitant) community action. Elaborating on this new role, Bell writes that

> Black power—economic and political—has replaced integration as the goal of CORE's activities. Nonviolence has given way to the assertion of the right of self defense. Direct action has been largely replaced by community and political organization in the ghetto. The membership of CORE has become predominantly Negro and increasingly working class.[28]

As CORE became more radical, the national director, James Farmer, an aggressive liberal, turned over the reins of leadership, in 1965, to Floyd McKissick, whose posture and philosophy were much more militant. The latter, in 1966, climaxed a speech at the CORE convention in Baltimore with the following words:

> The black man's cup is run over. I think the philosophy of nonviolence is a dying philosophy . . . No longer can you ask Negroes to adhere to nonviolence unless you call on whites to be nonviolent.[29]

[27] Inge Powell Bell, *CORE and the Strategy of Nonviolence* (New York: Random House, 1968), p. 10.
[28] Ibid., p. 17.
[29] The Los Angeles Times (July 3, 1966), p. 20.

## Southern Christian Leadership Conference

In 1957, Martin Luther King founded the Southern Christian Leadership Conference (SCLC) which, like NAACP and the National Urban League, stands forthrightly for nonviolence as it crusades around the clock for Negro rights. Germinated in the 1954 Montgomery bus boycott, it has sponsored sit-ins, resisted Bull Conner in Birmingham, participated actively in the 1963 march on Washington, and survived the death of its leader in 1968. It is now under the aegis of The Reverend Ralph Abernathy. At the time of its creation, the membership of SCLC consisted primarily of clergymen, black and white. Since that time, it has opened its doors also to nonclergymen. Its budget approximates a million dollars annually.

## Student Nonviolent Coordinating Committee

At the urging of Martin Luther King in 1960, approximately 200 Negro youths, leaders of the sit-in movement in the South, brought into being the Student Nonviolent Coordinating Committee, commonly known as SNCC or Snick. Throughout its brief history, its overriding goal has been to supervise, or at times to direct, the activities of local civil rights protest groups. Segregated lunch counters were its first target. Segregated ballot boxes and the war in Viet Nam have been its more recent targets.

From the birth of SNCC in 1960 until 1966, it was, true to its name, basically a nonviolent organization. John Lewis, a Martin Luther King adherent, was its leader during this early period. In 1966, Stokely Carmichael replaced Lewis, a change that mirrored the mounting militancy in the organization. With Carmichael's ascendancy, SNCC became the most militant of the Big Five organizations. Black power and black nationalism shoved integration into the background. The federal government became a *bête noire*. And the war in Indochina became the white man's vendetta against foreign blacks, a war that SNCC counseled American blacks to avoid. Why, it asked, should we fight oppression elsewhere when we are oppressed here at home? Illustrative is the following:

> Our work, particularly in the South, has taught us that the United States Government has never guaranteed the freedom of oppressed citizens, and is not yet truly determined to end the rule of terror and oppression within its own borders.[30]

SNCC's radicalism began to consume itself in the late 1960's. And Carmichael, proving to be more of a political liability than an organizational

---

[30] SNCC, "The U.S. Government Has Deceived Us" in Paul Jacobs and Saul Landau, *The New Radicals* (New York: Vintage Books, Inc., 1966), p. 34.

asset, relinquished his position of leadership to H. Rap Brown. The latter is in jail at the time of this writing. SNCC lost ground for reasons other than its own radicalism: ironically it was unable to compete with the growing radicalism of the Black Panther Party that was on the rise at the decade's end.

## TACTICS OF THE BLACK REVOLUTION

The Negro revolution being waged throughout the country today has two major purposes. One is to secure for Negroes the civil rights that, because they are first-class citizens in a democratic society, they are entitled to have. The second is to build their psyches to a point where they will be able to accept themselves as human beings of the highest order. In pursuit of either or both of these two purposes, Negroes have employed, among others, the following tactics: (1) reason, (2) rejection, (3) rhetoric, and (4) violence.

### Reason

Negroes have no trouble building a strong rational case for the social inequities and injustices that impinge on them at almost every turn. Despite legal dictums to the contrary, they do not have fair vocational opportunity. They have had, for instance, little access to such occupational avenues as finance, manufacturing, construction, utilities, and transportation. Managerial jobs are only beginning to open up for them. And corporate control is only a gleam in their collective eye. They have been shortchanged educationally. Open housing still falls short of reality for them. And health care is not nearly as accessible to them as it is to whites.

The problem, however, is not whether Negroes can or can not build a rational case for their plight. It is, rather, whether the white community will respond rationally to it. To date, the response has fallen short of reasonable expectations.

### Rejection

Frustrated by the slowness of fact and logic to ameliorate their lot, Negroes have recently turned to the tactic of rejection of the white culture. This manifests itself, among other ways, in dress and grooming, language, and separatism. Simply stated, an increasing number of blacks today, particularly the younger ones, are automatically rejecting whatever their white counterparts espouse. And they are substituting their own modes and mannerisms in lieu.

In the area of dress, the dashiki (tunic-type robe), the au naturel hairdo, the single earring for the male, and Afrosheen makeup for the female are all instances of rejection by Negroes of white modes. In the area of language, many blacks accept, only approximately, the standard language of the white community. These individuals make a fetish of employing the word ain't. They customarily use plural subjects with singular verbs. They employ indiscriminately such hackneyed terms as the man and honky. And they intersperse four-letter vulgarisms freely. We refer here not to illiterate blacks but to literate ones who deliberately flaunt the conventional language standards of the white culture.

Outright separatism is probably the most dramatic form of rejection of whites by blacks. It manifests itself symbolically when racial integration is held in contempt and when such slogans as black power and black nationalism engorge a given literary piece. It manifests itself in a more tangible way when blacks isolate themselves at an athletic contest, insist on living together in a college dormitory or residence wing, demand that certain college courses be closed to white students, and post illegal signs on store windows reading "For Blacks Only."

## Rhetoric

Rhetoric joins reason and rejection in the revolutionary repertory of blacks. We employ the term rhetoric here in the special meaning of language deliberately conceived and used to influence reader or listener opinion. Blacks employ rhetoric for the specific purposes of building black pride, deprecating white pride, keeping whites off balance, gaining social concessions, and arousing fear. It assumes the following forms.

*Color Language.* Illustrative are such statements as "We should be fighting City Hall not the Viet Cong," or "To tear down is to build," or Carmichael's "If the white man plays Nazi, we aint playing Jews."[31]

*Slogans.* Illustrative are such expressions as "Black is beautiful," "We shall overcome," and "The time for talk is over."

*Threats.* Cases in point are these: "Meet our demands or else," "Back down or we will back you down," and "If you like where you live, give us our rights."

*The Sweeping Generalization.* This device, as old as propaganda itself, takes the form, for instance, of the following: "All institutions of the white community are illegitimate," "Everything in America is racist," and "To be a cop is to be a pig."

*Contrasts.* This device takes the form of "You are evil and I am good," or "I have compassion and you do not."

[31] From a speech delivered by Stokely Carmichael to a Black Power Rally in South Park, Los Angeles, November 26, 1966.

*The Reverse Stereotype.* This tactic is one of taking traditional stereo-types and reversing them. Thus "White is beautiful" becomes "Black is beautiful." And the white stereotype of female pulchritude as a woman with fair or olive complexion, classical nose, silky hair, and thin lips converts to a woman with black skin, broad nose, kinky hair, and moderately thick lips.

*Demand for Improbable Concessions.* The intent of this tactic is to get a star by asking for the moon. Thus blacks in many colleges and universities have asked for a no-grading system in hopes of being evaluated more gener-ously under an existing one, or have asked for two or three times the amount of financial aid that they expected to receive. After building sit-ins, blacks have consistently requested amnesty. Interestingly, it has often been granted; and even when not, the request for it has generally tended to mitigate the punishment finally meted out.

*Refusal to Defend or Explain.* This tactic of blacks is customarily em-ployed when they make impossible demands. It turns the spotlight away from their own vagueness or unreasonableness and focuses it on the occasional confusion and discomfiture of the opposition. The message is essentially this: "We have stated the problem; it is your job to decide what we mean and to come up with a solution."

## Violence

When reason, rejection, and rhetoric fail their intended purposes, violence may become the tactic of last resort. This is not to imply that Negroes are a violent people because basically they are not. It is to imply, however, that when denial reaches an intolerable level, violence sometimes becomes in-evitable. When it has taken place, its locus generally has been the larger cities of the country in which ninety-eight percent of the Negro population growth is currently occurring.

Violence is endemic in certain Negro groups, no more than episodic in the Negro community as a whole. It is endemic, for instance, in the Black Pan-ther Party, a nationwide organization with a penchant for violence. It is also endemic at local levels in, for instance, the Black P. Stone Nation (a local federation of many Chicago street gangs), or in the hundreds of lesser street gangs in the many city ghettos throughout the country. Violence is episodic when it crops up unexpectedly, as it has many times in the past decade, in such places as Watts, Newark, Chicago, New York, Detroit, and Cleveland.

Violence is the result of both personal and social pathology. When the result of the latter, it rarely disappears without the social causes responsible for it first being eradicated. Thus violence on the part of at least a sizeable minority of Negroes will not abate—and may even worsen—until Negroes see victory in sight in their crusade for personal identity and social justice.

## ANTI-NEGRO ELEMENTS

Deterrents to victory in the aforementioned crusade are numerous, residing collectively in the conservative element of the social order which, on many fronts, is opposing Negro progress. Deterrents within the official establishment are giving ground slowly. Many outside the official establishment are giving ground even more slowly. A case in point is the Ku Klux Klan. A post–Civil War racist organization that reached its peak in the 1920's, it is still very much alive today. That it is giving ground at all is the result of a hardening of national sentiment, a growing assertiveness of federal power, and a liberalization of local attitudes in selected southern communities.

Other deterrents to Negro progress consist of private clubs with white-only memberships, the bias that exudes from the American Council of Churches, the right-wing racist fulminations that come from certain mass-media personalities, hate literature dispensed widely in the mails, and research that blinds itself to evidence.

In respect to racist literature, the National Putnam Letters Committee, headed by Carleton Putnam, has been active for the better part of two decades "documenting" the inferiority of Negroes. In 1954, Putnam resigned as Board Chairman of Delta Air Lines to enter the literary field. Since then, he has written a biography of Theodore Roosevelt and two rather widely publicized books on race: *Race and Reason* and *Race and Reality*, which purport to prove that Negroes are genetically inferior to whites. Putnam sneers at what he calls "soaps of the equalitarian ideology." He draws heavily from a study made by Dr. Wesley C. George who, in 1961, was designated by Governor George Wallace of Alabama to prepare a report on the biological aspects of the races. From this and related studies, Putnam concludes that Negroes are biologically inferior beings; that major "race stocks have evolved from subsapiens ancestors"; and that the brain of the average white person is approximately eight percent greater than that of the average black person.

The Patrick Henry Press, located in Richmond, Virginia, is a well known example of publishing firms that specialize in racist literature. Its publication list includes *The Wallace Story* by Bill Jones, the Putnam books already cited, *Desegregation: Fact and Hokum* by Henry E. Garrett, *The Biology of the Race Problem* by the aforementioned Wesley C. George, and *The Testing of Negro Intelligence* by Audrey M. Shuey.

The author of this last named book is Chairman of the Department of Psychology at Randolph Macon College. Without deprecating her scholarship in other areas, I hold that she concludes one-sidedly on the issue of race. Her research embraces almost every book or article that depicts Negroes as being innately inferior to whites while giving short shrift to or ignoring the literature that advances an opposing position.

## VALUES OF THE NEGRO COMMUNITY

We conclude this chapter with a frontal consideration of the question: Just what values do Negroes in the United States regard most highly? And while conceding that Negroes are not a unitary but a diverse social entity, we hold that a definable hard core of values applies indiscriminately to all of them. Interestingly but not surprisingly, it is a hard core shared by whites as well, consisting of the following values: (1) identity, (2) self-esteem, (3) social esteem, (4) self-actualization, (5) citizenship, and (6) altruism.

These combine into an admittedly idealized prototype which, if personalized, might lead to the ensuing kind of self-analysis. I am William Olson, secure in the knowledge that because I am a human being I am a very important person. I know who I am and accept myself for what I am: a person 29 years of age, black skinned, passively religious, college educated, three generations removed from slavery, junior executive, and married. I look hopefully for esteem from others because without it my self-esteem diminishes. My aim in life is self-actualization: what I *can* be I *must* be.[32] I move toward this goal in a democratic society whose constitution and laws guarantee me certain basic rights and freedoms. These include the rights of all free men including personal autonomy, privacy, security, protest, the franchise, and due process. These documents also guarantee me certain freedoms including freedom of religion, speech, press, and assembly. I unapologetically claim these rights and freedoms because the society has guaranteed them to me.

For me, however, to lay claim to my rights of individualism commits me to accord them also to others. Even more, it commits me to pursue the elusive goal of altruism. Self-actualization, in fact, leads me inexorably toward this goal, for I cannot truly become a complete person in a social vacuum.

As blacks crusade for the ultimate values that constitute the core of the above sketch, the means-end dilemma confronts them at almost every turn. To what extent, if any, do they have the moral right to desert that core of values in their struggle to attain it. The more militant and embittered blacks today claim to have clear-cut right to do so. Thus for white Ku Klux Klanism they are substituting black Klanism of a type. Disillusioned with vagaries of due process, they are substituting lawlessness. Recoiling for centuries from white racism, they are caught up in the throes of black racism. The less militant blacks today are working to bring about social change without sacrificing their cherished values. In the process, they avoid the means-end dilemma.

---

[32] Abraham H. Maslow, *Motivation and Personality* (New York: Harper and Row, Publishers, 1954), p. 91.

## THE AUTHOR'S PREROGATIVE

I end this chapter with a point of view. It starts with an admission that the American society has, until recently, been a white-dominated society. This is a fact of history. As a white-dominated society, it has perpetrated countless indignities and offenses against Negroes. This too is a fact of history. Today, however, white racism is fading, albeit slowly, as the black civil rights movement gains momentum. In this transitional period, blacks and concerned whites should guard carefully against unleashing any forces of short-sighted expediency that might slow up that momentum.

The racial revolution in America is currently at the crossroads. One way to resolve it is for polarized radicals, black and white, to match hatred, violence, and bloodshed, neutralizing in the process the help that concerned liberals in both camps might otherwise render. The problem of a tactic such as this is the likelihood of hate becoming a way of life. In any event, it crowds out love and brotherhood by keeping the fires of bigotry ablaze. Another way to resolve the revolution is for all committed citizens, black and white—and these constitute a sizeable portion of the country's population—to march together in the common cause of racial equality and justice.

At the moment, a major deterrent to this march of unity is the need felt by Negroes to stand psychologically tall. This, in great part, explains the rhetoric and associated practicalities of black nationalism, black power, and black is beautiful. Hopefully, however, Negroes are passing through one phase that will soon lead into another in which the terms black and white will be, not pejorative, but merely descriptive. If racial wounds are to heal, the ultimate goal of both groups has to be neither white racism nor black racism but nonracism.

For this goal to assume reality, the society should take a harder look than it has to date at the so-called Kerner Report of 1968.[33] This includes the following recommendations:

1. Increase federal and state government aid to cities.
2. Bring into being neighborhood task forces wherever needed.
3. Establish and implement grievance procedures against improper police behavior.
4. Include ghetto residents in the formulation of public policy.
5. Hire more Negro policemen.

[33] The Report of the *National Advisory Commission on Civil Disorders* (Washington, D.C.: Government Printing Office, 1968), pp. 15–27.

6. Assign the best trained policemen to ghettos.

7. In the case of riots, muster and apply law enforcement.

8. Train policemen in the prevention of disorders.

9. Speed up legal justice.

10. Hire more Negroes in the mass communications media.

11. Remove all barriers to jobs, education, and housing.

12. Take all steps possible to alleviate the powerlessness of Negroes.

13. Keep communications channels open at all times.

14. Create in the federal government new jobs, as required, to compensate for unemployment.

15. Reimburse the rural poor so that they will remain rural.

16. Eliminate de facto segregation wherever possible.

17. Improve the quality of adult education and early education for the disadvantaged. Subsidize higher education for the economically disadvantaged.

18. Increase state aid to disadvantaged communities.

19. Change the welfare system by increasing incentives and guaranteeing a living wage for all who cannot work.

Readers will undoubtedly differ widely over the validity of these recommendations. They should not differ, however, over the towering need of the society to wage a relentless crusade for social equality and justice.

# Bibliography

Anthony, Earl, *Picking Up the Gun: A Report on the Black Panthers.* New York: Dial Press, Inc., 1969.

Aptheker, Herbert (Ed.), *A Documentary History of the Negro People in the United States.* New York: The Citadel Press, 1951.

Baldwin, James, *Go Tell It on the Mountain.* New York: The Dial Press, Inc., 1968.

Barbour, Floyd B. (Ed.), *The Black Power Revolt.* Boston: Porter Sargent, 1968.

Bell, Inge Powell, *Core and the Strategy of Nonviolence.* New York: Random House, Inc., 1968.

Benedict, Ruth, *Race: Science and Politics.* New York: The Viking Press, Inc., 1943.

Bloch, Herman D., *The Circle of Discrimination.* New York: New York University Press, 1969.

Buswell, James O. III, *Slavery, Segregation, and Scripture.* Grand Rapids, Mich.: William B. Eerdmans Publishing Company, 1964.

Clark, Kenneth B., *Dark Ghetto; Dilemmas of Social Power.* New York: Harper and Row, Publishers, Inc., 1965.

Cleaver, Eldridge, *Post Prison Writings and Speeches* with an appraisal by Robert Scheer. New York: Random House, Inc., 1969.

Cleaver, Eldridge, *Soul on Ice.* New York: McGraw-Hill Book Company, 1969.

Cohen, Jerry and William S. Murphy, *Burn, Baby, Burn!* New York: E.P. Dutton and Co., 1966.

Davis, John P., *The American Negro Reference Book.* Englewood Cliffs, New Jersey: Prentice-Hall, Inc., 1969.

Drotning, Philip T., *A Guide to Negro History in America.* Garden City, New York: Doubleday and Company, Inc., 1968.

DuBois, William E. B., *Souls of Black Folk.* New York: Peter Smith Publisher, 1903.

Dunbar, Ernest (Ed.), *The Black Expatriates.* New York: E.P. Dutton and Co., Inc., 1968.

Editors of *Ebony, The Negro Handbook.* Chicago: The Johnson Publishing Company, Inc., 1966.

Eisenstadt, Murray, *The Negro in American Life.* New York: Oxford Book Company, 1968.

Ellison, Ralph, *Invisible Man.* New York: Signet Books, 1953.

Fullinwider, S. P., *The Mind and Mood of Black America.* Homewood, Illinois: The Dorsey Press, 1969.

Good, Paul, *Cycle to Nowhere.* Washington, D.C.: U.S. Commission on Civil Rights, 1968.

Grier, William H. and Price M. Cobbs, *Black Rage.* New York: Basic Books, Inc., 1968.

Hayden, Tom, *Rebellion in Newark.* New York: Random House, Inc., 1967.

Hughes, Langston, *Famous Negro Heroes of America.* New York: Dodd, Mead and Co., Inc., 1965.

Hughes, Langston and Milton Meltzer, *A Pictorial History of the Negro in America.* New York: Crown Publishers, 1963.

Jones, LeRoi, *Blues People: Negro Music in White America.* New York: William Morrow and Co., 1963.

Katz, William Loren, *Eyewitness: The Negro in American History.* New York: Pitman Publishing Corporation, 1967.

Katz, William Loren, *Teachers' Guide to American Negro History.* Chicago: Quadrangle Books, 1968.

King, Martin Luther, *Why We Can't Wait.* New York: Harper and Row, Publishers, Inc., 1964.

Lomas, Charles, *The Agitator in American Society.* Englewood Cliffs, New Jersey: Prentice-Hall, Inc., 1968.

Lubell, Samuel, *White and Black: Test of a Nation.* New York: Harper and Row, Publishers, Inc., 1964.

Malcolm X, *The Autobiography of Malcolm X.* New York: Grove Press, Inc., 1966.

Mannix, Daniel P. and Malcolm Crowley, *Black Cargoes: A History of the Atlantic Slave Trade, 1518–1865.* New York: The Viking Press, Inc., 1962.

Muse, Benjamin, *The American Negro Revolution: from Nonviolence to Black Power.* Bloomington: Indiana University Press, 1968.

Myrdal, Gunnar, *The American Dilemma.* New York: Harper and Row, Publishers, 1944.

*The Report of the National Advisory Commission on Civil Disorders* [The so-called Kerner Report]. Washington, D.C.: Government Printing Office, 1968.

Parsons, Talcott and Kenneth B. Clark (Eds.), *The Negro American.* Boston: Houghton Mifflin Company, 1965.

Pettigrew, Thomas F., *Profile of the Negro American*. Princeton, New Jersey: D. Van Nostrand Company, Inc., 1964.

Putnam, Carleton, *Race and Reason: A Yankee View*. Washington, D.C.: Public Affairs Press, 1961.

Reddick, L. D., *Crusader Without Violence: A Biography of Martin Luther King, Jr.* New York: Harper and Row, Publishers, Inc., 1959.

*Report of the President's Commission on Civil Rights*. Washington, D.C.: Government Printing Office, published yearly.

Roberts, Joan I. (Ed.), *School Children in the Urban Slums*. New York: The Free Press, 1967.

Rudwick, Elliott M., *Propagandist of the Negro Protest*. New York: Atheneum Publishers, 1969.

Scheer, Robert, *Eldridge Cleaver; Post-Prison Writings and Speeches*. New York: Random House, Inc., 1969.

Shuey, Audrey M., *The Testing of Negro Intelligence*, 2nd edition. New York: Social Science Press, 1966.

Smith, Arthur L., *Rhetoric of Black Revolution*. Boston: Allyn and Bacon, Inc., 1969.

Washington, Booker T., *The Future of the American Negro*. New York: Haskell House Publishers Ltd., 1968. (First published 1899).

Wills, Gary, *The Second Civil War*. New York: New American Library, 1968.

Wright, Richard, *Native Son*. New York: Harper and Row, Publishers, Inc., 1941.

Young, Whitney, *To Be Equal*. New York: McGraw-Hill Book Co., 1964.

# 9

## A Value Synthesis

In the first eight chapters, we have exposed and assessed the fundamental values that make up the fabric of our society today. By almost any standard, they constitute a potpourri. Idealistic for the most part, they have a strong leaven of materialism. Claiming impartiality to all citizens, they favor some more than others. In general, even the more idealistic ones have greater nobility in theory than in practice. The fact of their imperfection, however, is not surprising. For one reason, they were created by imperfect people; and once created, they have consistently mirrored the imperfections of those responsible for implementing them. Thus anyone assessing them needs to do so not on an absolute but on a relative basis. For a second reason, they carry the burden of having to serve two masters at the same time: the individual and the social group. As stated by one writer, they have to "join men into societies, and yet . . . preserve for them freedom which makes them single men."[1] This is no easy task.

The country's value system is, unquestionably, in a state of confusion and transition. Until the last generation or two, most people took the American Dream quite literally. It was a dream of individual sanctity, social equality, limitless opportunity, peaceful resolution of conflict, justice, and racial equality. It was a dream of hope, majestically symbolized in Emma Lazarus' sonnet engraved on the Statue of Liberty.

### The New Colossus

Not like the brazen giant of Greek fame,
With conquering limbs, astride from land to land;
Here at our sea-washed, sunset gates shall stand
A mighty woman with a torch, whose flame

---

[1] Bronowski, J., *Science and Human Values* (New York: Julian Messner, Inc., 1956), p. 70.

Is the imprisoned lightning, and her name
Mother of Exiles. From her beacon-hand
Glows world-wide welcome; her mild eyes command
The air-bridged harbor that twin cities frame.
"Keep, ancient lands, your storied pomp!" cries she
With silent lips. "Give me your tired, your poor,
Your huddled masses yearning to breathe free,
The wretched refuse of your teeming shore.
Send these, the homeless, tempest-tossed to me,
I lift my lamp beside the golden door!"

The American Dream has resisted satisfactory implementation for two centuries now, leading to a mounting cynicism by many of those left out of the dream. And these outsiders are not necessarily starry-eyed literalists. They generally are realists with a vision of the benefits that would be theirs if the society became more serious about translating its ideals into action.

The American Dream has lost much of its luster, and so too has the Judeo-Christian (or Protestant) ethic, whose tenets, as covered partially in Chapter 2, consist of the following.

1. A supreme deity—personal, omnipotent, omniscient, omnipresent, and noncontingent—involves himself around the clock in the affairs of men. This God figure operates both outside as well as inside the frame of natural law.

2. The concept of life as a purposeful phenomenon tolerates no opposition.

3. Man can "will" himself to become almost anything he chooses: good or evil, bright or dull, industrious or slothful, affluent or indigent.

4. God honors hard work by granting material rewards. These, in effect, are spiritual bonuses.

5. If the poor worked hard enough, they would not have to be poor.

6. Man is to respect and obey familial and civil authority.

7. The United States, favored by God, is to be loved and fought for.

8. The Golden Rule, the Ten Commandments, and the Sermon on the Mount constitute the explicit core of the ethic.

The Judeo-Christian ethic, while not completely abandoned, has lost its absolute hold on the society. The Christian church and the Jewish synagogue are no longer the holy citadels that they traditionally were. Science and relativism have made substantial inroads on supernaturalism. The materialism of organized religion is a growing target of attack. Theology that splits hairs while ignoring the social problems of the world is becoming increasingly suspect. And the upstart "God is Dead" movement is, to say the least, provoking widespread controversy. The forerunners of this movement—including, selectively, H. Richard Neighbur, Gabriel Vahanian, Bishop J. A. T. Robinson, and Harvey Cox—are not, as the term "God is Dead" would imply, atheists. Rather, they hold suspect the simplistic mysticism of a personal God communicating day in and day out, in a close one-to-one relationship, with those of the more than three billion inhabitants of the world who are deemed worthy of His attention.

The ethic is going into eclipse because its qualities of absolutism, simplicity, and inflexibility have become increasingly inappropriate for a world that is relative, complex, and dynamic. Nor is it the only creed that is going into eclipse, for, in the words of Michael Harrington, the accidental revolution of this century "has unsettled every faith and creed in the west."[2] The psychiatrist Carl Jung speaks in the same vein when he says that "as for ideals, the Christian Church, the brotherhood of man, and international social democracy . . . have failed to stand the baptism of fire."[3]

We have posited that the American Dream has fallen far short of its potential and that the Judeo-Christian ethic has been tried and found wanting; these are indicators of needed change in the country's value system. Other indicators consist of the following: people have become hypercritical of our established social institutions and patterns, many feel powerless to effect given change in the social order even when agreement has been reached that such change is essential, people fear technology—its tendency to deface and power to destroy, and the United States no longer beacons its idealism to an expectant world.

The foregoing enditements constitute a mandate for the country to assess its values critically and even revolutionize them if necessary. The specifics of such a revolution can, understandably, never be blueprinted at any given point in time. Yet the blueprint should evolve progressively and satisfactorily if individuals and groups who toil in this important arena of value assessment and revision adhere to the following principles.

1. Man should not attempt to return to any early idyllic state, because such a state probably did not exist in the first place. Once he has left the Garden, he has to go forward. Thus he will need to accept certain facts of twentieth century life as inevitable—controlled bigness, technology, and social complexity, among others. These are prices he has to pay for a style of living that only a few would trade for its counterpart of

[2] Michael Harrington, *The Accidental Century* (New York: The Macmillan Company, 1965), p. 41.
[3] Carl G. Jung, *Modern Man in Search of a Soul* (New York: Harcourt, Brace and World, Inc., 1933), p. 104.

yesteryear. My thesis is that, because man is in the twentieth century, his task is to eradicate the major ills of the century while reaping its benefits.

2. Microcosmic endeavor never eradicates macrocosmic malaise. Thus nothing but a massive effort on a national scale will suffice to bring about the many changes needed in the values of the emerging society.

3. The country's most compelling imperative is less to innovate in the arena of values than to fulfill the commitments it obligated itself for in 1776 and 1787. As stated by Archibald MacLeish, the problem is "not to discover our national purpose but to exercise it."[4] We exercised it in industrial and economic, but not in racial, matters in the eighteenth and nineteenth centuries. We exercised it politically in World War I by "making the world safe for democracy" and then rested on our laurels. We eradicated the threat of Hitler's inhumanity to man in World War II but did nothing about our own inhumanity to man. We became fat and complacent in the Roaring Twenties and even more so in the affluent fifties and sixties, forgetting the important fact that important human values have to be fought for relentlessly and unceasingly. The country's major task, then, is to give unflagging attention to the promises it has been making to its citizenry for two hundred years.

4. Because human beings have inviolable worth, the United States needs to underwrite for all its citizens a life style that is decent and respectable. Our culture fails to do this when it condones hunger amid plenty, allows disease to go unattended, allows ignorance to go uneradicated, and breeds insecurity by practicing bigotry, hypocrisy, and corruption.

5. The principle of peaceful resolution of conflict, of consensus as opposed to violence, is fundamental as the concerned society struggles to get its values in order. This principle was central in Thomas Jefferson's dream of a social order in which every man would have (a) a natural birthright to freedom and equality, and (b) the right to enjoy, without fear, the harvest of his birthright. Both parts of Jefferson's dream are in jeopardy today.

6. The final principle is that reason leavened by feeling will need to characterize the value crusade of the present and future. I emphasize here that rationality never exists in an emotional vacuum, for mind and emotions are interlocked. Thus the person who is truly rational is also

[4] Archibald MacLeish, *A Continuing Journey* (Boston: Houghton Mifflin Company, 1967), p. 86.

the one who is emotionally mature. Conversely, no person can be truly rational who is not emotionally mature.

As the country continues to assess and revise its values in the coming years, I envisage the following evolving outcomes: (1) a new concept of individualism to take shape, (2) a new social ethic to unfold, (3) the political order to become both more sensitive to the plight of the have-nots, and more world conscious, and (4) the system of formal education to become more value oriented. These will now be elaborated. And because this chapter is a synthesis, I make no apology for repeating a few selected ideas and concepts developed elsewhere in the book.

## INDIVIDUALISM

As highlighted in Chapter 2, the concept of individualism has been a lode star in our nation's ideology from colonial days to the present. And it is a noble concept straight from the combined sources of Judaism, Christianity, Anglo Saxon political traditions, selected literary works, and pioneer living. It communicates the message that individual man, because he is man, has intrinsic worth and accordingly merits the respect of all mankind and a place of importance in the universe. The trait of individualism has, throughout history, been a legitimate and effective counter to tyranny in high places, ideational absolutism, and even, at times, majority rule.

Inherent in the trait, however, is its insidious tendency to get mired in egocentricity. Once it takes this course in any given person, the result is hyperindividualism and thus infantilism. Yet, strangely, our culture has historically worshipped at the shrine of hyperindividualism—euphemistically called rugged individualism. Generation in and generation out, it has bred self-centered and socially insensitive people. The "Old Adam of excessive individualism,"[5] to use Stewart Udall's term, has historically sired such unsavory offspring as searing poverty, vulgar affluence, bigotry, narcissism, social complacency, and pathological competitiveness. That these have been condoned and allowed to prosper reveals the society's value system as more than a little muddled.

In consequence, an imperative for the years immediately ahead is for the society to redefine individualism, framing it this second time around in a context of emotional and social responsibility. A desperate need in this regard is for the mental-health movement to work its way into every facet of the social order, leading the way to the following outcomes—each of which we have elaborated in the first person.

[5] Stewart Udall, *1967: Agenda for Tomorrow* (New York: Harcourt, Brace and World, Inc., 1968), p. 10.

### Self-Identity

I know who and what I am.

### Self-Acceptance

I am able to accept myself at any given point in time.

### Emergence

My goal is optimum growth. Thus, I shall maximize my positive attributes and eliminate or lessen as many of my shortcomings as I can.

### Autonomy

I shall act and live independently, relying on others for social fulfillment, but I shall not exploit them.

### Social Relatedness

My goal is to relate comfortably and warmly to associates, with altruism my ultimate aim.

### Freedom from Guilt

I shall not dissipate my psychic resources by worrying about past errors of omission or commission. Rather, keeping those resources intact, I shall employ them in the pursuit of positive causes.

### Flexibility

I shall avoid rigidity in reacting to life's problems.

### Consistency

My goal is to avoid compartmentalization, applying my values consistently to life along its many fronts.

### Frustration Tolerance

I shall assess frustrating situations realistically and relate to them authentically, not magnifying them out of proportion to their importance.

### Openness

I shall look life in the face, understanding as much as I can of it and accepting the rest.

The foregoing composite is admittedly too idealized for mere mortals to achieve. Realizing this, we presented it to encourage relative progress toward it and, just as fundamentally, to emphasize in the context of this section that individualism which has true value has to have a mature emotional base. In contrast, individualism that is egocentered and uncontrolled can be destructively negative, sometimes beyond description. In our own country, it has been responsible in great part for such unsavory outcomes as the following: power madness in high places, insensitive materialism, character assassination, ecological abuses, medicine forgetful of the Hippocratic oath, dishonesty that has become endemic in international politics, sadism as a way of life among radicals, and hypocrisy as almost a universal administrative tactic.

If these are products of individualism, they reveal a time-honored value in serious need of reinterpretation. When redefined, it should emerge as a socially laden value, and the rightful possession of none but emotionally healthy, responsible individuals. Individualism needs to imply shared purposes, vigorous responsibility, and moral commitment. The existentialist imperative is appropriate in conclusion here, namely, that every person needs to act at all times as if he were doing so for the entire human race. Individualism at its best is a quality that has to be worked for and earned.

## AN EMERGENT SOCIAL ETHIC

As the rugged-individual ethic slowly recedes, a social ethic seems to be slowly emerging to fill the created vacuum. In effect, it is the ethic of individualism cleansed of much of its egocentricity in the arena of human concerns. Although similar in certain respects to the Judeo-Christian ethic, it differs in that it is oriented more in the here and now, in self-assessment, in self-fulfillment, and in the need for the social order more nearly to approximate its potential. I do not mean to imply that the social ethic has become epidemic, for to do so would falsely imply a miraculous change in humanity. What I mean to suggest, rather, is that more of the nation's citizens than ever before are becoming concerned about those social evils which, if not soon alleviated, will ultimately corrode and destroy our nation. Racial inequality, substandard living conditions, and lack of integrity in officialdom are three important instances of these evils.

Support for the social ethic resides in practical as well as idealistic motives. The defense on practical grounds is one of selfish enlightenment, going something like this: If the country's (and also world's) major social ills are not cured or, at least, significantly alleviated, the favored "haves" of the era of rugged individualism will lose their favored status. President Kennedy said essentially this in his inaugural address to the nation in 1960. President Franklin Delano Roosevelt said it in only a slightly different vein in his "Economic Bill of Rights" message to Congress in 1944:

> We have come to a clear realization of the fact that true individual freedom cannot exist without economic security and independence. . . .
> People who are hungry and out of a job are the stuff of which dictatorships are made.

The case for the ethic on idealistic grounds is at least as old as Christianity and the brotherhood-of-man concept. Justice Learned Hand, relating the ethic specifically to the concept of freedom, spoke out majestically for it in 1944.

> Liberty lies in the hearts of men and women. . . . While it lies there it needs no constitution, no law, no court to save it. . . . What then is the spirit of liberty? . . . [It] is the spirit which seeks to understand the minds of other men and women; . . . which weighs their interest along its own without bias; . . . the spirit of liberty is the spirit of Him who . . . taught mankind that lesson it has never learned . . . that there may be a kingdom where the least shall be heard and considered side by side with the greatest.[6]

President Lyndon B. Johnson aligned himself with the social ethic in his defense of the Civil Rights Bill of 1964.

> Its purpose is to promote a more abiding commitment to freedom, a more constant pursuit of justice, and a deeper respect for human dignity. . . . it is not enough just to open the gates of opportunity. All our citizens must have the ability to walk through those gates. . . .
>
> We seek not just freedom but opportunity. We seek not just legal equity but human ability, not just equality as a right and a theory but equality as a fact and a result.[7]

Arthur J. Goldberg is yet another champion of the social ethic, as the following excerpt from a United Nations address attests.

> . . . Indeed, human rights and economic rights are but a single interwoven and inseparable strand. In striving for both simultaneously, we in this Council [Economic and Social] embrace the aspirations of a better life and a great society of all men in which human misery and discrimination will one day be banished, not because of our limited nationality but out of our common humanity.[8]

The social ethic, in actuality, incorporates the best in humanism but translates it into the following basic imperatives for today's world: (1) the brotherhood-of-man concept must leave the musty pages of theory and find its way into practice; (2) all, not just a favored few, must have the abundant life here and now; and (3) altruism must win out over egocentric individual-

---

[6] Irving Dilliard (Ed.), *The Spirit of Liberty: Papers and Addresses of Learned Hand* (New York: Alfred A. Knopf, Inc., 1954), pp. 189–191.

[7] *Public Papers of Presidents: Lyndon B. Johnson* (Washington: U.S. Printing Office, 1965), pp. 842–844; also Commencement Address delivered at Harvard (Washington: U.S. Printing Office, 1965), pp. 635–644.

[8] Address made to the 41st session of the United Nations at Geneva, July 6, 1966.

ism. It is understatement to say that progress toward these goals can be assessed only in relative terms.

## VALUES AND THE POLITICAL ESTATE

If the social ethic is to become a force of power in the country, it will need to work its way into, and reshape the values of, the political estate. And we refer here to internal revision of, not a major change in, the estate. In this connection, modern nations have lived under four political systems: absolute monarchies or dictatorships, communism, socialism, and capitalism—one or a combination of these. The first of the four, hopefully, is anachronistic. The other three have histories spotted with successes and failures. Our founding fathers fought for democratic government because it promised the greatest amount of freedom to its citizens. And to all but a dissident few today, the choice was a good one. Although not a panacea, the system has worked moderately well. Yet a number of shortcomings are becoming increasingly acerbated and, if not ameliorated, may ultimately cripple or destroy the system. To prevent this eventuality, the country should, in my opinion, take the following action.

### Polarities of Wealth and Poverty

First in priority, the country needs to narrow the distance that now exists between tasteless affluence at one end of the economic continuum and subhuman poverty that exists at the other end. As developed in Chapter 3, the laissez faire system of free enterprise, that went almost uncontrolled until the Sherman Antitrust Act of 1890, nearly became victim of its own voraciousness. Adam Smith's thesis that private effort promotes public welfare had not been sustained. The system allowed material possessions to accumulate in unbelievable amounts in the persons of a select few and to be almost nonexistent in the persons of a sizeable minority. And political power followed in the wake of economic wealth.

Since 1890, the federal government has been increasingly active in the arena of economic affairs seeking the twofold outcome of narrowing the distance between poverty and affluence and lessening the likelihood of cyclic recessions and inflationary periods. However, it is my opinion that the government has not gone far enough. It allows, even as of today, 30 million people to eke out existences on an annual income of $4,000 for a family of four (or its equivalent for larger or smaller families) while the majority of the nation's population live comfortably or affluently. If the social ethic becomes truly operational, the magnitude of this disparity will have to be significantly lessened.

The problem is not only economic but also psychological and political. It is economic in respect to the material facts of the case. It is psychological in that it involves a hard core of traditionally held attitudes: for instance, that the poor do not have to be poor, that the poor are contented with their poverty, that the ultraaffluent have a moral as well as a legal right to their one-sided affluence, and that, social efforts to the contrary, the poor will always be with us. These unvalidated attitudes will have to be changed by education if humanism is to permeate the economic estate.

The problem of gross economic disparity is political in that the government will have to act more vigorously than it ever has before if the economic gap is to be narrowed enough to prevent disaster. An essential first step is equitable tax legislation slanted in favor of those in greatest need of benefit. The more affluent in the society would obviously have to bear the cost of this step. A related second step is guaranteed employment for all and, by implication, full production at all times. The procedural avenues to these outcomes might be any of the ones sketched in Robert Theobald's interesting book of 1966, the first three of the following four being illustrative.[9] The fourth is the author's.

1. Full employment, maximum production, and an equitable income for all, guaranteed by the federal government (Leon Keyserling).

2. The government as an employer of last resort of people to work in such worthy and needy institutions as hospitals, schools, libraries, parks, forests, and so forth. (Garth Magnum).

3. The government to pay incentive bonuses, inversely related to salary, to the poorly employed or nonemployed.

4. The corporate structure to develop a more value-oriented conscience, leading to more extensive employment of the socially disadvantaged.

In respect to this last recommendation, the conclusion reached several decades ago by Charles Beard, the then eminent historian, is still valid today.

If corporations cannot provide employment for the millions of the proletariat—for such we have, in spite of all claptrap to the contrary—can corporate persons expect to protect themselves forever, through Constitutional and judicial processes, against the distresses and distempers of natural persons twisting and turning in their search for the rights of life, liberty, and property declared in the American creed?[10]

[9] Robert Theobald, *The Guaranteed Income* (New York: Doubleday and Company, Inc., 1966).

[10] Charles Beard, "Corporations and Natural Rights" *Virginia Quarterly Review*, Volume 12 (July 1936).

We cite the above as illustrative only, leaving to others the task of blue-printing a sociably workable, comprehensive, viable plan.

## Office Holding and Personal Wealth

As expounded in Chapter 4, almost all important positions in government are filled either by individuals who themselves are affluent or by others who rode to high office on the shoulders of affluence. Thus government serves the interests of the nation's less affluent masses uncertainly and inadequately; those of the more affluent few, surefootedly and adequately. This state of affairs dulls the glitter of democratic ideals. The need, once more as stated in Chapter 4, is for the government to subsidize election campaigns thereby neutralizing, at least in considerable part, the make-weight influence of wealth. The social revolution of the day is currently backing this proposal.

## Quality Goals for Quantity Goods

It is also backing at the national level a redirection of emphasis from economic, to broad social, causes. Caught in the crossfire of public opinion is the system of capitalism. The latter, despite governmental attempts for almost a century to curb its economic onesidedness, is still slave to the profit motive. Capitalism has served the country well in many respects, but its record is not an unmixed one. Its earmarks, among others, are these: lack of a social philosophy, degrading poverty, excessive wealth, urban slums, deface-ment of the environment, exploitation of the socially disadvantaged, colonial-ism, competition allowed to become pathological, unethical advertising, and widespread unemployment. In simple terms, capitalism has worked well but not well enough.

The need of the future is a way of life "where men are more concerned with their goals than their goods," where mankind opts "to sacrifice for the common good rather than . . . scramble for private gain."[11] Admittedly this is an ideal that any cultural group can only approximate. Yet our nation can make significant progress toward it under the following three conditions. *It can make significant progress* if the mental health of its citizens becomes a serious national concern. As established in an earlier context, the mentally healthy person is able to project beyond himself into the psyches of others. Anyone capable of doing this will inevitably place a higher priority on social than on materialistic concerns. *It can make significant progress* if the con-science of the corporate society develops to a point where it too demonstrates

---

[11] Michael Harrington, "A Subversion of the Great Society" in Herman D. Stein (Ed.), *Social Theory and Social Invention* (Cleveland: The Press of Case Western Reserve University, 1968), pp. 49, 68.

serious concern for social welfare. It is showing slight signs of such development today in its hiring and educational policies and practices. These signs
need to shine more brightly in the future, however. *It can make significant
progress* also if the federal government escalates its efforts to assure welfare
rights to all its citizens. These include not only the rights and freedoms
promised in the Constitution but, additionally, the rights *not to be* hungry,
subservient, unnecessarily diseased, uneducated, fearful, or segregated. The
government at the time of this writing is currently deescalating rather than
escalating the national social-welfare effort. This, in my opinion, is merely a
temporary setback, however, which social pressures will soon reverse. The
thesis here is not that capitalism is a dying institution; rather, that it is an
active one in critical need of modification and control. Its close alliance with
materialism makes it particularly vulnerable. We terminate this section with
Heilbroner's assertive conclusion, namely, that

> The "self regulating" economy that is . . . [capitalism's] highest social
> achievement stands condemned by its absence of meaning and intelligence.
> . . . In the end, capitalism is weighed . . . and found wanting, not alone
> as a system but as a philosophy.[12]

## Shrinking Nationalism

Nationalism, like capitalism, has also been weighed in the balance and
found wanting. The phenomenon of nationalism, conceptualized by Machia-
velli (1469–1527) in the context of the city states of Italy, was waiting in the
wings when the nation states of Europe sprang up shortly thereafter. The
underlying thesis of nationalism is that "in the absence of a rational, overall,
coordinating source of authority everything . . . [will be] determined by a
struggle for power."[13] This thesis was a logical lead into the balance-of-
power concept that, for the past four centuries, has guided the thinking and
shaped the actions of national states. It has cast nations in the roles of
competitors vying for power: ideationally at times, politically always, and
militarily when other methods have failed.

As an historical political phenomenon, nationalism was inevitable. As a
political system for today's twentieth century technological world, its status,
to say the least, is vulnerable. Nationalism may even be an anachronism.
I make this admittedly controversial and assertive statement for the following
reasons. One is that any governmental arrangement that, in today's thermo-
nuclear world, depends for survival on competition threatens the entire human

[12] Robert L. Heilbroner, "The Future of Capitalism," *Commentary* (April 1966),
pp. 23–25.
[13] Harvey Wheeler, *Democracy in a Revolutionary Era* (Santa Barbara: The Center for
the Study of Democratic Institutions, 1970), p. 164.

race and thus is too dangerous to survive for long. A second reason is that the national state is failing functionally: it is no longer able, assuming it ever was, to give its citizens security. A third reason is that the more highly developed nations are channelling a disproportionate amount of their resources into warlike causes at the expense of humane, peaceful causes. And a final reason is that any system that perpetually divides rather than unifies individuals and social groups cannot be long-lived.

I am more comfortable in averring that nationalism in today's world (if the latter is to survive) will have to concede to some other organizational arrangement than I am in identifying or describing the specifics of that arrangement. Quite candidly, I make no pretense of knowing what they should be. Thus I generalize. The arrangement, I suggest, will need to be global in scope or at least more global than nationalism has proved to be; that cooperation will have to rise above competition; and that economic planning will have to take place at an international level to assure a more equitable distribution of the world's goods.

Possibilities such as these understandably come through with a utopian ring to many, but I personally hold that they are practical. They are practical because they are necessary. They are practical because existing institutions have proved incapable of coping with pressing world problems such as nuclear warfare, the population explosion, environmental erosion, racism, hunger, disease, and problems posed by the conquest of outer space. Thus if status quo political arrangements and institutional forms, including nationalism, have proved to be incapable of coping with the rising tide of world problems, arrangements and forms with the surface appearance of being utopian may, in the long run, prove to be the only truly practical ones. As stated relatedly by Harvey Wheeler, staff member of, and writer for, The Center for the Study of Democratic Institutions,

> The more practical and power-oriented politics is, the more shortsighted and static it tends to become. . . .

> Truly practical politics requires the adoption of . . . radical and visionary policies. . . . These are times when established institutions cannot adjust to change adequately enough. In such times the truly practical and conservative solutions to pressing problems always seem utopian and impractical. The world is at such a time today.[14]

## EDUCATION AND VALUES

With the country in a state of social turbulence, the goals and functions of formal education need to be reassessed and updated. The underlying thesis in

---

[14] Harvey Wheeler, op. cit., p. 205.

this connection is that education cannot operate on a business-as-usual basis at this critical time when the society is caught up in the throes of change. Avoiding pedagese, and deliberately condensing the substance of the presentation, I suggest that education needs to perform the following functions as it readies students to relate to the problems of today's world: (1) educate for emotional and social as well as for intellectual outcomes, (2) expose students in schools to the social facts of life as soon as they are ready for the exposure, (3) take learners, insofar as possible, into the pulsating society to give them a firsthand view of social problems, (4) teach learners to think critically.

## Education Broadly Based

The thesis of this section is that formal education, because a cultural extension of the homes of students, has an obligation to educate them broadly along lines of the intellectual, emotional, and social components, not just the intellectual one per se. Traditionally, schools have been cognitively oriented, most comfortable when teaching the basic skills, having students read "good" literature, and communicating to them through the so-called scholarly disciplines of the natural sciences, social sciences, and humanities. In the process, schools have generally assumed that cognitive learning results in the outcome of mentally healthy learners. And the assumption has a certain amount of validity.

Formal education, however, has carried the assumption too far. Does cognitive learning, for instance, lead surefootedly to the mental health outcomes identified previously in the chapter? Specifically, does it predictably lead to self-identity, self-acceptance, emergence, autonomy, social relatedness, freedom from guilt, flexibility, consistency, frustration tolerance, and openness? Scarcely! Thus I contend that schools need to meet the following specifications:

1. Be inviting, not forboding, places.

2. Set reasonable guidelines of student behavior.

3. Develop and implement well-conceived curriculums that relate specifically to the growth needs of learners without neglecting the needs of society.

4. Develop the extracurriculum on a broad social base, and motivate *all*, not just *middle-class*, students to participate in it.

5. Develop, give active support to, and staff adequately for a counseling program the goals of which are emotionally healthy students, careful educational programming, and equally careful job placement.[15]

---

[15] I have developed these in greater detail in *Maturity in High School Teaching*, revised edition (Englewood Cliffs, New Jersey: Prentice Hall, Inc., 1970), chapter 8.

## Education for Realism

Formal education not only has an obligation to educate learners as total organisms, but, at such time as they are ready for the exposure and when contextually appropriate, to reveal life to them as it is—not as dreamers would like it to be. The thesis is that improvement in the society will take place only when its members, old and young alike, see it realistically for what it is. Accordingly, if it can be substantiated beyond reasonable doubt that corruption in high places is rampant, if, as alleged by Philip M. Stern and Paul H. Douglas, tax legislation is habitually slanted to favor some more than others, if materialism is a dominant national trait, if ghettos are repellently subhuman, if racism prevails, and if our basic national documents grossly fail the test of implementation, formal education is remiss when sweeping unsavory facts such as these under the table. We emphasize once more, however, the importance of relating the "teach it like it is" approach to the stipulations cited at the paragraph's beginning.

At least one theoretical counter to the position taken in this section is that reality will unduly disturb the young. I contend, however, that if they are truly ready for the experience, they will welcome being disturbed. A practical counter to the position, although one not usually articulated, is that if the young see life as it is, they will crusade to upset the status quo. Conceivably it is just such a crusade engaged in by persons of all age levels and from all walks that the country desperately needs. Accordingly, we hold that lack of readiness, situational inappropriateness, and lack of taste should be the only major deterrents to truth taught in the many classrooms of the nation's schools.

## Schools and Communities

Education for realism requires concrete as well as theoretical implementation. Thus another contribution that formal education should make to the cause of value building is this: whenever curriculum goals dictate and logistics permit, teachers should take learners into local or nearby communities to acquaint them firsthand with life in action. Learning possibilities in urban centers are almost limitless; in small towns, generally extensive enough not to be ignored. Collectively, they include city halls, legislative chambers and associated activities, courts, libraries, embassies, civic centers, community houses, airports, museums, parks, slums, docks, factories, and so forth.

Traditionally, formal education's base of operations has been noticeably detached from the immediacies of the ongoing world. Nor in view of education's vast commitments is this a surprising state of affairs. Among other commitments, it is expected to tie the past to the present while looking to the future; instruct the masses, not just the few; educate youth broadly, not narrowly; produce learners who think critically, not memorize by rote; in general, turn youth away from the provincial, leading them toward the cosmic. Sensitive to the impact of these demands on professional time and energy, formal education has leaned heavily, and understandably so, on theory as a way out of the dilemma. In the process, learning opportunities inherent in "life out there" have tended to be ignored. Thus such social problems and affronts as justice emasculated, squalor of ghettos, bumbling inefficiency and graft in politics, and substandard life styles too often remain academic.

My intent here is not to deprecate theory in formal education; it is rather to call for a better balance between theory and living reality. Each needs the enforcement of the other. And in the process of effecting such a balance, education dulls the edge of many social injustices by exposing them to view, while authenticating at the same time the value systems of learners who came in contact with them.

Formal education, I realize, cannot, nor should it, make the world its classroom. Logistics and the importance of theory are two important reasons why. But neither should formal education function too far removed from living reality. The issue, actually, is not one of either—or but of what constitutes a defensible blend of both.

## Critical Thinking

The noblest service that formal education can render to value building is to cultivate in learners the ability to think critically. Critical thinking in the best traditions of problem solving commits individuals to acquire knowledge, analyze it, integrate it, postulate about it, conclude from it, and reflectively assess it at every point of contact with it. Critical thinking reaches its zenith in those persons who, because emotionally healthy, unafraid, and autonomous, are able to look all of life in the face and have an open encounter with any given aspects of it. It sinks to its nadir in their opposites who, because emotionally inadequate and dependent, meander through life slavishly dependent on others for ideas and values.

To the question of whether critical thinking can be taught, I answer as I did in an earlier publication.[16] It can be taught "(1) by a teacher's removing the blockages which stand in the way of learning," by allowing the psychic energy of learners to have relatively free outlet, by treating learning as a process more of release than injection. It can be taught "(2) by a teacher's stimulating an environment of learning" in such a way that he makes the classroom warm and attractive, provides a rich assortment of learning

[16] Inlow, op. cit., pp. 99–100.

materials, keeps the learning atmosphere alive, works with a meaningful curriculum tailored to each individual learner, and encourages autonomy. It can be taught "(3) by a teacher's helping . . . [learners] to proceduralize . . . [their] thinking." The method of this third approach is one of instructing directly for problem-solving outcomes by communicating the traditional steps of problem solving and supervising the learning situation closely to make certain that they are followed.

## A CLOSING WORD

As stated at the book's beginning, values are the determiners of life's choices and thus of man's behavior. They are products of myriads of influences, past and present. Some are hand-me-downs from previous generations. Other are original products forged at a given point of time in the crucible of social living. They flow from the culture and into the culture. And most fundamental of all, they are dynamic.

Today's foment in the society constitutes a mandate for intensive value assessment and resulting social change. The hope for this book is that it will advance these outcomes in some distinguishable way.

# Bibliography

Boulding, Kenneth E., *The Meaning of the Twentieth Century*. New York: Harper and Row, Publishers, 1964.

Carr, William C., *Values and the Curriculum*. Washington, D.C.: National Education Association, 1970.

Commoner, Barry, *Science and Survival*. New York: The Viking Press, Inc., 1966.

Congressional Quarterly, Inc., *Editorial Research Reports on Modern Man:* Washington, D.C.: Congressional Quarterly, Inc., 1971.

Cornuelle, Richard C., *Reclaiming the American Dream*. New York: Random House, Inc., 1965.

Deutsch, Karl W., *Nationalism and Its Alternatives*. New York: Alfred A. Knopf, Inc., 1969.

Fletcher, Joseph, *Situation Ethics*. Philadelphia: Westminster Press, 1966.

Fromm, Erich, *Escape from Freedom*. New York: Avon Book Division, The Hearst Corporation, 1964.

Gustafson, James M., *The Sixties: Radical Change in American Religion*, The Annals, 387 (January 1970).

Harrington, Michael, *The Accidental Century* (New York: The Macmillan Company, 1965).

Harrington, Michael, *Toward a Democratic Left*. New York: The Macmillan Company, 1967.

Harris, Fred R., *Alarms and Hopes, A Personal Journey, A Personal View*. New York: Harper and Row, Publishers, 1968.

Heilbronner, Robert L., *The Limits of American Capitalism*. New York: Harper and Row, Publishers, 1967.

Mumford, Lewis, *The Human Prospect*, edited by Harry T. Moore and Karl W. Deutsch. Carbondale, Illinois: Southern Illinois University Press, 1955.

Myrdal, Gunnar, *Challenge to Affluence*. New York: Pantheon Books, 1963.

Seligman, Ben B. (Ed.), *Poverty as a Public Issue*. New York: Free Press, 1965.

199

Sheldon, Eleanor B. and Wilbert E. Moore, *Indicators of Social Change.* New York: Russell Sage Foundation, 1968.

Starkey, Margaret M. (Ed.), *The Education of Modern Man* (New York: Pitman Publishing Corporation, 1966).

Stein, Herman D. (Ed.), *Social Theory and Social Invention.* Cleveland: The Press of Case Western Reserve University, 1968.

Theobald, Robert (Ed.), *Social Policies for America in the Seventies: Nine Divergent Views.* Garden City, New York: Doubleday and Company, Inc., 1968.

Udall, Stewart L., *1976: Agenda for Tomorrow.* New York: Harcourt, Brace and World, Inc., 1968.

Wheeler, Harvey, *Democracy in a Revolutionary Era.* Santa Barbara, California: The Center for the Study of Democratic Institutions, 1970.

# Index